BOMBER COUNTY

A History of the Royal Air Force in Lincolnshire

BOMBER COUNTY

A History of the Royal Air Force in Lincolnshire

Terry Hancock

MIDLAND
An imprint of
Ian Allan Publishing

Bomber County
A History of the Royal Air Force in Lincolnshire
© 2004 Terry Hancock
ISBN 1 85780 129 6

Published by Midland Publishing
4 Watling Drive, Hinckley, LE10 3EY, England
Tel: 01455 254 490 Fax: 01455 254 495
E-mail: midlandbooks@compuserve.com

Midland Publishing is an imprint of
Ian Allan Publishing Ltd

Worldwide distribution (except North America):
Midland Counties Publications
4 Watling Drive, Hinckley, LE10 3EY, England
Telephone: 01455 254 460 Fax: 01455 233 737
E-mail: midlandbooks@compuserve.com
www.midlandcountiessuperstore.com

North American trade distribution:
Specialty Press Publishers & Wholesalers Inc.
39966 Grand Avenue, North Branch, MN 55056
Tel: 651 277 1400 Fax: 651 277 1203
Toll free telephone: 800 895 4585
www.specialtypress.com

Printed in England by
Ian Allan Printing Ltd
Riverdene Business Park, Molesey Road,
Hersham, Surrey, KT12 4RG

Half title page: *These Lancasters of 50 Squadron, roaring over Skellingthorpe for the press, c1944, are just a few of some 700 Lancasters which the Lincolnshire-based squadrons could muster by the end of the war — truly a bomber county.* Via John Lintin

Title page: *Vulcan B1 XH481 of 101 Squadron sits on its dispersal at Waddington, c1960. The white gloss finish, to reflect the heat from a nuclear explosion, was surely one of the RAF's most attractive colour schemes.* Charles Parker

Below: *The Phantom was very much a Lincolnshire aircraft, entering service with the RAF at Coningsby in 1968 and remaining there for 19 years. It was initially used in the strike/attack role but 41 Squadron, one of whose aircraft is seen here in 1976, also specialised in reconnaissance. The aircraft's recce pod is just visible.* Phil Becker

Contents

Introduction

This book is an amalgamation of my previous books, *Bomber County* and *Bomber County 2*, with additional material which brings the story of military flying in Lincolnshire up to the year 2004. The year 2012 will see the 100th anniversary of the formation of the Royal Air Force's predecessor, the Royal Flying Corps, and since that date military aircraft have become a common sight over our county. The rapid progress in aeronautical design is well illustrated by the difference between those early machines at Killingholme and today's Tornado F.3s and Sentry AEW.1s but the RAF itself has also seen many changes, not least in the years since the end of the Cold War. In 1978, when *Bomber County* was first published, ten operational squadrons were based in Lincolnshire, six of which were equipped with the mighty Vulcan; early in 2004 there are just two, neither of which is a bomber unit, so that the title of this book is now an anachronism but one which reflects those stirring and dangerous days of 60 years ago.

In this book I have tried to capture the flavour of the different periods by including eyewitness accounts taken from published works, and letters kindly sent to me by people who served in the pre-1974 traditional county of Lincolnshire and its post-1974 and 1995 successors. While researching and writing, it became even more obvious to me that war is a miserable business, the only redeeming feature of which is that to overcome it brings out some of the best human qualities, some of which

I hope are covered in this book. I humbly dedicate it to all those airmen and airwomen, air and groundcrew, who served in Lincolnshire from 1914 to 2004, and especially to those whose 'last home' was in this county.

Acknowledgements

I am extremely grateful to the people and organisations listed below, all of whom gave generously of their time to contribute to this book:

Group Captain Dowling, Flight Lieutenant Ferrill, Flying Officer Heath and Squadron Leader Hughes, RAF Swinderby; Squadron Leader Tait, Flight Lieutenant Edmunds and Flying Officer Stone, RAF Binbrook; Flight Lieutenant Rees, Flight Lieutenant Wade, Flight Lieutenant Goff, Flight Lieutenant Stevens, Squadron Leader Leeming, Flight Lieutenant Costin, Flight Lieutenant Withers, Squadron Leader MacDougall, Squadron Leader Fonfe, Flight Lieutenant Guy, Flight Lieutenant Ratcliffe and Mrs Jacqui Wheeler, RAF Waddington; P/O Foy, RAF Nocton Hall; Flight Lieutenant Gray, RAF Donna Nook; Flight Lieutenant Sneller, RAF Holbeach; Flight Lieutenant Curtis, RAF Wainfleet; Mrs Jean Buckberry, RAF College Librarian, F/O Cable, Flight Lieutenant Hodson and Ms Ruth Vernon, RAF Cranwell; Flight Lieutenant Weaver, Flight Lieutenant Rose and Flight Lieutenant Smith, RAF Coningsby; Squadron Leader Hammond-Doutre and Flying Officer Townsend, RAF North Coates; Squadron Leader Masefield and Squadron Leader Steenson, RAF Scampton; Flight Lieutenant McGran and Flight Lieutenant Ratcliffe, RAF Digby; Public Records Office, Kew; Air Historical Branch, MoD; Fleet Air Arm Museum; RAF Museum; Air Britain (Historians); Strike Command Public Relations; Lincolnshire Aviation Society; Lincoln Central Library; Keith Shooter and Ray Evans, BAE Systems; Mike Craven, Hunting Contract Services; Ms Heather Deacon, Babcock Defence Services; D Allison, K Ansell, M Applegarth, Roger Audis, Barry Barnes, Maude Baxter, M Beattie, E G Boulton, Chaz Bowyer, Pip Brimson, Herman Brooks, Graham Chaters, Fran Cooper, Peter Corbell, T H Crow, Tony Cunnane, Beryl Czornyj, R Drury, John Edmunds, E M Evans, Robin Fletcher, Tony Foster, Geoff Gardiner, Jeff Hadfield, D Hamilton, S Harker, Flight Lieutenant Hendry, Mike Hodgson, Tony Holland, Ray Hooley, Ted Hooton, Pat Horton, G/C Howie, Tim Hudson, Mike Ingham, R A Lord, Gill and Terry Lowe, Sally McIntosh, Brian Martin, Terry Millward, Trevor and Vicki Muhl, Roy Conyers Nesbit, Bill Newton, Owen Northwood, Brian Orrell, Wally Phillips, N R Portass, S F Porteous, R A Price, V D Price, A Proud, R Raynor, W Reeves-Bilson, J A Richardson, T J Sour, E Sower, Perry Sparkes, L A Thomas, G A Todd, Margaret Trickett BBMF, A Tyson, Steve Vessey, John Walls, Rod Wetton, ACM Sir Neil Wheeler, Jack White, Harold Willars, M Williamson and G P Young.

Particular thanks are due to Peter Green, Dave Langlands and Charles Parker; and, of course, to Mary, Lorna and Phil.

Chapter One

World War One

Royal Naval Air Service

The first airfields of the RAF's antecedents, the Royal Flying Corps (RFC) and Royal Naval Air Service (RNAS), were established around military training areas on Salisbury Plain and in Hampshire, or near naval ports such as Chatham and Portsmouth. The first landings in Lincolnshire by military aircraft were those made in transit from the south to Montrose, in Scotland, or to the coastal air stations of the RNAS, as promulgated by the Admiralty in August 1913. One of these was to be at Cleethorpes but this was changed first to Immingham and then to Killingholme before work actually started.

On the outbreak of war in August 1914 the RNAS had a system of aerial patrols around the south and east coasts based on eight seaplane stations: Calshot, Fort Grange (Portsmouth), Eastchurch, Isle of Grain, Felixstowe, Great Yarmouth, Killingholme and Dundee. However, as Killingholme was not quite ready for operations Wing Commander Samson, a famous pioneer airman of the RNAS, was ordered to establish a base at Skegness, on 10th August 1914, and to take charge of air patrols from the Humber to Cromer, including the defence of the Admiralty fuel tanks at Immingham. His Eastchurch Squadron, now a 'Mobile Squadron', left the Isle of Sheppey on 9th August, and consisted of two BE.2s, a Bristol TB8, a Bleriot XI, a Short (Admiralty No.3) and a Sopwith Tractor Biplane. Of these, the Short, with its pusher engine behind the crew, carried a Maxim gun in the front cockpit but the other aircrafts' only armaments were the pilots' and observers' pistols and some hand-grenades.

Squadron Commander Richard Bell-Davies, whose subsequent career was closely tied to Killingholme, flew the Sopwith up to the Humber and had 'to land on plough' near Lincoln owing to engine failure. A blocked petrol feed pipe was cleared and Bell-Davies took off into driving rain to land again, when lost, on 'a good grass field' and spend the night in a farm. The next morning he flew on to Killingholme where three of the other aircraft had already arrived; from there they flew to Skegness, where their camp was established on a field on the south side of the Burgh road.

Three patrols were flown daily from Skegness during its brief existence: Patrol A was Skegness-Cleethorpes-Mablethorpe-Skegness; Patrol B was Skegness-Cromer-Skegness; and Patrol C was Skegness-six miles north of Mablethorpe-Skegness-The Wash-Skegness. On 24th August the squadron returned to Eastchurch on the south coast, leaving Killingholme to take over its task.

Killingholme had flown its first patrol on 21st August but was still a very makeshift airfield and it was December before hutted accommodation was provided and the road to the station metalled. A typical patrol flown in the early months of World War One was that of Sub-Flight Lieutenant Adams, on 18th November. (The aircraft is given as a DFW Mars Arrow, a German-designed biplane purchased by the Admiralty pre-war.) He '...left Killingholme at 0730, turned at Donna Nook, 0810, landed Killingholme 0845. Altitude 2,000ft, vis 10m, weather good, conditions some showers. Area clear'. Bad weather, of course, stopped flying.

Various aircraft were flown in the period 1914–15, including Sopwith Spinning Jennies (in which a Killingholme pilot, Lieutenant Brooke, was reputed to have been the first airman to deliberately put an aircraft into a spin and, more importantly, the first to recover from such a manoeuvre!). Also on strength were Avro 510 seaplanes, BE.2cs, Caudron GIII seaplanes, Sopwith Schneiders and White & Thompson Bognor Bloaters.

One of Killingholme's duties was that of air defence against Zeppelins, the dreaded German airships greatly feared by the civilian population, but air interception was an art still very much in its infancy, as is witnessed by the following official report by the Commander-in-Chief, Nore, on a Zeppelin raid carried out on the night of 6th June 1915:

'At 5.07pm a Zeppelin was reported 100nm off Humber East. At 8.00pm 2 miles NNE Happisburgh (Norfolk) going to W.Nr L9. At 8.30 it passed over Cromer very high. It thence followed the line of the Coast, passing Sutton 9.50 and off the Spurn 10.10. Accidentally or intentionally it then went along the coast passing Withernsea at 10.40. At Bridlington possibly Flamborough Head was sighted and it then, at 11.12, turned SW, making a good line for Hull arriving there at 11.45. At Hull, bombs were dropped in large numbers, a timber yard was destroyed, 40 to 50 homes and 24 persons were killed. The bombardment lasted about 15 minutes, the Zeppelin acting with great deliberation and apparently selecting marks for its bombs. As each bomb dropped, the ignition of the fuse lit up the Zeppelin clearly. HMS *Adventure* fired but without effect.

'It then went down the river and was apparently careful to avoid places where danger lay. Thus the guns and air station at Killingholme was avoided, also the excellent objective of the oil tanks there, and the docks and

This Bristol TB8, serial 153, was part of the Eastchurch Mobile Squadron, Royal Naval Air Service, and was on its way to Killingholme when it suffered engine trouble and had to land at Well Beck Farm, Alford, on July 28th 1914. The pilot Capt I T Courtney, Royal Marine Light Infantry, was a well known pre-war aviator. Geoff Hadfield via Charles Parker.

One of the various aircraft used in Killingholme's early days was this German design, the DFW Mars Arrow, serial 154. This photo was taken after it force-landed near Donna Nook in May 1914, but it carried out patrols until dismantled in October, the fact that it was German being a distinct disadvantage! Grimsby Library, via P H T Green

stores at Immingham, as well as the WT station at Cleethorpes, both well defended, were, for this reason, untouched.

'Fire was opened from HMS *Kale* off Immingham, and also from the pom-pom at the docks, but the target was too difficult.

'It then came down from 6000' and dropped bombs on Grimsby at 12.45. Thence went seaward to the SE. Surface fog prevented the Killingholme machines from ascending. Two machines from Eastchurch, one from Yarmouth and one from Grain went up in connection with this attack.'

Thus, the Zeppelin's position had been known from 8.00pm until 12.45am, a total of almost five hours, and yet it had bombed Hull with impunity; little wonder that there was a public outcry about these early Zeppelin raids. On the credit side, as the report pointed out, military targets known to be defended were not damaged; but was this accidental? Perhaps the 'surface fog' obscured them?

This was the situation faced by Commander Bell-Davies when he was appointed district commander of air stations in the north of England in January 1916 (having been awarded the VC in the Dardanelles since his earlier sojourn at Skegness). He was responsible to the Admiral East Coast at Immingham and his HQ was at Killingholme, which he described thus in *Sailor in the Air:* (Peter Davies, 1967):

'The landing ground was a small field bounded on one side by the Humber, on another by the oil tanks with their surrounding unclimbable fence, on a third side by a railway line complete with telegraph wires and signals and on the fourth by a disused claypit. On this unsuitable ground ab-initio training with a Bristol Boxkite was being carried on. I had the training transferred to Redcar (Yorks) where the aerodrome was adequate. The other activity was seaplane training on the Humber. There was a small single-engined flying boat of French make called by the mystic letters FBA, a Sunbeam-engined Short tractor, quite good but underpowered, and a number of Sopwith seaplanes called Schneiders.'

Davies also had some realistic comments in his official report on night flying in case of a Zeppelin attack:

'The Air Station is on very low ground on the Humber shore – there is a constant haze even when clear inland, which increases the difficulty of landing at night and finding the aerodrome.

'The BE.2cs of the War Flight have very poor rate of climb, 35 minutes to 6000', so their chance of catching a Zeppelin is very small. Therefore, it is of no use to send pilots up at night after Zeppelins except under exceptionally favourable conditions and subject to your approval I have given orders accordingly. The War Flight is being used to give experience to pilots.

'I therefore submit that Killingholme Air Station is of little value as a War Station for land machines, that it may be of value as a War Station for seaplanes but at present it is not sufficiently developed and the pilots not sufficiently trained for it to be considered as anything more than a school.' (Ibid)

Vice-Admiral Ballard, Admiral East Coast, agreed to these proposals, but made a suggestion: the Zeppelins were often sighted out at sea, where they obtained an accurate fix on their position in daylight, waiting for darkness before heading inland to their targets; if the Schneiders could be got out to sea they could attack in daylight. Bell-Davies then looked at the Humber ferries, paddle steamers built with large open decks to carry sheep, but which could equally well carry four Schneiders. Thus the PS *Killingholme* was requisitioned and a mast and derrick fitted to lower and recover the seaplanes, while a scratch crew was made up from the Air Station personnel. Bell-Davies recalls the operation:

'We took our craft down the Humber from Hull to Immingham and secured her in the basin. With her shallow draught and double rudders steering was extremely tricky and she was apt to take wild steers. There was a compass but I found that the north point was always directed at the funnel.' (Ibid)

A binnacle, with other navigational equipment, was obtained from a redundant cruiser, HMS *Forth*, and some of the PS *Killingholme's* original crew joined; the ferry then set off for the Dogger Bank:

'The *Killingholme*'s performance at sea was unusual to say the least. Each time she rolled, the overhang of the deck hit the surface with a bang which shook the ship and made the funnel wobble. We carried on through the night, got a latitude sight at noon the next day, and in the afternoon picked up soundings with the hand lead on the Dogger Bank. The *Killingholme* was evidently not the sort of ship which could ride out a hard blow at sea. I made up my mind that if it came to blow, we would make for the Humber.' (Ibid)

Come on to blow it did and the *Killingholme*'s port paddle wheel (designed to break easily if it hit the shallow bottom of the Humber) broke and the vessel had to be taken in tow by an armed trawler, which kept her head into the sea so that

'...it was possible to put a man into the sponson to cut away the broken floats... casting off the tow, we set off again for the Humber... If the vessel steered badly before, she steered now like nothing imaginable. We had to use both wheels to keep her headed even approximately in the right direction. Early the next morning we made Spurn Head and anchored under its lee. I demanded a tug to take *Killingholme* up the river as the Humber was not wide enough to allow for her erratic steering'. (Ibid)

After this episode the ship was fitted with hardwood paddles and some other improvements. A full crew was appointed and

'...at the next new moon she was again sent off to the Dogger with her Schneiders, but the Germans evidently knew all about her. A number of Scandinavian ships used the port of Hull and it seems probable that German intelligence managed to make use of them. Two apparently inoffensive fishing trawlers approached her during the night and fired torpedoes at short range. One torpedo was seen to pass right under her, but another hit a paddle wheel blowing it and the overhang deck overboard. The hull remained intact; no one was killed but several of the crew were hurt'. (Ibid)

Bell-Davies' memory seems to have played him false here as records show that the *Killingholme* was mined rather than torpedoed and, sadly, three of her crew were killed by the explosion, on 27th April 1916; in addition, one of the ship's Sopwith Babies was reported 'wrecked' on this date with its crew of two listed as 'killed in action' but it is not clear if this was also a result of the mine. This seems to have been the last use in this role by the hardy *Killingholme* but she

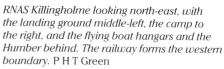

RNAS Killingholme looking north-east, with the landing ground middle-left, the camp to the right, and the flying boat hangars and the Humber behind. The railway forms the western boundary. P H T Green

survived to take part as a barrage balloon ship in World War Two.

Commander A H Longmore took command of Killingholme Air Station in June 1916, an event recorded in his autobiography (*From Sea to Sky 1910–1945*; Bles, 1946) and where he found that

'...some recently built sheds were waiting to house the new large American flying boats which had not yet been delivered. Short float-seaplanes with single 225hp Sunbeam engines and a few Sopwith Scout seaplanes were in use, the former for patrols and the latter for interception of Zeppelins. Up to date they had not been very successful and it was not a well-placed station for operating seaplanes on account of the strong tide in the estuary and the large rise and fall which made slipway work difficult'.

Despite the misgivings of its senior officers, Killingholme went on to become one of the leading seaplane stations, whilst still retaining its small land aerodrome. Its complement was 900 sailors and it was a seaplane school as well as an operational North Sea patrol and anti-Zeppelin base; at times there were as many as 100 aircraft there and some of these would have flown against the Zeppelin raids of September 1916, when L22 bombed Humberston, L13 Owmby and Gainsborough, and L23 Boston.

The large flying boats, responsible for patrolling towards Denmark and the mouth

PS Killingholme in her original role of Humber ferry; the large upper deck comfortably carried the Sopwith Schneiders or Babies and with these the vessel had a brief career as a seaplane carrier. Grimsby Library, via P H T Green

of the Baltic, were initially Curtiss H-12 Large Americas and a major task was to watch for German warships entering the North Sea from the Kiel Canal or the Kattegat, another being the interception at sea of incoming Zeppelins. The H-12s suffered from poor seaworthiness and so a Royal Navy officer, John Porte, redesigned their hull, giving rise to the excellent Felixstowe F.2A which in due course began to replace the H-12s. By May 1918 Killingholme had an establishment of eleven F.2As and ten H-12 Large Americas, and US Navy personnel were beginning to appear prior to the Americans taking over Killingholme Air Station in July 1918. It was on 10th May that the four years of anti-Zeppelin efforts were apparently crowned with success, as described in this report by Captain Munday:

'Reports indicated that a Zeppelin was on a course to be intercepted. Felixstowe F.2A N4291 left Killingholme at 1320. Capt. Pattinson, pilot; Capt. Munday, 2nd pilot; Petty Officer Stubbington, engineer and Air Mechanic 1st Grade John, W/T Operator.

'At 4.30 I observed a German Zeppelin of the latest type on our port beam. It was about 1,500 feet above our machine and approximately 1 mile from us and proceeding due east in the direction of Heligoland. I pointed it out to Capt. Pattinson and he at once put the machine at its best climbing angle. I went to the forward cockpit and tested the gun and tried the mounting and found everything worked satisfactorily. The engineer rating immediately proceeded to the rear gun cockpit and tested both port and starboard guns. At this time our machine was at a height of 6,000 feet. The hostile craft had evidently seen us first and was endeavouring to get directly over us in order to attack us with bombs. When at a height of 8,000 feet and the Zeppelin had climbed to 9,000 feet I opened the attack and fired about 125 rounds of explosive ammunition. The engineer rating also opened fire and fired about the same number of rounds. The Zeppelin was about 500 yards distant. All our fire appeared to hit the craft and little spurts of flame appeared all over the envelope. I noticed much that appeared to be water ballast and many articles being thrown overboard and then the nose of the hostile craft went up a few degrees from the horizontal; this was, apparently, soon checked by the occupants as the craft righted and commenced to climb as much as possible. I had a gun stoppage and spent many minutes clearing it, being obliged to take the breech of the gun to pieces.

'The Zeppelin continued to climb and gain on us slightly and again endeavoured to get directly over our machine. The enemy succeeded and dropped five or six bombs. The engineer rating reported to the pilot (Capt. Pattinson) that seven hostile destroyers were circling around beneath us. We were now at a height of 11,000

feet and the Zeppelin's height was approximately 12,500 feet. I opened fire again and fired another 130 rounds of explosive and tracer bullets. I noticed the propeller of the Zeppelin's port engine almost stop and the craft suddenly steered hard to port. I concluded that the port engine had been hit by our gunfire as well as other parts of the craft as the envelope and gondola seemed a background for all the flashes of the explosive and tracer bullets. There was much more outpouring of ballast and articles and considerable smoke. I concluded that we had finished the Zeppelin and informed Capt. Pattinson that we had bagged it, but the craft again headed for Holstein in a crabwise fashion emitting much smoke. I had other gun stoppages and one bad jamb. One of the explosive bullets exploded in the gun and flashed into my face and on to my hand but outside of a few scratches I received no injury. Our port engine commenced to give slight trouble and the engineer investigated. He reported that an oil feed pipe had broken and that it would not be long before it would break in two.

'As soon as I had cleared my gun of the trouble caused by the exploding of the explosive bullet I signalled to Capt. Pattinson that I was ready to re-attack and looked for the enemy craft. I saw it still proceeding due east in a crabwise fashion. It was losing height and emitting smoke which was of a black variety though parts of it were pure white. The hostile destroyers underneath opened fire on us and owing to engine trouble, lack of petrol for our return journey, and being only about 60 miles off Heligoland we gave up the attack at 5.35, having been attacking for one hour and five minutes.

'The oil pipe broke in two and we were forced to glide and land on a rough sea. The engineer quickly climbed out on top of the engine and repaired the break with tape. Fifteen minutes later we took off. As the machine was difficult to control Capt. Pattinson asked me to get out and endeavour to ascertain whether we had damaged the rudder or elevators in taking off and in looking back I observed the German destroyers steaming with all speed in our direction. 4291 landed at Killingholme at 8.50.'

HMPPS Killingholme *in Immingham Dock, showing the damage caused by the mine on 27th April 1916. Note the Sopwith Baby on deck – was this the one reported as wrecked?* Grimsby Library, via P H T Green

A Curtiss H-12 Large America flying boat on one of Killingholme's slipways, 1918. P H T Green

The Zeppelin they had attacked has since been officially identified as L62, which German records say was struck by lightning on 10th May, and it was on this information that British intelligence supported Munday and Pattinson's claim after the war. However, the American aviation historian Douglas Robinson, in his book *The Zeppelin in Combat*, shows that the airship attacked was, in fact, L56, which reported that it was attacked by a British flying boat on 10th May, the combat lasting from 4.15pm to 5.40pm. L56 was not damaged, but jettisoned its bombs and three tons of fuel, thus making it abandon its patrol.

Captain Munday's report illustrates extremely well the hazards of operational flying in World War One. The F.2A's top speed, it should be noted, was 95.5mph, and its official ceiling, exceeded in this case, was 9,600ft. Its manoeuvrability is shown by the fact that it is recorded that a student pilot at Killingholme was reprimanded for 'not flying by the book' when he looped an F.2A over the station!

A second Zeppelin contact was made by Lieutenant Robinson and Ensign Hodges, of the US Navy, again in N4291, on 30th May and they engaged it for ten minutes; no damage was observed but the Zeppelin jettisoned its bombs and some fuel to gain height so that its attack was aborted. There was better luck for the anti-submarine

patrols, with one probable sinking by a Curtiss H-12b on 9th July 1918, another by the indefatigable Captain Munday who saw 'oil and bubbles' after an attack 15 miles east of Spurn on 8th June 1918, and three other attacks by F.2As during 1918. In addition the US Navy, after taking over Killingholme Air Station, made one attack off Scarborough on 20th July and claimed U156 as sunk after an attack by a Short 320 floatplane on 25th September. These were some of the out-of-the-ordinary events from the 540 patrols flown from Killingholme in the period February to November 1918. When the Royal Air Force (RAF) was formed from the RNAS and the RFC on 1st April 1918, the flying boats became 320, 321 and 322 Flights, RAF, but were disbanded when the US Navy took over in July.

Whilst at Killingholme the Americans had a plan, vaguely reminiscent of HMS *Killingholme*, whereby flying boats would be loaded on to lighters which would then be towed across the North Sea to a position off the north German coast; here the flying boats would be lowered into the sea, take off and bomb German naval targets, land back on the sea and be hoisted aboard the lighters for the trip home. Although this plan never came to fruition, lighters were used to carry RAF Sopwith Camel fighters from Harwich to attack Zeppelin sheds in Germany later in 1918.

One of Killingholme's Felixstowe F.2As, N4465, showing its open cockpit (most were covered) and nose gun position; the midships position is less visible, just behind the lower wing. The black and white stripes on the nose are an example of one of many colourful schemes carried by North Sea patrol flying boats, to aid their recovery if force-landed on the sea.
P H T Green

When the US Navy left Killingholme in January 1919, the Station housed the cadres of 228 Squadron (Curtiss H-12s) and 249 Squadron (Short 184s). This continued until October 1919, after which it became a stores depot until closure in 1920. So ended the career of a little-known base which had its fair share of 'alarms and excursions!'. Today, little remains at the site, but one of the hangars now forms part of Grimsby's bus garage.

When the RAF was formed on 1st April 1918, Killingholme came under the control of 18 Group whose HQ was at Birmingham, but in June 1918 this moved to North Killingholme rectory which, to avoid confusion with the Air Station, was called Habrough; renamed 18 (Operations) Group in August, then 18 (Naval) Group in June 1919, the HQ finally disbanded in October 1919.

Just down the coast at Immingham the RNAS had established 8 Kite Balloon Section

(KBS) in late 1917, on the docks 'conveniently near the destroyers' anchorage'. Kite balloons were similar to the RFC's observation balloons used on the Western Front, having a wicker basket slung beneath for the crew; their naval use was for trailing from escort ships, where from 3,000ft the

horizon visible was 63 miles in clear weather, and the observer watched for mines, torpedo tracks, submarines and, if necessary, spotted for the ships' gunners. Balloons from 8 KBS equipped the Humber-based escorts which took the convoys up to North Queensferry or Scapa Flow, and one of its observers spotted a mine ten feet below the surface in July 1918. Otherwise Immingham balloons had no great claim to fame, although kite balloons were responsible for the sinking of two U-boats during World War One. From 1st April 1918 Immingham, like all other RNAS stations, became part of the RAF and was retitled 8 Balloon Station.

The RNAS had other 'stone frigates' in Lincolnshire. During 1915 Rear-Admiral Vaughan-Lee put forward a plan to centralise RNAS pilot training on aeroplanes,

balloons and airships. A site at Cranwell was selected for three reasons: it had lots of room for expansion, newly qualified pilots could be posted easily to the RNAS east coast air stations and there were no outstanding natural features which would act as guides to enemy raiders. An advance party arrived on the 3,000-acre site in December 1915 and the RNAS Training Establishment, part of HMS *Daedalus*, opened on 1st April 1916, the first Commandant being Commander Godfrey Paine RN. It was an enormous camp, even by today's standards, with two airfields, one north and one south of the camp itself. On the northern edge of North Aerodrome was the Airship Station, the first shed for a kite balloon being completed in March 1916. The station was still having many new buildings added and conditions were primitive. In the

Daedalus magazine *Piloteer* it was suggested that 'In view of the wholesale roadway and pathway improvements on the Station, a selected area of the true, original, MUD we have known and endured should be preserved and perpetuated in a framework of glass'.

So large was Cranwell that a single track railway was built from the main line at Sleaford; it was completed in 1917 and used by two locomotives, built by Manning Wardle. The railway station is now the main guardroom, but the line was not finally removed until 1957, by which time a diesel locomotive was working it. Perhaps the railway helped to alleviate the problems of the sailor who wrote a lament sold on postcards at Cranwell in 1916, the first verse of which ran as follows:

'There's an isolated, desolated spot I'd like to mention,
Where all you hear is "stand at ease", "quick march",
"slope arms", "attention".
    'It's miles away from anywhere, by jove it's a rum 'un,
A man lived there for 50 years and never saw a woman.'

Be that as it may, King George V and Queen Mary visited the camp in July 1916. Apart from the flying training there was also an Electrical and Wireless School, a Boys' Training Wing and a Physical Training School. The large influx of sailors had the expected effect on surrounding Lincolnshire and *Piloteer* recorded the first

RNAS wedding at Sleaford when, on 16th June 1917, CPO 'Taff' Gibbons married an unnamed bride at Quarrington Church and the happy couple were towed through the streets by a party of petty officers.

Naval airmen would have done their basic flying at either Hendon or Chingford before moving to Cranwell for what we would now call 'advanced' training. Sub-Flight Lieutenant Rochford subsequently described the training he received in his autobiography (*I Chose the Sky*; Kimber, 1977):

'The day after my arrival I reported to Flight Lieutenant A R Cox who was in charge of the Avro Flight on the North Aerodrome. Although I had already flown solo for nearly two hours on the Avros at Chingford, Cox took me up for a dual control flight to satisfy himself that I was competent. We landed after 25 minutes in the air and two days later I made three solo flights. After a further five flights, on one of which I made a spiral descent from 5,000 feet, I was transferred to the Curtiss Flight commanded by Flight Lieutenant R B Munday on the South Aerodrome... towards the end of August, Munday took me up one evening for three short flights and on the third one we practised landing in a field adjoining the aerodrome. Two days later, following some further circuits and landings with Munday, I was allowed to fly the Curtiss solo for the first time.'

Rochford was then moved to the BE.2c Flight and after familiarising himself with the type

'I flew my first cross-country, a compass and map-reading course, Horncastle, Skegness and Frieston, landing at the aerodrome at Frieston, and later returning direct to Cranwell. The following day, in the morning, I made another cross-country flight to Bourne, Sutton Bridge, Boston and back to Cranwell'.

The last hurdle was training on the Bristol Scout, a fighter which had been replaced in France by more modern types, and then Rochford received his coveted 'Wings'.

Airship pilots and 'balloonatics' followed a different path, doing their basic flying on engineless balloons at Wormwood Scrubs and undertaking navigational and gunnery training before being posted to Cranwell. The common perception of World War One airships is of the German Zeppelin but it is a lesser known fact that the RNAS also made great use of airships, though for different duties, being used for anti-submarine work where their endurance of 4–20 hours, according to type, was extremely useful.

The first RNAS patrol airship stations opened in 1912 and by 1915 they were being erected all around the coast, more particularly in the north and west as the airships were very vulnerable to attacks by enemy aircraft over the North Sea. No operational airship stations were built in Lincolnshire, the nearest being at Howden, just north of the Humber, but Cranwell was their training base, and was also responsible for patrolling the Wash – not many submarines were found! British airships were mainly 'non-rigid', i.e. they were gas-filled envelopes without the metal framework of the Zeppelins; in the early Sea Scout classes, the three crew were carried in old aircraft fuselages suspended beneath the envelope but the Coastal and North Sea classes which came into service in 1917–18 had enclosed gondolas for crews of up to ten.

Some rigid (Zeppelin-like) airships were also built for the RNAS though these were not very successful and saw little operational use. However, crews for them needed to be trained and a very large shed (700ft long, 150ft wide and 100ft high) at Cranwell came into use in June 1917. Eventually there were two of these large sheds and three smaller ones at Cranwell, the based rigid being the R25.

The training airships at Cranwell numbered about 11, mostly of the S.S. Sea Scout

King George V (front left) and Queen Mary visit the RNAS Training Establishment, Cranwell, on 20th July 1916. The party is walking across the railway line to the airship station and the gap between the sheds is the present-day Lighter-than-Air Road. RAF Cranwell, via P H T Green

Although serving with the RNAS at Cranwell, Avro 504A 2930 was originally an RFC aircraft, fitted with a finless rudder; the RNAS converted it to 504B standard (their version of the 504) by adding the fin of 3307, a 504B which was written off at RNAS Redcar in June 1916. D S Glover via P H T Green

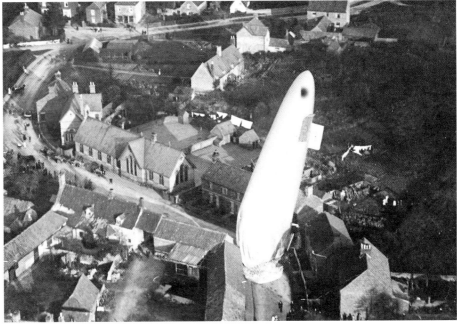

Class; single-engined with an aircraft fuselage for the crew, who had four hours of instruction before going solo on their unwieldy craft and then undertaking intensive flying. Even crashes were usually fairly gentle affairs, one such being S.S. 39 which nosed into the main street at Thurlby, near Bourne, whilst on its way to Cranwell from Wormwood Scrubs in November 1916. S.S. 39 proved something of a 'rogue' as she force-landed in a tree in May 1917 and then in July broke away from her handling party whilst landing at Cranwell; the CO of the Airship Wing, Wing Commander Waterlow, and two others of the party did not let go of the ropes in time and were carried aloft, eventually falling to their deaths. Wing Commander Waterlow is buried at Leasingham. Generally speaking, though, the airships were very safe, only 46 crew being killed in World War One.

Over 200 airships served with the RNAS and more than proved their worth as no surface ships were sunk whilst being escorted by an airship. Despite this there was no place for the non-rigids in the post-war RAF and they quickly disappeared, Cranwell's airship site having been demolished by the mid-1920s and being used subsequently for Officer's Married Quarters, reached via 'Lighter-than-Air Rd'.

Aeroplane pilots underwent a further stage of training before leaving Lincolnshire and that was to turn them into military pilots, as Sub-Flight Lieutenant Rochford recalled in his autobiography:

'From Cranwell I attended a short course at the bombing and gunnery school at Frieston where Flight Lieutenant Morrison was the CO. This was a small RNAS Station under the control of Cranwell and was situated at the mouth of the Wash, the bombing being carried out in BE.2cs on its large area of sandy beach. There were three stages in the bombing course: first, flying over the mirror; secondly, dropping dummy bombs; thirdly, dropping live bombs. The gunnery course was entirely on ground ranges.' (Ibid)

Frieston was inspected in early 1917 and its training found to be unsatisfactory; a new syllabus was drawn up and adopted and this gave more realism and much better preparation for actual combat. Scout (fighter) pilots performed the following tasks over the mudflats of the Wash:

1. One flight giving four runs over the bomb-dropping mirror at 2–4,000ft.
2. Six runs of camera-gun aiming practice against a kite or other well-defined object, two photos to be taken on each run.
3. One flight firing 100 Lewis gun rounds at a kite.
4. One flight firing 100 Vickers gun rounds in a dive at an aeroplane silhouette.
5. One flight on the Vickers gun clearing jambs – 30 rounds containing seven clearable jambs, the belt to be emptied.
6. A camera-gun flight against another machine, taking 12 photos.

Together these flights totalled three to four hours. Non-scout pilots (i.e. bombing or flying boat) had a different set of exercises:

1. One flight of six runs practising course setting over the mirror at 2–4,000ft.
2. Three flights of 12 runs bomb-dropping over the mirror at 2–4,000ft.
3. One flight of four runs dummy bomb dropping at 800–1,200ft.
4. One flight of four runs 'surprise' dummy bomb dropping – the pilot was not to attack until signalled by Aldis lamp after which he was to attack at once irrespective of the direction of flight.
5. One flight of four runs dropping live bombs at 2–6,000ft.
6. One flight firing 100 rounds from Lewis or Vickers gun at a kite.

Total flying time 4¾ hours.

After these fairly short periods the pilots were considered fit to join a squadron where, no doubt, their CO made sure they had more practice, depending on the ferocity of the air war at that particular time. Several from each course would not have made it that far, because learning to fly aeroplanes was a dangerous business as the following record of fatal crashes at Cranwell, from August 1917 to November 1918, illustrates:

August (2), October (1), December (2), January (2), February (1), March (4), April (2), May (3, including 1 at Frieston), June (2), July (7, including two US Navy), August (5), October (2), November (2); a total of 35. Pilots were not the only ones at risk. A mechanic was killed by walking into a revolving propeller in June 1918.

On 1st April 1918 the RNAS was merged with the RFC to form the RAF. But, as the *Piloteer* observed in its April 1918 issue, this historic event seemed, in the main to pass the affected sailors and soldiers by:

'The first act of the great amalgamation has been witnessed and, really, there was nothing fearfully exciting about it. On the first of April the Flagstaff flew a different pennon, but no mysterious and abrupt transition into khaki had occurred. We were all quite normal – members of the RAF in the habilements (or togs) of the RNAS.'

Things weren't quite that simple, though, as the first party of (ex) RFC Boys found when they arrived at Cranwell from Halton on 6th April. They heard sneers and very uncomplimentary remarks about the RFC, the first encounter of many such incidents that followed, showing the deep feeling of jealousy between the two Services which took some time to iron out and heal.

The Royal Flying Corps

The Zeppelin raids over Britain during 1915, as illustrated in the section on RNAS Killingholme, caused much concern among the civilian population and though by the end of 1916 such attacks were more rare, the slow, unwieldy and highly inflammable 'Zepps' still flew over Britain for as long as eight or nine hours, dropping bombs at random. As Lincolnshire was a favourite entry point, being clearly defined by the Humber and the Wash, it received its share of raids, bombs falling at such diverse places as Humberston, East Halton, Alford, Anderby, Fiskerton, Uffington, Welbourn, Skellingthorpe and Metheringham. One of the worst attacks was a hit on an army billet at Cleethorpes on 1st April 1916, which killed 31 members of the Manchester Regiment.

To counter these sorts of attacks the Government reviewed Britain's air defence organisation. Until this time the RNAS had responsibility for air defence, the RFC being, for the great part, in France supporting the Army, of which it was a part. Under the new organisation the War Office took over air defence (then called Home Defence) from the Admiralty in 1916 and set up a network of aerodromes, anti-aircraft guns, searchlights and observers stretching up the east coast from Kent to Edinburgh. Home Defence aircraft squadrons were formed, initially equipped with aircraft which were obsolescent for service in France. One such unit was 38 Squadron, commanded by Captain A T Harris, which moved its HQ to Melton Mowbray in Leicestershire in September 1916.

The HQs of these Home Defence squadrons were normally situated in a large house in a town, the aircraft being allocated to three Flights, each at its own aerodrome which had to be sited so that its aircraft could cover a section of eastern Britain, overlapping with its neighbours. Apart from this requirement, it was up to the COs to find suitable sites, and the late Marshall of the Royal Air Force Sir Arthur T Harris was kind enough to describe to me, in a letter of 4th August 1979, how he did it:

'I looked for airfield sites partly from the air, partly from maps and partly by car and the simple criteria in those days were to find a field flat enough, big enough and with a reasonable grass surface to be used either as a Squadron or Flight Airfield or an Emergency Landing Ground. In those days the War Office seemed to show a peculiar reluctance in undergoing the expense of removing a few trees or flattening a few hedges and ditches for such purposes so one's choice was somewhat restricted. As an example, I could quote such airfields as Leadenham and Waddington, etc.'

Leadenham was one of 38 Squadron's aerodromes, housing 'C' Flight, with 'A' Flight at Stamford (later called Wittering and thus in Northamptonshire) and 'B' Flight at Buckminster in Leicestershire (the aerodrome for which was just over the border in Lincolnshire). During its time here, 38 Squadron flew BE.12s, BE.2es and FE.2b/ds. Captain Harris was succeeded by Major Twistleton-Wykeham Fiennes just after the squadron moved to Lincolnshire.

To the south 51 Squadron, with its HQ in Norfolk, stationed its most northerly ('B') Flight at Tydd St Mary near Sutton Bridge. To the north 33 Squadron had its 'A' Flight at Brattleby (later called Scampton), 'B' Flight at Kirton-in-Lindsey and 'C' Flight at Elsham; the HQ was in a house called 'The Lawn' in Gainsborough and its aircraft types were generally the same as those of 38 Squadron.

The late Mr Perry Sparkes was 33 Squadron's armoury sergeant, also responsible for ground gunnery training and was stationed in Gainsborough. He recalled operational life on the squadron in a letter to the author in 1978:

'We were under canvas until Christmas when we were stationed in a wing of Gainsborough workhouse (very gruesome!). There was quite a lot of flying done at night but not many Zeppelin alerts. Each Flight was given a certain area to patrol in training. I do not remember any Zeppelins sighted in Lincoln. One night, with one of the very few alerts, an officer pilot with his gunner took an old FE.2 up and crashed before leaving the landing ground; he, the pilot, was burnt to death and his gunner, a young 2nd Lt, sustained a broken collar bone but he followed the pilot to the grave next morning, the pilot being a Jew. We were very well treated by the Gainsborough people, so much so that quite a few of our chaps found wives in and around Gainsborough, myself included. My wife had two brothers, both chemists in the town, but she lived at Kirton, her father being a chemist, N Boon, a well known citizen of North Lincolnshire.

'You query in your letter why was our HQ in Gains-

Winterton Emergency Landing Ground

Eastfield Farm

A
B

To Winterton

440 yards

550 yards

Ermine Street

Measurements are approximate

Winterton Emergency Landing Ground, c.1917.
Mr Fletcher

borough and not at a flight station. The only reason I can account for this was it was much more comfortable and convenient than out on a flight station.'

The squadron's workshops were across the road from the old workhouse (now an Aldi supermarket), in hangars only recently demolished to make way for the local Focus DIY store. Aircraft were towed to and from the workshops to fly from a small field (called Layne's Field) just across the Trent, sometimes also used for operational patrols.

The late Lieutenant Reeves-Bilson, commissioned into the Leicestershire Regiment and transferred to the RFC when serving in France, recalled his time with 'B' Flight 33 Squadron in a letter to the author in 1980:

'[I] was posted to England for night-flying training, firstly to No.1 School of Aerial Gunnery at Hythe and then to Reading for engines, and finally to Kirton-in-Lindsey on FE.2b aircraft. However, on 26th April 1918 my flying career was cut short when, flying with Lieutenant Van Staden, we crashed in flames in FE.2B B407. Poor Van Staden, who had married a Gainsborough girl some three weeks previously, was burned to death; but I must have been thrown clear, as I remember hitting the ground but was picked up some 50 yards away and rushed to the John Coupland Hospital in Gainsborough...

After convalescence, I was put on as an instructor on every subject imaginable, from navigation, gunnery, use of the course and distance aids, up to the use of the Constantinesco interrupter gear (not much use on pusher aircraft), and travelled up and down the airfields from Elsham, Kirton-in-Lindsey, Scampton, Harpswell, Leadenham and Buckminster. Finally, a remarkable coincidence! When living in Devon some years ago, my wife and I were driving into Tiverton and picked up an elderly man who, to my surprise, was wearing an RFC tie. The usual questions elicited the fact that he served in the transport section at Kirton-in-Lindsey and actually drove the ambulance which took me to hospital.'

Mr Bilson queried if his was the crash seen by Mr Sparkes but it seems more likely that this was FE.2b A5656, piloted by Lieutenant Solomon, which crashed on take-off from Gainsborough at 7.56pm on 19th October 1917. The graves of the pilots mentioned are found in Gainsborough Cemetery.

The Flight Stations of the Lincolnshire-based Home Defence squadrons were situated someway inland, thus giving their aircraft the time to take off and climb when Zeppelins were first spotted over the coast. Between them and the coast were situated several small Emergency Landing Grounds which could be used for refuelling or the inevitable forced landings. These were at Anwick, Blyborough, Braceby, Bucknall, Cockthorne, Cuxwold, Gosberton, Greenland Top, Grimsthorpe, Kelstern, Market Deeping, Moorby, New Holland, North Coates, Swinstead, Willoughby Hills and Winterton.

I am indebted to Mr Fletcher of Winterton for the plan of the landing ground there. The L-shape was comprised of 5-gallon drums filled with cotton waste which, when lit at night, showed the landing direction, along the long arm, with the short arm at the upwind end; pilots were instructed to land 100 yards out from this short arm. The limestone circle marked the LG's position and also its centre, and was a feature of all British World War One aerodromes. One hut housed the two or three airmen who manned the LG and the other was the petrol store. (A resident of Market Rasen recalls that when the airmen moved into Cockthorne ELG all the girls of the town went off to see them!). It is still possible to see the L-shapes of some of the ELGs, as at Winterton and Bucknall, and at Winterton it is still called Aerodrome Field.

In May 1918 38 Squadron was sent to France, just after its HQ at Melton Mowbray moved to Buckminster; it was replaced by 90 Squadron with the ubiquitous FE.2b, these being replaced by the Avro 504K (NF) in August 1918, but the squadron subsequently disbanded in June 1919. Another unit to move its HQ to a Flight Station was 33 Squadron, in this case to Kirton-in-Lindsey in June 1918, re-equipping with Bristol Fighters and then Avro 504K (NF)s before the war ended. (It should be noted that, as explained in Lincolnshire Airfields Since 1912 (Midland Counties, 1984), the World War One Kirton-in-Lindsey was situated north of the village, near Manton, and not on the World War Two site.) The squadron then moved again, to Harpswell, then disbanded in June 1919.

In February 1918 the Home Defence squadrons were organised into wings and 48 Home Defence Wing, controlling 33 and 90 Squadrons, was established in Gainsborough in a house called 'North Sandsfield', near the Grammar School. As for 51 Squadron, it received more potent aircraft in the shape of Camels and BE.12bs, before moving south in May 1919.

The full story of the Home Defence operations is told in the standard work on the subject, *The Air Defence of Britain 1914–18* by C Cole and E F Cheesman (Putnam, 1984), but it is interesting to note those occasions on which Lincolnshire RNAS and RFC units were sent up to intercept Zeppelin raids, which were as follows:

15th June 1915
Attack on Tyneside. Two Spinning Jennies from Killingholme.

11th September 1915
Attack on London. One sortie from Killingholme.

30th July 1916
Attack on London. One Sopwith Baby from Killingholme.

31st July 1916
Attack on eastern England. Two Sopwith Babies and one Short 184 from Killingholme.

2nd August 1916
Attack on eastern England. Three Sopwith Babies from Killingholme; one BE.2c and one Bristol Scout from Cranwell.

23rd September 1916
Attack on northern England. One BE.2c from Cranwell.

25th September 1916
Attack on the Midlands. One BE.2c from Cranwell.

1st October 1916
Attack on the Midlands. One BE.12 from 38 Squadron, Leadenham.

27th November 1916
Attack on the Midlands. Two BE.2cs from Cranwell; two BE.12s from 33 Squadron, Kirton (one crashed on take-off); one BE.12 from 33 Squadron, Scampton (crashed on take-off); one BE.2c and one BE.12 (crashed on take-off) from 33 Squadron, Elsham; three BE.2es from 38 Squadron, Leadenham, and one BE.2e from 38 Squadron, Buckminster.

To expand on this particular attack: the BE.12 which managed a safe take-off from Kirton was piloted by Lieutenant Brophy who actually sighted a Zeppelin (probably L21) and chased it from Beverley to Flamborough Head where he abandoned the chase; he was airborne for three hours on this cold November night, flying at heights of between 8,500 and 13,000ft.

23rd May 1917
Attack on northern England. Three Sopwith Babies and two Short 184s from Killingholme.

21st August 1917
Attack on northern England. One Curtiss H-12 from Killingholme; one BE.12, two FE.2b and one FE.2d from 33 Sqn, Scampton; one BE.2c and one FE.2d from 33 Sqn, Kirton; one BE2e and two FE.2b from 33 Sqn, Elsham; two FE.2b and one FE.2d from 33 Sqn, Gainsborough.

24th September 1917
Attack on the Midlands. One BE.2e from Cranwell; two FE.2bs and one FE.2d from 33 Squadron, Scampton; one BE.2e and three FE.2ds from 33 Squadron, Elsham (one crashed and killed observer); one FE.2d from 33 Squadron, Gainsborough; one BE.2e from 38 Squadron, Leadenham; one BE.2e and one FE.2b from 38 Squadron, Buckminster; two FE.2bs from 51 Squadron, Tydd St Mary.

19th October 1917
Attack on northern England. One BE.2e from Cranwell; one BE.2c from Frieston; two FE.2bs and two FE.2ds from 33 Squadron, Elsham; two FE.2ds (one crashed, pilot killed) from 33 Squadron, Gainsborough; two FE.2bs (one force-landed) from 38 Squadron, Leadenham; two FE.2bs from 38 Squadron, Buckminster; two FE.2bs from 51 Squadron, Tydd St Mary.

12th April 1918
Attack on Midlands. One FE.2b and one FE.2d (force-landed) from 33 Squadron, Scampton; one FE.2b from 33 Squadron, Elsham; one FE.2b (crashed at Coventry) from 38 Squadron, Buckminster; two FE.2bs and one FE.2d from 51 Squadron, Tydd St Mary.

August 3rd 1918
Attack on Midlands. One FE.2b from 33 Squadron, Scampton; one FE.2b from 33 Squadron, Kirton.

5th August 1918
Attack on the Midlands (and the last Zeppelin attack). One Bristol F.2b (crashed, pilot killed) from 33 Squadron, Scampton; one FE.2b and two FE.2ds from 33 Squadron, Kirton; two Bristol F.2bs from 33 Squadron, Elsham; one FE.2b from 38 Squadron, Leadenham; one FE.2b from 38 Squadron, Buckminster; two FE.2bs from 51 Squadron, Tydd St Mary.

The Lincolnshire squadrons only saw one or two Zeppelins, and attacked just one, but the courage of the Home Defence pilots should not be underestimated – they went up at night with only very primitive flying instruments and without radio, yet they flew whenever asked, and were so successful that the Zeppelins found it much too costly to operate over Britain after August 1918.

Training
In early 1916 the RFC was greatly expanding; urgently required new squadrons were forming and pilots were needed for these. In addition the RFC was badly in need of replacement pilots as casualties began to mount on the Western Front, owing largely to the appearance of the Fokker Eindecker, a monoplane fitted with a machine gun firing through the propeller arc, meaning that it could be aimed by line of flight. The RFC had no immediate answer to this and the slow two-seater reconnaissance aircraft, mainly BE.2cs, were easy prey. The situation improved in the late spring of 1916 when RFC squadrons equipped with the Airco DH.2s arrived in France, but in July the RFC was thrown into the Battle of the Somme and, when this ended in November, had lost nearly 700 pilots and observers.

Training units and airfields were thus desperately needed and Lincolnshire's open countryside, sparse population and lack of industrial haze soon came to the notice of the airfield planners, as did the Lincoln escarpment – it is no accident that many of the World War One airfields were situated along the Cliff, where the prevailing southwest wind gave added lift to aid take-off. Flying training had, by this stage of the war, progressed to a more formal programme compared with the early days. Trainee pilots were sent to Reserve Squadrons, where they were required to fly a minimum number of 15 hours solo, carry out some night flying and also receive instruction and practice in bombing, air fighting and formation flying.

In November 1916 five of these Reserve Squadrons moved into newly opened airfields in Lincolnshire; 37 Reserve Squadron to Scampton, 44 to Harlaxton, 45 to South Carlton, 47 to Waddington and 49 to Spittlegate (Grantham). The aircraft were a mix-

Another Tydd St Mary conversion, with the front cockpit simply covered over and two Lewis guns for the pilot to operate; the clear view forward and upward afforded by these 'pusher-engined' FEs is plain to see.
Via Chaz Bowyer

E3033 was an Avro 504K of 33 Squadron at Kirton-in-Lindsey (Manton) in 1919. The 504Ks were the last equipment of the Lincolnshire Home Defence squadrons and the true nightfighter conversion was a single-seater with a Lewis gun and extra fuel tank on the upper wing; this aeroplane seems to be a standard two-seater, used for training pilots in night flying. 33 Squadron

ture of Avro 504s, BE.2s, Henri and Maurice Farmans, and Armstrong Whitworth FK3s. In December came a further increase in pilot qualifications when the minimum hours to be flown solo were 18, raised to 20–28 depending on the type of aircraft.

The Lincolnshire Reserve Squadrons came under the control of Northern Group Command at York. In May 1917 it was realised that the title Reserve Squadron was not really appropriate and so they were renamed Training Squadrons. Some of these were posted away from Lincolnshire and replaced by others, but the training remained basically the same until the advent of the methods pioneered by Major Rupert Smith-Barry at the School of Special Flying, Gosport. The casualty rate during training was severe, some 8,000 of the 14,000 British pilots killed during World War One losing their lives during training. This was partly due to bad instruction and Smith-Barry actually trained the instructors so that all gave the same tuition, including how to recover from difficult manoeuvres, such as spinning, from which recovery had previously been largely a matter of luck and instinct. Further improvements were the fitting of voice pipes (the Gosport Tube) so that communication with the pupil was possible, and the gradual standardisation on the Avro 504 trainer.

The airfields too were not always ideal, as evidenced by this memo from the OC 24th Wing to HQ Training Brigade, dated 10.1.17:

'Ref yr "Secret TB/809 dated 3.1.17" I was up at Harlaxton yesterday and am of the opinion that the Aerodrome is not fit to be classed as a Night Landing Aerodrome until the tree stumps on the aerodrome have been removed. Urgent application has been made to the contractors to do this'.

Presumably this had been done by the time Cadet Chapman was at 53 Training Squadron at Harlaxton in November of that year, from where he wrote to his mother, as recorded in *High Endeavour* (J I-Chapman; Leo Cooper, 1993):

'My Dear Mother, Please excuse pencil as I am writing this in bed at 11pm. I have had the most exciting day. In fact I've had my first crash (no one hurt) on that foolproof bus, a DH.6. It happened like this. I asked my instructor if I could take a bus up this morning and he said I had done so long on the DH.6 he would come up with me, sit in the front and give me some forced landings. I took him round for about a quarter of an hour, then he took control and started looking down for fields; all of a sudden he throttled back his engine and shouted to me to land the bus... I spotted what looked like a nice field, spiralled down but overshot it and all of a sudden found we were running into a huge, great tree. I tried to zoom up over it but my engine wouldn't take it so my instructor avoided the tree by making a vertical bank and side slipped on to the ground, hitting it with our left wing first. She went up on her nose and stuck there. All we did was to climb down out of the machine. The damage was two bottom planes, an undercarriage, one or two struts and a prop... It is a most extraordinary thing but I have just realised I've cost the government just about £500 today. Oh how I wish I had it in cash. I must go to sleep now, so cheerio and good night, Ron.'

Not suprisingly, this appears to have rather worried Mrs Chapman as the cadet's next letter shows, though it is doubtful if it would have appeased her worries:

'I don't want you to get upset by that crash of mine, because minor things like that are of everyday occurrence at an aerodrome. I have been extraordinarily lucky not to have had a dozen or more similar ones in the 32 hours I have put in the air. In fact only yesterday a fellow went up in a machine and his engine cut out just above a wood and he landed in a tree with bits of branches sticking through the planes in all directions. The machine stuck up there and it was quite a time before the pilot could get down... needless to say, he wasn't hurt in the slightest.'

A fire on either occasion would have resulted in a different story, but young Chapman's love of flying was not diminished as this letter written in December shows:

'Now I must tell you of 2 hrs 20 mins that I did in the air today. My Flight Commander told me to go on my cross country flight test in a DH.6. Two others started also but one lost his way and had to make a forced landing. We had to report at the aerodrome at South Carlton about five miles north (the far side) of Lincoln and at Spittlegate (Wing HQ) about 3 miles away just outside Grantham. I took the lead and followed the railway line up to Lincoln flying over an RNAS Aerodrome at Cranwell and also Waddington (Freddie's Squadron). From Lincoln I could see South Carlton. I landed there – made a top hole landing – reported and flew back with the other fellow just behind me as far as Grantham where for some unknown reason he left me and lost his way and was not heard of until late tonight. He also had a forced landing. I landed at Spittlegate and reported to Wing and returned to base just in time for lunch at 1. I was in the air for 2 hrs and 40 mins and enjoyed it tremendously. The ground was a mass of white; it was quite calm and brilliant sunshine. I was flying at 3,000 feet and could see for miles and miles. I could see the Great North Road stretching ahead for miles. There was a ground mist over Lincoln and I came down to about 1500 feet and seemed to be about 50 feet above the cathedral spire (sic) but in reality I was more like 1200 feet above it. It was beautifully clear and I traced my whole course on the map as I went along (one hand on the joy-stick and one holding the map). I had a splendid engine which gave me full revs the whole way and did not miss once...'

Cadet Chapman was perhaps fortunate that he was not training in the early part of 1917 when the training squadrons were again under pressure as the Imperial German Air Service gained ascendancy in the air over France and Flanders. In April 1917 the RFC lost 131 aircraft – one third of its strength there – and 316 airmen; not for nothing was this period known as 'Bloody April'. The arrival of the Sopwith Camel, SE.5a and French Spads once more swung the war in the Allies' favour, allowing the training squadrons to once again concentrate on turning out pilots with training that would help them to survive the air fighting. This was in sharp contrast to spring 1917, when pilots were so desperately needed that they were sent to the Western Front with very little flying experience and thus fell victim to the German Albatros scouts. The next period of excessive losses came when the RFC was thrown piecemeal into the battle to stop the German spring offensive in March 1918.

A further reorganisation in the RFC's training structure came in the summer of 1917 when the flying training establishments were redesignated Training Depot Stations (TDS). The purpose of this was to speed up the training process by housing at the TDSs squadrons which would train pilots on aircraft like the Avro, and then teach them to fly operational aircraft as these were delivered to the squadron. The reorganisation also reduced the number of new airfields required, as several TSs moved to each TDS, thus saving essential agricultural land. The Training Depot Stations in Lincolnshire were 34 TDS (Scampton), 39 TDS (Spittlegate), 40 TDS (Harlaxton), 46 TDS (South Carlton) and 48 TDS (Waddington). In addition 59 TDS formed at Scopwick (later called Digby) in September 1918.

On 1st April 1918 the Royal Air Force was formed by amalgamating the RFC and the RNAS, and further TDSs were formed from the RNAS Training Establishment at Cranwell. Initially these were numbered 201, 202 and 213 TDS, but to bring them into line with the titles carried by the former RFC TDSs they were soon changed to 56, 57 and 58 TDS respectively. Cranwell also had a Wireless School, and the armament training school at Frieston became the RAF's 4 School of Aerial Fighting, later 4 Fighting School, responsible for training scout pilots in gunnery and combat techniques. At Harpswell 199 and 200 Squadrons were established to train pilots and observers for the night operations which were now being flown by the Independent Force, RAF, over Germany; they disbanded in June 1919.

Training did have its lighter moments, young pilots being rather foolhardy. At Scampton it is recorded that a favourite trick after take-off was to disappear down the Cliff, thus bringing the crash tender along at full speed. Several airmen already famous, or later to become so, served at the Lincolnshire training airfields. At Scampton, 11 Training Squadron was commanded by Captain Robert Saundby, who was deputy to Air-Marshal Harris at Bomber Command in World War Two. At Grantham, 24 Training Wing was commanded by Lieutenant Colonel Charles Portal, Chief of the Air Staff in World War Two, who married Joan Welby of Denton Manor in July 1919 at Grantham Church. At South Carlton, 23 Training Wing, responsible for 34 and 46 TDSs, was in early 1918 commanded by Lieutenant Colonel Louis Strange, who had earlier gained fame when he was thrown from the cockpit of his spinning Martinsyde

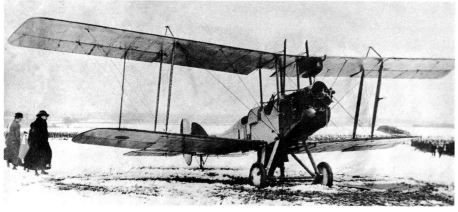

Although not a Harlaxton-based aircraft, this 23rd Training Wing Airco DH.6 at Scampton shows well the angular lines of this basic trainer, the first type to be designed as such. Many parts, including the four wings, were interchangeable, for easy repair after exploits like Cadet Chapman's. Norfolk and Suffolk Aviation Museum, via P H T Green

The BE.2e was widely used by the Lincolnshire training squadrons; this unidentified example was forced down near Apley on 11th April 1917 by a blizzard. The pilot was believed to be an Italian and seems to have made a perfect landing. The event brought out the locals. Via Stewart Scott

S1 over France, hung on to the Lewis gun mounted on the upper wing, flipped the aircraft right way up and landed back in the cockpit! In *Recollections of an Airman* (John Hamilton, 1933), Strange had this to say about life in 23 Training Wing:

'There were not enough pupils or instructors to make good use of the total number of machines on the establishment and yet there were so many machines under repair that we were continually up against a shortage. The workshops were well organised and well run but they had too many jobs to cope with. The instructors too were hopelessly overworked and I said we must have more of them (Strange soon changed matters)... with the result that we made a mighty effort to meet the monthly demand for pilots for overseas work and at the same time keep back a number of promising pupils as future instructors.

Work on a Training Wing was no joke. The write-off of one machine for every 140 hours flying meant the loss of something between 30 and 40 machines a month, in addition to some 70 or 80 minor crashes. In May of 1918 for instance, we had sixteen fatal accidents in the 23rd Wing... but the work had to go on at a still more feverish pace in order to cope with the overseas requirements, for at that time the monthly output of pilots from Home Establishment was well in the neighbourhood of 400.

'There was, however, a lighter side to our strenuous days at Lincoln. The keen competition between ourselves and the neighbouring Wings gave us many opportunities of letting off steam... Early one morning Waddington turned out to find a few nice healthy young ash saplings flourishing on their aerodrome, the implication being, of course, that they grew there because the aero-drome was never used.'

The typical World War One training airfield was a grass square with 2,000ft sides. It had three pairs of hangars (of brick or wood), plus one single, all 180ft x 100ft, and up to 12 Bessoneaux canvas hangars. Air-

Only senior instructors were allowed the privilege of having their aircraft in special colour schemes, and this red and white Camel, 'Dimps III' of No. 4 Fighting School, Frieston, in 1918, was probably the mount of the Chief Instructor. E7232 was a Ruston Proctor built aeroplane. Terry Treadwell

Crashes were everyday occurrences at the Lincolnshire training aerodromes, but were often survivable, as with Lieutenant Lobley, the pilot of Maurice Farman MF.11 'Shorthorn' 1724 at South Carlton, in 1918. Farman was one of the many French manufacturers which supplied aircraft to Britain during World War One and the MF.11 was a popular training type. A T Dickinson via P H T Green

South Carlton aerodrome in March 1918, when it was home to 46 TDS. Hallifers Wood is in the foreground and the present-day A15 Ermine Street runs diagonally across the top of the photo, with Tillbridge Lane (the A1500), also a Roman road, crossing it at right angles. P H T Green

craft of this period were still wooden-framed with linen coverings and thus very susceptible to weather damage if kept in the open. Living quarters, stores, offices and workshops were all in wooden huts. World War One hangars, albeit in a dilapidated state, could still be seen at Bracebridge Heath in 2000, and at South Carlton a heavily rebuilt hangar and some huts still survive.

Aircraft Manufacture

For every pilot killed or wounded during World War One there was an aeroplane written off or badly damaged, and here again Lincolnshire played a large part in providing replacements. Lincoln was, during the war, one of the largest aircraft manufacturing areas in the world and the full story is told by John Walls and Charles Parker in their excellent book *Aircraft made in Lincoln* (SLHA, 2000).

Suffice it to say here that three Lincoln firms, Ruston Proctor, Robey, and Clayton & Shuttleworth, plus Marshalls of Gainsborough, were engaged in aircraft production; only Robey had (unsuccessful) designs of their own and the others, plus Robey subsequently, built other companies' designs under licence. To receive these aircraft into service the RFC established, in 1917, 4 Aircraft Acceptance Park on West Common, Lincoln, later restyled 4 (Lincoln) AAP. It was to here that the manufacturers delivered their aircraft, whereupon they were tested and any Service modifications incorporated. If deemed satisfactory they were then collected by RFC or RNAS pilots and flown to their squadrons. Sub-Flight Lieutenant Rochford again:

'On Boxing Day (1917) Harold Ireland and I went to London by train on our way to Lincoln where we were to collect two Sopwith Camels, built by Clayton & Shuttleworth, from the Acceptance Park. These we were to deliver to RNAS Dover. We stayed overnight in London and the following morning continued our journey by train to Lincoln and arrived at the Acceptance Park in time for some lunch. Afterwards we collected our Camels and took off. We had no maps and knowing the compasses in our machines were far from accurate we decided to follow the railway line towards London.' (Ibid)

Rochford later picked the wrong railway line out of Peterborough and became lost, an incident which illustrates the rudimetary navigation methods being used at that time. As for 4 (Lincoln) AAP, it moved to Robeys' airfield at Bracebridge Heath in 1918 and the sheds which had been erected on the Common were soon dismantled. The living accommodation had been in the racecourse grandstand and a remarkable mural of the RFC's 'Wings', dating from 1917, can still be seen in that building. However 4 (Lincoln) AAP's stay at Bracebridge Heath was short, the unit disbanding in 1920. Bracebridge was, briefly, also the home of 120 Squadron from August to November 1918, with a variety of aircraft.

Aircraft built in Lincoln and Gainsborough included Sopwith 806s, 1½ Strutters, Camels and Triplanes, Royal Aircraft Factory BE.2cs, Handley Page 0/400s and Bristol F.2b Fighters. The very large (for their day) Handley Pages were built by Clayton & Shuttleworth and flown from what became known as Handley Page Field, by their factory on the River Witham just east of Lincoln, where sheds can still be seen.

It might be thought that all examples of an aircraft type, wherever built, would be the same but, according to *The Camel File* (R Sturtivant and G Page; Air Britain, 1993) 'Ruston Proctor Camels were markedly inferior in performance, in particular heavy, sluggish and exceptionally tail heavy'. Be that as it may, the firm produced 1,575 Camels, 28 per cent of the total and the largest number built by any one manufacturer; in the first two weeks of July 1918, for example, it delivered 30 Camels (E1502–E1532). One of these, E1531, was delivered to 4 (Lincoln) AAP on West Common on 13th July, but force-landed near Croydon on 19th August, the cause being 'the front spar of the starboard lower frame failing, followed by a collapse of the leading edge. The timber of the spar was defective, being cross-grained'. Fortunately the pilot was unhurt.

In contrast to this level of production, the first five aircraft built by Ruston-Proctor were BE.2cs which were delivered over the period 5th July to 30th August 1915. It is possible to ascertain these facts by consulting the three hand-written ledgers 'Record of Aeroplanes', held by Ray Hooley, the archivist of Alstom (the successor to Ruston-Proctor). The first volume reveals much fascinating detail, as the following examples illustrate:

'2670. Delivered by rail July 5th, 1915. Inside trailing corners of bottom planes cut away to enable pilot to see vertically downwards. Machine arrived (at destination) with fuselage broken, rebuilt fuselage despatched 27/7/15. Machine completely erected by Wolfe 10/8/15. Engine No. 21943.

'2671. Delivered to aerodrome (West Common) 18/7/15. Flown from Lincoln 28/7/15 3.30pm by Captain Tennant. Pilot reported that Machine held up on account of porous crank case. Left wing down. Mr Ramsey went up. Engine No. 22045.

'2672. Delivered to aerodrome 6/8/15. Flown from Lincoln 13/8/15 at 10.50am by Lieutenant Rowden. Washout in mainplane eliminated for future. Extra rib on elevator embodied. Hole added in bonnet for filler cap. Large landing wheels 700m/m x 100m/m introduced. Pilot reported tail heavy and left wing down. The propeller seams opened up in one lamination during the flight to Farnborough. New propellor despatched. Engine No. 21998.

'2673. Delivered to aerodrome 14/8/15. Flown from Lincoln 17/8/15 at 4.30pm by Lieutenant Porter. Circular devices introduced on top of top planes and sides of fuselage. Also red, white and blue stripes on rudder. Union Jacks omitted. Pilot reported left wing down. Engine No. 21963. [Added in red ink to this entry later was: 'Flown by Lieutenant W. L. Robinson VC on October 3rd 1916 when he brought down at Cuffley the first hostile airship to be destroyed on British soil.']

'2674. Delivered to aerodrome 22/8/15. Flown from Lincoln at 1.20pm by Lieutenant Brown. Pilot reported OK for trim on planes. Engine No. 22037.'

Leefe-Robinson's BE.2c was not the only Ruston-Proctor aircraft with a claim to fame as Camel B7270, flown by Captain Roy Brown, was involved in the shooting down of Baron Von Richtofen on 21st April 1918.

A further back-up RFC/RAF unit in Lincoln

This mural of an RFC Pilot's Brevet was painted in 1917 above the fireplace of the Officer's Mess of No. 4 (Lincoln) AAP, which was under the grandstand of the then Lincoln racecourse on Lincoln's West Common. Remarkably it survived post-war racing, World War Two army occupation, and dereliction, and is now preserved in the Lincoln City Council's Community Centre which occupies the old grandstand. Dave Langlands

A busy scene at No.4 AAP on West Common as a Lincoln-built Camel gets ready for a test flight. A mechanic is about to swing the propeller and two more hold down the tail; in the background is the Lincoln Cliff.
Via Chaz Bowyer

In 1978 this was almost certainly a unique sight, a three-bay hangar erected in 1917–18 at Bracebridge Heath for No.4 AAP when it moved from West Common; the site was used for commercial purposes from 1920 but these hangars, regrettably, were demolished in 2001. One single example remains, together with the bungalows for the workforce on the opposite side of the A15. Lincolnshire Library Services

was 6 (Lincoln) Stores Depot Park, on Longdales Road, which housed large quantities of aircraft spares and other equipment for the surrounding airfields. Now built over, the sports pavilion on the playing fields at the junction of Ravendale Drive may be one of its buildings.

Coastal Patrols

Although Killingholme's flying boats and those of the other seaplane stations, plus the airships, patrolled against U-boats out at sea, by 1918 these were becoming a menace in coastal waters too, especially on the north-east coast. Accordingly, in April, the RAF decided to patrol coastal shipping lanes at 20 minute intervals from land bases adjacent to the coast, and the aircraft chosen was the Airco DH.6, many of which were now surplus to their training role, having

been supplanted by the Avro 504. It was not a particularly suitable aircraft and could only carry light bombs if flown solo without an observer but, despite this, the patrols were a great success, only two vessels being attacked whilst under DH.6 escort.

To operate the patrols new squadrons were formed, each with three or four dispersed Flights and, not unexpectedly, a Flight was allocated to patrol the Humber estuary. The Flight, from 251 Squadron which formed at Seaton Carew, County Durham, in April 1918, took over the ELG at Greenland Top near Keelby; it was later given the identity 505 Flight, 251 Squadron, and its DH6s continued the patrols until the squadron disbanded in January 1919, by which time it had been joined by 404 Flight, 248 Squadron, whose HQ was at Hornsea in Yorkshire. The aircraft of 404 Flight operated

from the former ELG at North Coates until the unit disbanded in March 1919.

As previously mentioned, all the northen Lincolnshire stations by this time were under the control of 18 Group at Habrough, whilst those south of Lincoln came under 12 Group at Cranwell.

Thus Lincolnshire's part in World War One came to an end. Mainly a training area, the county had performed this vital if unglamourous role for two and a half years, while Killingholme, Greenland Top and North Coates had helped to keep enemy U-boats away from the convoys and the Home Defence squadrons had helped to defeat the once dreaded Zeppelins.

Between the Wars

The war-weary British people celebrated the end of 'the war to end wars' and the majority of airmen looked forward to 'demob'. Squadrons flew back from France to disband, some of them to Lincolnshire airfields, and during 1919 the Home Defence squadrons and most of the TDSs disbanded. Even so, there were new casualties, such as Flight Cadet Cecil Reid of Toronto, based at South Carlton, whose aeroplane, on 10th January 1919, was seen 'at eleven o'clock, to be flying at low altitude and suddenly nose-dived into the ground, near the banks of the Witham between St Catherines and Brace-bridge. The pilot was alive when pulled from the wreckage but died shortly afterwards'. (*Lincolnshire Echo*, 10th January 1919)

Flight Cadet Reid was buried with full military honours in Lincoln's Newport cemetery, and his grave was visited on the 80th anniversary of his death by his nephew, Vern Reid, also of Toronto.

By February 1920 all of Lincolnshire came under 3 Group at Spittlegate/Grantham, the units being Spittlegate itself, Scopwick, Frieston, Bracebridge Heath, South Carlton, Lincoln Stores Depot, Cranwell and Killingholme. By the end of the year only Cranwell, Scopwick and Spitalgate remained as active airfields, the others quickly reverting to farmland.

The RAF College

The infant RAF was the subject of covetous glances from generals and admirals anxious to regain control of their respective air arms. Trenchard was reappointed Chief of the Air Staff, having resigned during 1918 because of disagreements with the government of the day, and it was largely owing to his organisation and foresight that the threatened takeover was averted. For example, the generals and admirals suggested that future RAF officers should be trained at Sandhurst or Dartmouth, after which they would have flying training with the Air Force. It was also suggested that the RAF should use the other Services' medical, dental, engineering and other facilities.

Trenchard realised that the RAF must have its own traditions to survive and was faced with the choice, because of limited finance, between establishing a firm training foundation and few operational squadrons, or adopting the 'sharing' suggestion and having more squadrons. He chose the former course and his first step was the foundation of an RAF College on the lines of Dartmouth and Sandhurst, through which would pass the cadets destined for permanent commissions in the RAF. The site chosen for this college was Cranwell, described by Trenchard as 'an ideal place for the pur-

pose, with a large and excellent aerodrome and perfect flying surroundings'.

Trenchard's choice of Cranwell also reflected an additional motive, for its location was well away from the bright lights likely to distract these young men from their studies: 'Marooned in the wilderness, cut off from pastimes they couldn't organise for themselves, they would find life cheaper, healthier and more wholesome.' Career other ranks were to enter the Service through Halton, the technical training school. As Trenchard put it: 'I have laid the foundations of a castle. If nobody builds anything bigger than a cottage on them, it will at least be a very good cottage'.

The first cadet's course began on 5th February 1920 under the command of Air Commodore C A H Longcroft. The aircraft used were Avro 504Ks, with advanced training on DH.9s, Bristol F.2bs, Sopwith Snipes or Vickers Vimys, depending on the pupil's aptitude. Apart from flying there was great emphasis on ground training and the complete course lasted for two years. Until Halton was expanded, some of the first apprentices also trained at Cranwell and one of these was Frank Whittle, jet engine pioneer. His abilities as an engineer were obviously recognised by his instructors, for at the end of his three-year apprenticeship he was one of five awarded a cadetship in the College, in 1926.

In March 1920 the apprentice wing was renamed No 2 School of Technical Training (Boys) and by 1922 some 1,200 young hopefuls were housed in East Camp; but by 1926 Halton had been enlarged sufficiently to cope with these numbers and 2 SofTT closed, with the boys transferring to Halton.

Leslie Burch enlisted in the RAF as a Boy Mechanic in 1923 and later recalled those days in *The Flowerdown Link 1918-1978* (L Burch; Burch, 1980):

'...at Sleaford station we were transferred to "The Cranwell Express" where a diminutive locomotive (Manning Wardle) hauled coaches lacking in comfort with hard wooden seats along the light railway, straining at the gradients and slowing to a walking pace into camp... hundreds of uniformed figures assembled to

The crowded fitters' workshop at Cranwell, c.1919, gives some idea of the size of the station and, indeed, the size of the RAF as it began to run-down. RAF Cranwell

THE GATEWAY TO A BETTER LIFE

take a look at the assortment of newcomers and perhaps to greet them. The most disturbing thing was that they were all of mixed uniforms, khaki jackets and blue trousers or vice versa, or some all khaki... we were escorted along and through great ugly barrack blocks until our destination was reached, U2, a vast dormitory with fifty beds which were allocated by a leading boy... Later we were escorted to a building for medical inspection where my modesty was affronted by the crisp order to get my clothes off.'

[After successfully passing the medical] 'there followed the attestation, the swearing in, and I found myself standing at a small table under an electric light swearing allegiance to my King and Country and being prepared, if called upon, to fly in a kite, balloon, airship, aeroplane or seaplane or other such device without question. And so on 11 September 1923 I became a member of the 4th Entry of Boy Mechanics of His Majesty's Royal Air Force'.

This was not the end of boys' training at Cranwell however, as in September 1929, the Electrical and Wireless School moved up from Flowerdown, near Winchester, with the task of training boy entrants in these important roles. In the 1930s Westland Wallace and Vickers Valentia 'flying classrooms' were in use, being contacted by W/T from trainee wireless operators frantically tapping away from a series of small brick huts situated along the Cranwell railway line between the camp and the village.

As the RAF expanded in the 1930s, the school also started to train men recruits. As many as 3,000 men and boys were there, causing intense pressure on the camp, before further schools began to open, with the result that Cranwell became, in 1938, No.1 Electrical and Wireless School. A further unit on the camp was an RAF Hospital, serving the RAF camps in the area; and an essential part of the scene, vital to the splendid passing-out parades of officer cadets and apprentices, was the RAF College Band, formed in 1920. For many years this and the RAF Central Band at Uxbridge were the only two professional bands in the RAF. It is still in being in 2004.

The RAF Cadet College, as it was known until 1929, created great interest among foreign visitors as it was the first college in the world to train officers for permanent commissions in an air force. Flying took place from the South Aerodrome and in 1923 the aircraft line-up was as follows:
'A' Flight

Avro 504Ks (white wheels)
'B' Flight
Bristol F.2bs (blue wheels)
'C' Flight
Avro 504Ks (red wheels)
'D' Flight
Bristol F.2bs (black/white quartered wheels).

Each aircraft also carried its flight letter and aircraft number on its engine cowling.

Apart from flying there were also many other things to be learnt, including the workings of the internal combustion engine. To encourage interest in this subject each cadet was issued with a war-surplus P&M motorbike, which he was expected to keep in working order, with free oil and petrol issued for this purpose. The practice ceased when the Press publicised it as 'wasteful expenditure', which perhaps did the RAF a favour as more cadets were injured motorcycling than flying!

T E Lawrence (of Arabia) joined the RAF after World War One under the pseudonym of Aircraftsman Ross but was discharged

later and then joined the Royal Tank Corps. However, the RAF held more appeal for him and on 24th August 1925, as AC2 Shaw, he arrived at Cranwell, posted to 'B' Flight. Lawrence recalled his days at Cranwell with obvious affection in an autobiographical account of his time in the RAF (*The Mint*: Cape, 1955; quotations by permission of A W Lawrence):

'our hangar shelters a calm crescent of tarmac and grass and its open mouth is a veritable suntrap. Through the afternoon eight of us lay there waiting for a kite which had gone away south... and was overdue. Wonderful, to have it for our duty to do nothing but wait hour after hour in the warm sunshine, looking out southward'.

On another occasion Lawrence describes how, on his motorbike, he raced a Bristol Fighter

'from Whitewash Villas, our neighbour aerodrome [presumably Digby] along the Sleaford to Lincoln road. An approaching car pulled nearly into the ditch at the

Not many photos of ground training come to light so this training rig for the Automatic Pilot System (i.e. 'George'), at Cranwell's Electrical and Wireless School in 1937, is particularly interesting. P H T Green

A smart line-up of Avro 504K basic trainers and their instuctors, pupils and groundcrew, Cranwell, c1923. RAF Cranwell

A Bristol F.2b Type J (DC), alias a 'Biff', of 'D' Flight (signified by the black and white wheels), RAF College, basks in the sun at Cranwell, c.1929, when the 'Brisfit' (another nickname) was nearing the end of its long service with the RAF. P H T Green

Opposite page:

Siskin III (Dual Control) advanced trainers at Cranwell in the early 1930s; note the mouthpiece of the Gosport Tube intercom system protuding into the rear cockpit, a sure cause of facial injury in the event of a bad landing. RAF Cranwell

Cranwell's large airfield could support the long take-off run required by fuel-laden aircraft attempting to break the World Long-distance Flight Record. Fairey Long-range Monoplane J9479, seen here, was especially designed for this purpose and made the first non-stop UK – India flight of 4,130 miles, in April 1929. Later that year, on its way to South Africa, it crashed in Tunisia, killing its crew. RAF Cranwell, via P H T Green

sight of our race. The Bif was zooming among the trees and telegraph poles, with my scurrying spot only eight yards ahead... A long mile before the first houses I closed down and coasted to the crossroads by the hospital. Bif caught up, banked, climbed and turned for home, waving to me for as long as he was in sight'.

Flying was a more carefree occupation in those days!

By the early 1930s the Junior Term flew Avro 504Ns, the Senior Term having Armstrong Whitworth Siskins for those cadets destined for fighters and Atlases for the prospective bomber pilots. The Siskin was notoriously difficult to land because of its high angle of attack, resulting in several accidents and it was recorded that 'a Siskin lip and a bloody nose were regarded as honourable scars'. In fact, accidents were still fairly common, 56 RAF aircrew being killed in 1930, six of these at Cranwell, though from 1920–30 there were only eight fatalities at the College in 45,000 flying hours.

The South airfield was very large by the standards of the day and was used as the starting point for the RAF's long distance flights, the long take-off run being necessary for aircraft heavily laden with fuel. May 1927 saw a modified Hawker Horsley III bomber, piloted by Flight Lieutenant C R Carr with Flight Lieutenant L E M Gillman as navigator, leave for a non-stop flight to India, but it was forced down in the Persian Gulf after flying 3,420 miles. After this the Air Ministry purchased two Fairey Long-range Monoplanes, specifically designed for a record-breaking attempt on the World's Long-distance Record.

The first Long-range Monoplane, crewed by Squadron Leader A G Jones-Williams and Flight Lieutenant N H Jenkins, left Cranwell on 24th April 1929 and landed at Karachi on 26th April having flown 4,130 miles non-stop in 50 hours, 37 minutes. This aircraft crashed later in the year on a flight to South Africa. The second aircraft, piloted by Squadron Leader O R Gayford with Flight Lieutenant G E Nicholetts as navigator, finally gained the World Record for Britain, leaving Cranwell on 6th February 1933 and arriving at Walvis Bay, South Africa (now Namibia), on the 8th – 5,309 miles and 57 hours, 25 minutes later. France broke this record in August of the same year but three modified Vickers Wellesley Is regained it for Britain in November 1938 when, having left Cranwell for Ismailia in Egypt, they flew non-stop from there to Darwin in Australia – 7,162 miles in 48 hours.

Another interesting event was the building of the Cranwell series of light aircraft designed by Flight Lieutenant Comper and built by the Cranwell Light Aeroplane Club to take part in the Lympne Light Aircraft Trials; Comper later designed the famous Comper Swift record-breaking small biplane. The Napier Gloster, an entry for the 1925 Schneider Trophy race, was test-flown at Cranwell by a Mr Carter, but the under-

carriage unfortunately hit the ground and the machine crashed, seriously injuring its pilot. Training was Cranwell's real purpose, however, and this carried on unabated. Congestion at the main airfield meant that large fields in the neighbourhood were used as 'forced landing grounds', two of these being at Temple Bruer and Wellingore, sometimes called Welbourn.

In 1934 several changes took place; most notably the new College building, designed by James West, was officially opened on 11th October by the Prince of Wales (who had commanded the Boys' Wing in 1918). It was, and is, an impressive building much more befitting its role than the old World War One huts it partially replaced; the revolving light installed in the new tower flashed white every three seconds and was visible for 20 miles on a clear night. More modern aircraft also arrived, Avro Tutors replacing the old 504Ns, Bristol Bulldogs the Siskins and Hawker Harts the Atlases.

The RAF Expansion brought new units to Cranwell; the School of Store Accounting and Storekeeping in 1934 (becoming the Equipment Training School in 1936), a Supplies Depot in 1936, HQ 21 Group Training Command in 1938, and the School of Clerks (Accounting) in 1939. The Empire Air Day of 1937 gave Cranwell a chance to show the Lincolnshire public what the RAF could do and 9,000 people visited the station; the flying programme was opened by a formation of nine Harts and nine Tutors, followed by a message pick-up by a Hawker Audax, crazy flying by two Tutors, aerobatics by two Hawker Furies (which had replaced the Bulldogs), bombing by a Wallace, a flypast by three Valentias of the E & WS, bombing by three Harts, an attack on a towed-target by a Fury, and a massed flypast by 21 aircraft. In addition, the new Bristol Blenheim I bomber and Avro Anson coastal reconnaissance aircraft showed off their paces. A similar display at Waddington was marred by the fatal crash of a Fury from 2 FTS, Digby.

The Flying Training Schools
Having discovered the county's suitability for flying training the RAF decided, after World War One, that all the criteria still

applied and so established two of its six newly-titled Flying Training Schools here, No 3 at Scopwick and No 6 at Spittlegate. Their stay at these locations was short-lived however, 6 FTS, which had never received any aircraft, moving to Manston, Kent, in May 1921, leaving Spittlegate free for the arrival of two bomber squadrons, Lincolnshire's first; they were 39 Squadron (February 1921) and 100 Squadron (February 1922), both equipped with DH.9As but with 100 Squadron's 'D' Flight having Vickers Vimys – the only heavy bombers then based in the UK. 100 Squadron re-equipped with Fairey Fawns before leaving for Eastchurch in August 1924 and 39 Squadron retained it's DH.9As until it too departed in January 1929.

Meanwhile 3 FTS had disbanded at Digby in April 1922, Digby being the new name for Scopwick as the station was being confused with Shotwick in Cheshire which, to make doubly sure, was renamed Sealand. The CO of 3 FTS during its time at Digby was Squadron Leader A T Harris. A lodger unit for a brief period in early 1922 was 2 Squadron, whose 16 Bristol Fighters flew out of Ireland in February; they became lost over Grimsby so the CO landed at Walesby to ask the way and then led his men on to Digby!

Digby, having been vacated by 3 FTS, had a short period of what would become known as 'Care and Maintenance' before, in June 1924, it became the home of 2 FTS which flew in from Duxford, Cambridgeshire. It is interesting to note that by 1930 the RAF's Flying Training Schools were No.1 (Netheravon), No.2 (Digby), No.3 (Spittlegate, reformed there in April 1928), No. 4 (Abu Suier, Egypt) and No .5 (Sealand), once more emphasising Lincolnshire's suitablity for pilot training. At this time the only country strong enough, militarily, to be considered a threat was France and the RAF's operational squadrons were based in southern England to counter this. It was not until the resurgence of Germany as a military power, together with the development of longer-ranged aircraft, that LIncolnshire began to move into the RAF's front line.

Numbers 2 and 3 FTSs received two types of student: university entrants with permanent commissions, and recruits seeking short service commissions; the third type of entry was via Cranwell. Aircraft used for training were the ubiquitous Avro 504K, later replaced by the 504N (known as the Lynx-Avro because of it's change to the Armstrong Siddeley Lynx engine), Snipes, F.2bs, Siskins, DH.9As, Vimys and, later, Atlases.

Several officers later to gain high rank served at Digby in the 1920s; Wing Commander Tedder, later Marshal of the Royal Air Force Lord Tedder, was CO (the station school is named after him), and amongst the instructors were Flight Lieutenant F J Fogarty (later Air Chief Marshal Sir Francis Fogarty), and Flying Officer Frank Whittle, late of Cranwell. Whittle was chosen to take part in the popular 'crazy flying' event at the RAF Pageant at Hendon, the idea being for two pilots to fly as though it were their first time in an aircraft. During the rehearsals at Digby, Whittle was involved in two crashes, luckily escaping serious injury in both. What happened after the second crash is recalled in *Jet* (F Whittle; Muller, 1953):

'I was met by a furious Flight Commander who, his face flushed with rage, sarcastically demanded, "Why don't you take all my bloody aeroplanes into the middle of the aerodrome and set fire to them – its quicker!"'

Whittle later received congratulations on his performance at Hendon from the AOC 23 Group.

2 FTS began to run down during the early 1930s and eventually closed in December 1933. Meanwhile 3 FTS continued to operate at Spittlegate, later renamed Grantham, equipped with similar types of aircraft, but with the addition of the Hawker Tomtit and Bristol Bulldog TM. The RAF Expansion Scheme began to come into effect and a change in the training syllabus took place to cope with the much larger intake of trainee pilots; initial training was undertaken at civilian-manned Elementary and Reserve Flying Training Schools (ERFTS), on de Havilland Tiger Moths, Blackburn B.2s and, later Miles

A line-up of Hawker Harts (nearest the camera) and Hart Trainers (with the modified rear cockpit) at Cranwell in the early 1930s. Originally designed as a bomber, the Hart was a popular training aircraft right up until the early years of World War Two. RAF Cranwell, via P H T Green

Opposite page:

A charming photo of the varied aircraft types in service with 3 FTS, Grantham, in 1932. Leading the formation is the School's newest addition, a Tiger Moth I, K2573; on its right is an uncowled Tutor K2508, and on its right an Atlas TM, either K2520 or K2523. In the foreground is Siskin III (DC) J9236 and on its right is Tomtit K1779. Group Captain Howie

Silver-doped K2508, a Tutor basic trainer of 3 FTS; the Tutor was the standard RAF trainer from 1932 until World War Two, and was powered by an Armstrong-Siddeley Lynx radial engine usually, but not in this case, cowled. Group Captain Howie

Magisters. One of the ERFTS, No 25, was formed at Grimsby Airport in June 1938, but disbanded when World War Two started.

At the ERFTS pilots learnt the basics of flying and then came to an RAF FTS for advanced flying and instruction in Service matters, after which they were awarded their 'Wings', if successful. The course lasted for a very busy year. At Grantham (as Spittlegate was now known) in the mid-1930s, there were 15 flying instructors plus ground instructors, and each course had some 30 students (one third of whom were non-commissioned). The course was split equally into ground and flying instruction, and after starting the day with drill and PT, half the course flew in the morning, weather permitting, whilst the other had instruction on administration, navigation, armament, engines, discipline, meteorology, RAF history and organisation, rigging, wireless and aeronautical theory. After lunch they

swopped over and, to gain their 'Wings', each pilot had to successfully complete the following: four cross-country flights of not less than an hour to a point not less than 60 miles away, one of which was Sealand; climb to 15,000ft and stay there for 30 minutes; fly in cloud and 'rough' weather; make four 'forced landings' at the neighbouring forced landing grounds (Coleby, Wellingore, Nocton and Temple Bruer); perform aerobatics; and carry a passenger (normally one of the other students).

By this time the aircraft in use were Hawker Hart Trainers and Furies. Sport was mandatory on Wednesday and Saturday afternoons and at the end of the course those who passed out were posted to operational squadrons where they learnt more about military flying. Pilots passing out at this time were to bear the brunt of flying on operations early in World War Two and of the 33 students on the course which started in September 1935 only eight survived the war, including one Robert Stanford-Tuck. As for 2 FTS, which reopened in October 1934 at Digby owing to the demand for pilots generated by the RAF's expansion, it was now commanded by Group Captain T Leigh-Mallory (later Air Chief Marshal Sir Trafford Leigh-Mallory), while a star of the station rugger team was Flight Lieutenant George Beamish, who rose to the rank of Air Marshal.

By 1937 the RAF expansion was taking effect and the threat was plain to see – Hitler's Germany across the North Sea. Lincolnshire was therefore in the front line and airfields were needed for operational squadrons; consequently 3 FTS moved to a new airfield at South Cerney in Gloucestershire and 2 FTS, a month later, followed it south to Brize Norton in Oxfordshire. Flying training was not finished at Grantham however as, after a spell of just over a year as a bomber station, 12 FTS moved in to the airfield as one of four new FTSs opened during 1938.

FTS courses now lasted for only 22 weeks as the need for new pilots grew more urgent; but equally urgent was the need for more modern training aircraft: the British aircraft manufacturing industry was concentrating on building bombers and fighters and the only advanced single-engined trainer in production was the Miles Master, which could not be manufactured quickly enough to meet demand. The Air Ministry therefore sent a purchasing commission to the USA and there they ordered Lockheed Hudson reconnaissance bombers and some training types, chief amongst which was the North American Harvard. The Harvard was an ideal type for training pilots destined for fighters as it had such modern refinements as a retractable undercarriage, flaps, a variable-pitch propeller and a fair performance. It served with the RAF from 1938 to 1957 and 12 FTS was the first unit to use it, the residents of Grantham and the surrounding area soon being made aware of its presence thanks to its notoriously raucous engine sound, actually caused by the propeller tips going supersonic. However, the Harvard's time at Grantham was short as 12 FTS became a 'twin-engined' unit in 1939, and re-equipped with the Avro Anson.

Armament Training

The flying training establishments in Lincolnshire were aimed at turning out pilots who were also trained in elementary navigation, there being no navigators as such in the RAF in the 1920s and early 1930s. Air gunners were squadron groundcrew who volunteered for flying in addition to their 'day job'; training was required for these and once more Lincolnshire's geographical features made it the RAF's choice – this time for the mudflats of the Wash and the large sandy beaches of the North Sea coast. Quite simply, the RAF needed somewhere it could drop bombs and fire machine guns at targets without risk to civilians and in 1926–27 three Armament Practice Camps were

opened, at Catfoss in the East Riding, and at North Coates Fitties and Sutton Bridge in Lincolnshire. To these three camps, each year, came all home-based squadrons of the RAF and Fleet Air Arm for bombing and gunnery training.

The range for North Coates was on the sands at Donna Nook and that for Sutton Bridge on the mud near Holbeach St Matthew. At Donna Nook, in the early thirties, were three bombing targets, one of which could be illuminated at night, and ten gunnery targets. Two squadrons were detached at any one time to North Coates for approximately a month, and there was a Station Flight of Fairey Gordons which towed drogues for air-to-air gunnery. The APCs were open only during the summer months – Sutton Bridge, for example, generally operated from March to October/November, and was not officially placed on a permanent basis until March 1936.

In *High Endeavour* (J I-Chapman; Leo Cooper, 1993), Pilot Officer Chapman

Below: *Summer camp! North Coates Armament Practice camp basks in the sun, with a squadron of Fairey IIIfs or Gordons parked in front of the canvas hangars, c.1933.* P H T Green

Opposite page:

Not the Hyderabad flown by Flying Officer Chapman but a Hyderabad nevertheless, belonging to 503 (County of Lincoln) Squadron, and flying past the county's greatest landmark, c.1928. P H T Green

Siskin IIIa of 56 (Fighter) Squadron at Sutton Bridge for gunnery training in the summer of 1930; note the canvas hangar on the right. The Siskin ws the RAF's main fighter during the late 1920s and early 1930s. J A Richardson

remembers an unfortunate incident involving a Handley Page Hyderabad heavy bomber in 1926:

'I had every pilot's love for low flying and this stretch of sand (Donna Nook) was a constant temptation to which I often succumbed. One morning I was haring along the beach at nought feet and about 150 miles per hour without proper heed to what I was doing. The result was that I hit the ground a glancing blow with my undercarriage and bent it rather badly. Having bounced back into the air I was forced to do some quick thinking. A crash landing of some sort was now inevitable and it was beyond the resources of the Squadron to repair a damaged aircraft of this size. I had achieved what the manuals call a "Maker's rebuild".'

Chapman flew the damaged aircraft back to his home base of Bircham Newton where he crash landed 'ignominiously'.

By 1937 it was becoming evident that the new generation of RAF aircraft would require specialised aircrew other than pilots, and the observer's flying badge, last seen in World War One, was re-introduced. Groundcrew airmen had been receiving Observer training, to qualify them for part-time flying duties, since 1934, and an Air Observer School (AOS) opened at North Coates in January 1936, where a two-month course on bombing and gunnery was undertaken alongside the activities of 2 Armament Training School (ATS), the new title of the APC. 2 ATS and the AOS merged in 1937 to become 2 Air Armament School (AAS) and this in turn became 1 AOS in March, leaving for Wales on the outbreak of war. Sutton Bridge became 3 ATS, which also moved to safer territory in September 1939.

A third Lincolnshire station heavily involved in armament training was Manby, which opened in August 1938 as 1 AAS; it ran courses for armament officers, air gunners, bomb aimers, armourers and instructors, using a variety of aircraft such as Fairey Battles, Westland Wallaces and Hawker Hinds and Furies. The bombing and gunnery range at Theddlethorpe, opened in 1935, was taken over by Manby. The station was getting into its stride by September 1939 and, unlike the units at North Coates and Sutton Bridge, 1 AAS remained *in situ*.

Recruit Training

There were, of course, many more airmen in ground trades than there were aircrew and they too needed training, their sheer numbers during the expansion period presenting the RAF with the problem of how and where to train them. No 10 Recruits Sub-Depot opened at Scampton in the late 1930s. Mr M Applegarth of Leeds, along with 199 other recruits, arrived there after Attestation at West Drayton, having been met at St Mark's railway station by a Warrant Officer Fairey and a number of corporals. Then, as Mr Applegarth recalled in a letter to the author: 'We were quickly made to understand that discipline was of paramount importance'.

At Scampton the men were divided into squads of 30 and billeted in huts by the side of the parade ground, this becoming well known to them during their subsequent periods of 'square-bashing'. The recruits were segregated from the 'proper airmen' of 49 and 83 Squadrons, having their own cookhouse and canteen, and the punishment for looking up if the Handley Page Hampdens flew low over the square was an extra drill period! However, Mr Applegarth managed to get a flight in an old Vickers Virginia, which did go some way to compensate for all the drill. The segregation was relaxed when an IRA threat was countered by the recruits doing guard duty with squadron personnel, patrolling the bomb dump.

Whilst undertaking such a patrol with a 49 Squadron AC1 air gunner, Mr Applegarth was let into some of the secrets of a Hampden gunner's existence: the air gunner manned the under-gun position in the fuselage and when the grass was wet became soaked on take-off as spray came into the turret. The single Vickers K machine gun had a recoil which tended to jam the ball-bearings on which it traversed, and if this happened the gun could not be moved sideways; Mr Applegarth noted that the air gunner was also

'well aware of the problem which would accrue in the event of the pilot being incapacitated. I often wonder if he survived. I have since realised that John Hannah and Guy Gibson would be with 83 at this time, and it became apparent that 83 was "The" squadron on the station'.

After leaving Scampton Mr Applegarth was posted to Norfolk.

Operational Flying

In 1925, in an attempt to strengthen the RAF, the Auxiliary Air Force (AuxAF) was formed to support the regular squadrons: the AuxAF squadrons were based near large centres of population and were initially light bomber units. Alongside the AuxAF units were formed the Special Reserve squadrons, which differed from the auxiliaries in having one Flight composed of regular officers and airmen and the other of 'weekend' airmen, whilst the auxiliaries were manned largely by the civilian volunteers. The Squadron CO was also a regular officer, again unlike the AuxAF. Thus the Special Reserve, or Cadre Squadrons as they were called, were much more like Regular Air Force than part-time volunteer, although officially reserve units, and were distinguished by being numbered in the 500 series whereas the AuxAF squadrons were in the 600 range. The second Cadre unit to form was 503 Squadron, in

Left: This is the Fawn III light bomber in which Pilot Officer Allison, AuxAF, had his first flight with 503 Squadron. The Fawn was not a distinguished design and only a few squadrons flew it; of note are the two fuel tanks on the upper wing. John Walls

Opposite page:

A nice shot of two of 503 (County of Lincoln) Squadron's Hyderabads, showing the uncowled Napier Lion engines that distinguished it from its successor the Hinaidi, which had cowled Bristol Jupiters; note also the underwing bomb racks. J8319, the nearest aircraft, took off from Waddington in March 1930 with the control column in the rear cockpit locked and crashed, being written off. RAF Waddington, via P H T Green

Equipping many newly formed Lincolnshire bomber squadrons during the 1930s Expansion Period was the Hawker Hind. This example from 50 Squadron at Waddington in 1937 shows the underwing bomb racks and the trough in the fuselage side for a Vickers machine gun; the gunner in the rear cockpit was armed with a Lewis gun. K6741 eventually went to the South African Air Force. Via P H T Green

October 1926 and to house it Waddington (which had retained its buildings and airfield, unlike most of the other World War One stations) was re-opened.

Advertisments for 'weekend volunteers' to man 503 Squadron appeared in the local press and Mr Douglas Allison, born in Lincoln, applied to join it at the Lincoln recruiting office. He asked to be a pilot and was interviewed by three Regular officers who asked him what was the difference between a carburettor and a magneto – providing the correct answer, he was accepted on trial! He was given a trial flight in an Avro 504N and then became the first volunteer to be accepted and commissioned, starting flying training in earnest on 26th March 1927 with a flight in Fairey Fawn III J7980, piloted by Squadron Leader Oxland.

Dual instruction on the Lynx-Avro began on 26th April and continued at weekends and in the evenings until his solo on 31st May, after which he flew 503 Squadron's operational aircraft, the Fawn bomber, training in general flying, forced landings and bombing until his solo on the type in September 1927. When the Fawns were replaced by the much larger, twin-engined Hyderabads, the 503 Squadron pilots went solo on the completely different type after only three hours' instruction, a far cry from the long conversion courses of today. Mr Allison left Lincoln, and 503 Squadron, in 1930 to work abroad, but returned to flying as an instructor at Brough ERFTS in 1937, later commanding 14 EFTS at North Luffenham, Rutland, during World War Two.

Handley Page Hinaidis replaced the Hyderabads until 1935 when 503 Squadron returned to a day-bomber role with Westland Wallaces, replaced a year later by Hawker Harts. The squadron's first CO was Wing Commander Twistleton-Wykeham-Fiennes and in April 1929 the unit was officially named 503 (County of Lincoln) Squadron. Practice bombing was carried out over the airfield, the target being a chalk circle in the centre; 8lb and 11lb smoke bombs were used, the impact being plotted by two quadrants on the ground. The squadron suffered few accidents and only two fatal crashes are recorded.

In May 1937 503 Squadron was joined at Waddington by two new units of the rapidly growing Bomber Command, which had been formed on 14th July 1936 after a restructuring of the RAF. These new squadrons (50 and 110) were initially equipped with biplane bombers until the new types came into service; both units had the Hawker Hind, and a month after their formation 44 and 88 Squadrons formed, also with Hinds, the latter unit staying only a month before leaving for Boscombe Down, Wiltshire.

Back at Waddington, 44 Squadron was the first squadron at the base to receive the long-awaited new equipment when its Bristol Blenheim Is arrived in December 1937, but the other three units entered 1938 still

with their Hinds. More Blenheims soon arrived, this time for 110 Squadron, leaving 50 and 503 Squadrons feeling rather envious of their companion units. The Blenheim was a twin-engined monoplane with enclosed crew positions, gun turret, retractable undercarriage, and a maximum speed of 210mph. The Hind, on the other hand, was little changed from the World War One bombers: a single-engined biplane with open cockpits, the rear one with a Lewis gun, and a maximum speed of 186mph; if war had come with the Munich crisis of 1938 many RAF squadrons would have flown into battle with out-dated aircraft such as this.

However, 503 Squadron was not destined to receive the new equipment; having never attracted as many reserve airmen as the RAF hoped, it disbanded on 1st November 1938, a sad day for its personnel, although those airmen who so wished were transferred to its successor squadron, 616 (South Yorkshire) Squadron, AuxAF, at Doncaster. So Waddington became an all-Regular three squadron station until, under a type rationalisation, 110 Squadron and its Blenheims moved down to Wattisham in Suffolk to join all other Blenheim units in No 2 Group, whilst 44 and 50 Squadrons both re-equipped with Handley Page Hampdens, a type which was to play a significant part in early World War Two operations from Lincolnshire bases. Both 44 and 50 Squadrons were at Waddington when World War Two started.

In the meantime the RAF expansion had meant that additional airfields were needed in eastern England and it was natural for World War One sites to be examined for suitability. Scampton was selected and work began in 1935. There was some local resistance to this and a workmen's hut was burnt down, but by October 1936 the airfield was ready and 9 and 214 Squadrons arrived, both night-bomber units and equipped with biplane Handley Page Heyfords and Vickers Virginias respectively. Much of the accommodation was still under construction so tents were in evidence for the first months. The 'Ginny' as the Virginia was affectionately known, was obsolete, and in January 1937 214 Squadron re-equipped with the Handley Page Harrow, another interim type but at least a monoplane. The Harrow did not see much service in Lincolnshire as 214 Squadron moved to Norfolk to be replaced, in June, by the reformed 148 Squadron with the Hawker Audax, another elderly biplane, soon exchanged for a more modern type, the Vickers Wellesley. When 9 and 148 Squadrons left Scampton in March the two replacement squadrons, 49 and 83, were both Hind-equipped but by September 1939 they were operating Hampdens.

Hemswell was the second new station, built on the World War One site at Harpswell, its squadrons arriving in early 1937, 61 and 144 having Audaxes and Ansons until, in the autumn, Blenheims arrived for 144 with 61 receiving theirs in early 1938. However

the Hampden had been chosen as the type to be operated from Lincolnshire, and the two Hemswell squadrons re-equipped with these in 1939. Grantham, having lost 3 FTS, also became a bomber station, briefly housing 113 and 211 Squadrons with Hinds. During 1938 these two units were replaced by two Fairey Battle squadrons, 106 and 185, but these left in October 1938 and the airfield reverted to a training role, presumably because of its limited size.

The Lincolnshire bomber airfields were controlled by 5 Group HQ, Bomber Command; initially located at Mildenhall, it soon moved to its operational area when, in October 1937, it occupied a large house at the foot of Spitalgate Hill, Grantham, called St Vincents. On the outbreak of war 5 Group was commanded by Air Vice-Marshal A T Harris. One of its air weapon ranges was at Wainfleet, opened in August 1938 on the site of an artillery range used in the 1890s, and the other was at Holbeach.

The fact that Lincolnshire was a part of England near to Germany and suitable for mounting a bombing offensive against that country worked also in reverse. It was in reach of German bombers which would strike at the bomber airfields and also cross the county on their way to the industrial areas of the North Midlands, South Yorkshire and Lancashire. To counter this threat Fighter Command also moved into Lincolnshire, 12 Group establishing two squadrons at Digby in November 1937. Like those of the bomber squadrons their aircraft were elderly, 46 Squadron having Gloster Gauntlet IIs and 73 Squadron Gloster Gladiator Is, both biplanes. These aircraft, doped silver, carried the colourful markings of the between-the-wars fighter squadrons, 46 having a red arrowhead on the fuselage while 73 had a blue and yellow flash. The Munich crisis saw these markings disappear and when the two squadrons got Hurricane Is in 1938 their new mounts sported earth and dark green camouflage.

The airfields opened between 1935 and 1940, planned under the Expansion Scheme, were quite attractive, with brick buildings built to a set design so that as stations appeared very similar, airmen posted from one to another could quickly find their way about. The designs were approved by the Royal Fine Arts Commission and the Society for the Preservation of Rural England was asked for its views. The typical station of this period had a grass airfield with three large hangars which dwarfed the other buildings. The official test for a level surface was to drive a light car over the airfield at 20mph without experiencing 'serious discomfort' while for load-bearing a fully-laden three-tonner was driven slowly across. Barrack blocks were two-storey and married quarters were provided for officers and airmen, with large messes for junior ranks, senior NCOs and officers. Older airfields were usually (but not always) brought up to this standard and examples in Lincolnshire

61 Squadron would have been proud of its new Bristol Blenheim Is, as this smart line-up at Hemswell in 1938 shows; however, they kept them for only just over a year before 5 Group re-equipped with Hampdens, the Blenheims being concentrated with 2 Group in East Anglia. Note the small external bomb carriers under the rear fuselage, the main bomb load being carried internally. MoD H1510 via P H T Green

Just prior to World War Two this Vic of 5 Group's Hampdens fly over the Cathedral, the three towers of which were always a welcome sight to returning bomber crews. John Walls

can be found at Waddington, Scampton, Digby, Hemswell, Manby and Kirton-in-Lind-sey.

By 1939 Lincolnshire had become the home of 11 airfields and the amount of flying generated, together with a large influx of new and inexperienced pilots, created many accidents in the county. Those accidents listed below took place during that year and involved aircraft which were destroyed, not those which were repairable:

22nd Jan   Blenheim I, 61 Sqn, at Hemswell.
23rd Jan   Blenheim I, 144 Sqn, nr Kirton-in-Lindsey.
24th Jan   Wallace II, 3 ATC, landing at Sutton Bridge;
            Blenheim I, 44 Sqn, landing at Waddington.
30th Jan   Blenheim I, 44 Sqn, landing at Waddington.
7th Feb   Tutor I, RAFC, landing at Cranwell.
15th Feb   Blenheim I, 44 Sqn, at North Coates.
17th Feb   Tutor I, RAFC, landing at Cranwell.
24th Feb   Hurricane I, 46 Sqn, landing at Digby.
9th Mar   Hurricane I, 73 Sqn, landing Digby.
10th Mar   Hurricane I, 213 Sqn, 1 mile NW of
            Grantham.
14th Mar   Blenheim I, 110 Sqn, on approach to
            Waddington.
20th Mar   Hampden I, 50 Sqn, Boultham Baths,
            Lincoln.
21st Apr   Hurricane I, 73 Sqn, taking-off from Digby.
2nd May   Hurricane I. 32 Sqn, hit tractor at Sutton
            Bridge.
8th May   Hampden I, 44 Sqn, landing at
            Waddington;
            2 x Audax, RAFC, collided at Stubton.

9th May	Hurricane I, 73 Sqn, on approach to Sutton Bridge; Wallace II, 1 AAS, into sea off Theddlethorpe range.	
7th Jun	Blenheim IF, 29 Sqn, night landing at Sutton Bridge.	
19th Jun	Hurricane I, 46 Sqn, landing at Digby.	
26th Jun	Hart Trainer, 12 FTS, landing at Grantham.	
3rd Jul	Hampden I, 144 Sqn, landing at Hemswell.	
18th Jul	Hampden I, 44 Sqn, at Corby Glen.	
25th Jul	Hurricane I, 73 Sqn, landing at Digby; Blenheim IF, 23 Sqn, collision nr Grantham.	
1st Aug	Hampden I, 49 Sqn, overshot at night at Scampton.	
7th Aug	Hampden I. 83 Sqn, Take-off from Scampton.	
15th Aug	Wallace I, 2 RTS, landing at North Coates.	
16th Aug	Blenheim IF, 25 Sqn, landing at Sutton Bridge.	
24th Aug	Hampden I. 144 Sqn, landing at Hemswell.	
8th Sep	Oxford I, RAFC, at Cranwell.	
9th Sep	Hurricane I, 504 Sqn, at Metheringham.	
20th Sep	Audax, RAFC, take-off from Cranwell; Hart Trainer, RAFC, on approach to Cranwell.	
24th Sep	Harvard I. Grantham Station Flt, spun in at Newton.	
30th Sep	Hind I, Abingdon Station Flt, in fog 2 miles north of Cranwell.	
3rd Oct	Tutor I, RAFC, at Cranwell.	
6th Oct	Audax, 12 FTS, landing at Grantham.	
8th Oct	Blenheim IF, 23 Sqn, bellylanding at Digby.	
10th Oct	Audax, 12 FTS, take-off from Grantham.	
13th Oct	Battle I, 1 AAS, dived in at Theddlethorpe range.	

17th Oct	Hampden I, 50 Sqn, hit hangar at Waddington.
24th Oct	Hind Trainer, RAFC, landing at Cranwell.
27th Oct	Anson I, 608 Sqn, shot down by Hurricane over the Humber.
30th Oct	Hampden I, 83 Sqn, take-off from Scampton.
31st Oct	Hampden I, 50 Sqn, at Branston.
7th Nov	Hart Trainer, RAFC, on approach to Cranwell.
13th Nov	Fury II, 1 AAS, dived in at Theddlethorpe range.
15th Nov	Anson I, 12 FTS, undershot at Grantham.
23rd Nov	Hampden I, 49 Sqn, hit hangar on overshoot at Waddington.
29th Nov	Blenheim IF, 23 Sqn, dived in near Gainsborough; Hart Trainer, RAFC, landing at Welbourn LG.
1st Dec	Tutor I, 219 Sqn, nr Grantham; Tutor I, 219 Sqn, force-landed nr Grantham.
9th Dec	Battle I, 266 Sqn, bellylanding at Sutton Bridge.
13th Dec	Audax, RAFC, night take-off from Cranwell.
18th Dec	Hart Trainer, 12 FTS, night landing at Grantham.
19th Dec	Battle I, 1 AAS, at Cockerington Grange.
31st Dec	Battle I, 1 AAS, undercarriage collapsed at Manby.

As can be seen, most of these accidents occurred on or near an airfield during the tricky operations of taking-off and landing. Worthy of note is the wide variety of aircraft

Although belonging to 73 Squadron at Digby in 1938 these Gloster Gladiator I fighters are not, for reasons unknown, carrying the unit's colourful markings. The Gladiator was the RAF's last biplane fighter and was replaced by Hurricanes and Spitfires, though it acquitted itself well in action during the early years of World War Two. RAF Cranwell via P H T Green

types, both old and new. The number of crashes also indicates the large amount of flying undertaken in this crucial year. Even when the RAF got into its stride during World War Two, many airmen were still killed in accidents before ever seeing the enemy.

Chapter Three

World War Two –
The Early Years 1939-1942

The Bombers

By 1938 it was obvious to most servicemen that a war with Nazi Germany was becoming more and more likely but, although the RAF expansion was well underway, the equipment was often still lacking. No.49 Squadron had reformed at Bircham Newton in Norfolk in 1936 and moved to Scampton on 14th March 1938, flying Hawker Hind light bombers. Tragedy came shortly after the move when two Hinds collided, killing two airmen, but training continued and in April the squadron went to North Coates for armament training followed, a month later, by tactical exercises during which targets in Lancashire, Cheshire and Birmingham were 'attacked'. This intensive training continued in June with affiliation exercises against the very similar Hawker Demon two-seat fighters of 64 Squadron, another fatal crash occurring at Doddington on 19th June.

On 20th September 49 Squadron's first Handley Page Hampden I medium bomber arrived and the unit was heavily involved training on this new type, though it was December before the last Hind departed. By February 1939 the crews were familiar enough with their Hampdens to begin exercises, followed by armament training at Catfoss in Yorkshire and, on 22nd April, 'A' Flight moved up to Evanton in Scotland as an exercise. Five aircraft flew further afield on 25th July, showing the flag over France, and training continued at a high pitch until general mobilisation on 1st September, by which time 49 Squadron had 16 Hampden Is and 15 crews, with five Hampden Is and four Ansons in reserve. At 17:40 hours on the 1st, six Hampdens were detached to Newton in Nottinghamshire, in case of air attack on Scampton, but they returned home the next day.

Also at Scampton was 49 Squadron's sister unit, 83 Squadron, one of whose pilots was later to become Lincolnshire's best-known airman, Flying Officer Guy Gibson; he was on leave in Wales in late August 1939 when on the 31st he received a telegram which simply said 'Return to unit immediately'. What he found once back at base –

'Sunny Scampton we call it because it's in Lincolnshire and one doesn't see much sun up there.' – was recorded in *Enemy Coast Ahead* (G Gibson; Michael Joseph, 1946):

'...complete bedlam reigned... There were tractors driving round the perimeter roads in the sweltering heat, some with long bomb trailers bouncing along behind; others pulling out our Hampdens along cinder tracks far into the country to dispersal points fairly safe from enemy bombs. All round the airfield sandbagged gun emplacements were being put up by aerodrome defence squads, but there were not many guns. Gas officers were running round placing yellow detectors in the right places.'

This scene was being repeated at Waddington and Hemswell, while similar activities took place at Digby, Cranwell, Grantham, Manby, North Coates and Sutton Bridge. The preparations were not to be wasted as on 3rd September Prime Minister Neville Chamberlain addressed the nation and announced that Great Britain was now at war with Germany. This was at 11:00 hours; at 18:15 hours 49 and 83 Squadrons sent eight Hampdens to the Horn Reef Lightship to attempt low-level bombing of the German fleet. They saw nothing however and returned to base at 22:30 hours, Gibson recording that the pilots had never taken off with a full bomb load before! Nine Hampden Is of 44 Squadron at Waddington were sent to the Heligoland Roads at the same time.

The aircraft and personnel of 49 Squadron seemed to spend most of autumn 1939 moving backwards and forwards to Newton, interspersed with practice bombing on the range at Misson in Yorkshire; two aircrew were killed when Anson I N5096 crashed at Ratcliffe, Nottinghamshire on 4th October. However, in late November the situation stabilised somewhat and, in common with the other Lincolnshire units, 49 Squadron settled back into its base at Scampton. It lost Hampden I L4034 and its crew on 23rd November, practising approaches at Waddington, but on 2nd December 'B' Flight flew the squadron's second operation, a sweep over the North Sea, whilst nine aircraft took off to search for the battle cruiser *Deutschland* on the 21st, in company with three aircraft from 83 Squadron and 12 from 44 Squadron. The 24 Hampdens flew along the Norwegian coast to no avail and set course for Lincolnshire, but bad weather resulted in their flying in over the Scottish and Northumbrian coasts where one formation was intercepted by Spitfire Is of 602 Squadron from Drem which shot down L4089 and L4090 of 44 Squadron, mistaking them for German aircraft, despite the Observer Corps in the area and a Hurricane squadron making a correct identification. Such errors in aircraft recognition were to result in many unneccessary deaths during World War Two, and in this case one wireless operator/gunner was killed and one gunner wounded.

Hemswell too was flying these early operations, its first being on 26th September by 144 Squadron, which became the first 5 Group squadron to drop bombs in anger

The day war broke out! This comedian's catchphrase is completely true in this case as these are Waddington's Hampdens dispersed by the A15 on 3rd September 1939. They still seem to be a tempting target! W Baker

when three of its Hampden Is bombed two German destroyers in the Heligoland Bight. However, as can be seen from the above, operations were of a low intensity compared with later in the war, though the Hampdens, Vickers Wellingtons and Armstrong Whitworth Whitleys operating with Bomber Command in 1939 were paving the way for these.

Operations did intensify during 1940 as raids were carried out on docks and shipyards housing invasion barges after Dunkirk. Neither side, at this stage, was bombing civilian targets and severe losses during daylight raids had dictated that Bomber Command now operated almost entirely at night, a policy which remained throughout the war, although daylight raids did increase after 1944. Because the Hampdens were the only aircraft in RAF service during the years 1939–41 able to carry sea mines, they were often employed to sow these in addition to their normal bombing role.

The number of bomber stations in Lincolnshire rose to four when Binbrook opened in June 1940, its first units being 12 and 142 Squadrons equipped with Fairey Battle light bombers, just returned from France where these light bombers had suffered heavy losses during the air offensive against the advancing Germans. (The first Victoria Crosses of World War Two had been awarded, posthumously, to Flying Officer D E Garland and Sergeant T Gray of 12 Squadron for their bravery in pressing home an attack on a bridge over the Albert Canal near Maastricht on 10th May 1940.) Despite the Battle's obvious vulnerability, the fear of invasion was such that the two squadrons took part in attacks on the Channel ports which housed the build-up of German invasion barges.

Binbrook came under the command of 1 Group, Bomber Command, and as the invasion scare receded in the autumn of 1940, 12 and 142 Squadrons re-equipped with Vickers Wellington IIs, the bomber with which 1 Group was to standardize. 1 Group's second Lincolnshire station opened in August 1940 when Swinderby received 300 and 301 Squadrons of the Polish Air Force, the county's first association with these expatriate Europeans, an association which was to last right through the war and led to many Poles settling in Lincolnshire when their homeland was annexed by Russia. Although under RAF command, the Poles had their own uniforms and ranks, and were responsible to the Polish Government-in-Exile in London. Like Binbrook's units, the Poles initially flew Battles, their first operation being to Boulogne on 14th September, but after 85 sorties up to 18th October, they began to receive Wellington Ics. With these they bombed Berlin in February 1941 and gained fame from their frequent mentions in the media, 'Polish squadrons' being immediately identifiable to local residents.

Bad weather affected all five Lincolnshire stations in early 1941 and several were attacked by the Luftwaffe. Coningsby received its first unit in February 1941, this being 106 Squadron with Hampden Is. The Hampden had borne the brunt of all 5 Group operations for 18 hard months, and Waddington was the first station to receive its replacement, the Avro Manchester I; 207 Squadron, formed there on 1st November 1940, becoming the first squadron to operate this twin-engined heavy bomber. The squadron took its Manchesters into action for the first time on 24th February 1941, when six aircraft attacked a German cruiser in Brest naval dockyard. Although German naval ships continued to attract the attention of Bomber Command, the targets were increasingly becoming German cities and

A Handley Page Hampden of 49 Squadron being bombed up at Scampton in readiness for a raid on Germany early in World War Two. The Hampden was very much a Lincolnshire type, being based at several county airfields from 1939 to 1942.

industry, partly in retaliation for the Blitz, partly because the accuracy of navigation and bombing at night demanded large targets.

The initial delight within 207 Squadron at getting the new bomber must have soon turned to disappointment as the Manchester proved to be singularly unsuccessful, plagued as it was by trouble from its under-developed Rolls-Royce Vulture engines throughout its short operational career. In mid-November the squadron moved to Bottesford, Leicestershire (though part of the airfield crossed into Lincolnshire). Later that month, on the 22nd, Pilot Officer Hills took a Manchester for a short visit back to Waddington, an eventful flight described in *Avro Manchester* (R Kirby; Midland Publishing Ltd, 1995):

'For part of the flight they followed the Lincoln to Boston canal [actually the River Witham] which ran alongside a high embankment carrying the Lincoln to London main railway line. The crews at times got a kick out of flying along the canal at the same height as the bank waving to surprised engine drivers as they overtook them at the same level.'

Hills, however, suffered an all too familiar failure in the port engine and, on opening the throttle on the starboard Vulture to gain height, this failed too, meaning an inevitable forced-landing straight ahead:

'By great good fortune there was flat open ground bordering a small tree-lined lake slightly to their left...Hills shouted "Hold on!" to warn the crew, raised his feet from the rudder bars, bracing them on the instrument panel and yanked hard back on the stick just before the aircraft hit the ground. The nose rose sharply and the tail hit the ground first. The severity of the impact resulted in the rear fuselage and tail unit breaking off immediately forward of the crew entry door. The triple fin unit, fortunately unoccupied, tumbled away to come to rest on the edge of the lake.

'Twenty tons of uncontrollable, disintegrating, screeching Manchester slithering on its belly was bearing down on the lake at almost 100mph. The scene in the flooded disused quarry now known as Fiskerton Lake could not have provided a more marked contrast – a fishing match was in progress. Competitors were distributed around its margin and one of the organisers was out on the lake in a flat-bottomed punt. For this group the afternoon epitomised peace, solitude and an escape from warwork.

'In an instant the careering Manchester appeared over the bank and pitched forwards into perhaps 10ft of water, throwing up a massive tidal wave as it did so. Fishermen turned and ran as the wave broke upon the bank, whilst the unfortunate occupant of the punt had a grandstand view before the advancing wall of water swept over his craft, rocking it violently and sending cascades of water over its gunwhales. Within a few seconds the Manchester had settled and the waves were dissipating, leaving the boatman standing unscathed, soaking wet and transfixed with fear ankle-deep in water, his sandwiches bobbing gently around him.'

In this crash the crew suffered only minor injuries and the incident brings a smile to the face of the reader, but many Manchester crews were not so fortunate;-for example, L7310 of 207 Squadron was taken up for an air test from Waddington on 21st June 1941, with Flying Officer Les Syrett and Sqn Ldr

The Hampden's replacement was to be the Avro Manchester and the first squadron to be equipped was 207 Squadron at Waddington, one of whose aircraft, L7284, is seen here. However, the Manchester's engines proved to be very unreliable and only 200 of the type were built, This particular aircraft was one of the lucky ones which survived to be scrapped, but 66% were lost in accidents or on operations.
Avro via P H T Green

Charles Kydd as pilots and Sergeant Arnott as wireless operator, no other crew members being required. Robert Kirby relates what happened next:

'They commenced their take-off run towards the south, parallel to the Sleaford road... which took the aircraft between the old First World War hangars on the south side of the airfield and the bomb dump. L7310 became airborne about in line with the hangars and the bomb dump and had achieved perhaps 150ft above the boundary when the port engine failed...

'It was the single most critical moment of the whole flight. The port airscrew was immediately feathered. Paape [pilot of an already airborne Manchester] saw a wisp of smoke and heard the clipped voice of Kydd, "Returning to base, engine failure." Everyone looked on with bated breath as L7310 fought a battle for precious speed and height. Syrett had 10 degrees of flap on and had retracted the undercart, but as the aircraft was only 5mph above stalling speed he could neither take off the flap nor lower the wheels or even change course. The aircraft was descending almost as fast as it was going forward. Within seconds, Paape and all in radio contact heard Kydd's final transmission, "Losing height, have to go down." Paape, in helpless frustration, called into the radio, "Be careful, Charles." It was not to be. L7310 had run out of options.

'Syrett headed for a field which was guarded by a row of trees directly in his path. Unable to increase speed or climb to clear the trees, Syrett called to the other two to brace themselves.

'The aircraft flew into and through the trees, stalling as it did so. It crashed heavily into the field beyond, where its forward motion was further checked by a grassy bank. The deceleration forces and impact were tremendous. They were on the east side of the Sleaford Road at Dunston Pillar.'

Pilot Officer Syrett was very badly injured, the others killed. Despite many crashes like this, the Manchester was in production and the Hampdens were getting old, so re-equipment of squadrons and the formation of new ones with Manchesters went on. At Waddington, 97 Squadron, a resident at the base during World War One, reformed there on Manchesters in February 1941, moving next month to Coningsby, but 44, 49, 61, 83, 106 and 144 Squadrons soldiered on with Hampdens throughout that year.

In December 1941 a significant event took place at Waddington; the Manchester, having been redesigned to take four Rolls-Royce Merlin engines, re-emerged as the Lancaster, an aircraft which was to become forever associated with Lincolnshire. It fell to the recently officially titled 44 (Rhodesia) Squadron – a quarter of its strength coming from that country – to become the first Lancaster-equipped unit. The first operation with the new bomber was on 3rd March 1942, laying mines in the Heligoland Bight, while on 28th April a low-level raid against the MAN diesel works at Augsburg gained Squadron Leader J D Nettleton the VC. The squadron soon became the envy of 5 Group, and Coningsby became the next Lancaster station, 97 and 106 Squadrons converting during January and May 1942 respectively. Their stay was brief though, 97 moving to the new airfield at Woodhall Spa in March and 106 to Syerston in September, allowing Coningsby to close in order to have concrete runways laid.

The early wartime-built stations, from late 1940 on, were temporary affairs, accommodation being hutted and, together with bomb dumps, hangars and workshops, distributed around the perimeter of the airfield and in the surrounding countryside. Runways were not provided until the arrival of the Manchester, Lancaster, Halifax and Stirling made them essential if operations were to be carried out during the winter months.

At the other 5 Group stations changes were also taking place, with Hemswell transferring to 1 Group, the HQ of which was now at Bawtry Hall, near Doncaster; its two Hampden squadrons, 61 and 144, left in July 1941 and were replaced by the Wellingtons of the Polish squadrons, 300 and 301, from Swinderby. At Waddington, 207 Squadron left in November and was replaced by a Canadian unit, 420 (RCAF) Squadron, still with Hampdens. At Scampton, 1942 saw 49 Squadron, one imagines reluctantly, receive Manchesters in April (though Lancasters replaced these in June), while 83 Squadron left in August to be replaced by the Lancasters of 57 Squadron. Thus the Hampdens departed from the station, pilot Flight Lieu-

Another Manchester, this time of 50 Squadron at either Swinderby or Skellingthorpe in July 1942, by which time most had been retired to conversion units. On 30th May 1942, F/O Leslie Manser was awarded (posthumously) the third VC given to Lincolnshire based bomber crew, flying from Skellingthorpe. 50 Squadron

tenant R A B Learoyd of 49 Squadron and wireless operator/air gunner Sergeant J Hannah of 83 Squadron having both been awarded the VC for Hampden operations whilst stationed at Scampton.

Lancasters equipped 467 (RAAF) Squadron at Scampton in November 1942, but the squadron left the same month for Bottesford. Two new 5 Group stations were opened in Lincolnshire during 1942, namely Woodhall Spa and Skellingthorpe, the latter serving for a period as a satellite of Swinderby after opening in late 1941. Another Hampden unit, 50 Squadron, transferred to 5 Group and Swinderby, the base having been vacated by the Polish squadrons in July 1941, together with 455 (RAAF) Squadron, also with Hampdens. The aircraft of 50 Squadron actually moved on the 18th and the squadron flew its first Swinderby operation on the night of the 20th, such was the intensity of bombing at this time (later, even two days to settle in was a luxury!). As for 455 (RAAF) Squadron, after some vicissitudes, it became operational in September and the two squadrons continued to raid Europe.

As at many other airfields, accommodation at Swinderby was strained and the weather held up building work. As a consequence, 50 Squadron moved to Skellingthorpe whilst runways were built, and 455 departed with its Hampdens in April 1942 to convert to a new role, torpedo dropping. The squadron had been the first Australian bomber squadron to form in Britain and two humorous stories are told of its personnel whilst at Swinderby; one disconsolate Aussie, surveying the steadily falling rain, exclaimed 'Jeez, if they cut the barrage balloon cables, the bloody place would sink', while a compatriot, appearing before Newark Magistrates, told the JP 'My grandfather was deported to Australia for poaching

and I'm hoping you'll give me the same sentence'.

This was a particularly worrying time for the Australians as their homeland was being bombed by the Japanese and an invasion seemed imminent. June 1942 saw the return of 50 Squadron to Swinderby as 'Skelly' had proved unsatisfactory. Whilst there the squadron had converted to Manchesters, and Flying Officer L T Manser received a posthumous VC for operations on 30th May 1942; a primary school built on the site of the former Skellingthorpe airfield now proudly bears his name. By October 1942 the squadron had been brought up to scratch and moved back to Skellingthorpe from Swinderby. Thus at the end of 1942, the 5 Group order of battle was as follows:

Waddington
9 and 44 Squadrons (Lancaster)
Skellingthorpe
50 Squadron (Lancaster)
Scampton
49 and 57 Squadrons (Lancaster)
Woodhall Spa
97 Squadron (Lancaster)

The northern Lincolnshire bomber stations had been taken over by 1 Group; at Hemswell the Poles had Wellingtons as did 12 and 142 Squadrons at Binbrook. July 1941 saw another former World War One airfield reopen, Elsham Wolds, which received 103 Squadron's Wellington Ics from Newton; the squadron was to stay at Elsham for the rest of the war, re-equipping briefly with Halifaxes IIs in 1942 before it was decided that the Lancaster should be 1 Group's aircraft. The next new station was Grimsby, built on the site of the pre-war flying club airfield at Waltham and still often known by that name; it opened in November 1941 for the Wellington IVs of 142 Squadron from

Binbrook, leaving just the Wellington IIs of 12 Squadron at that airfield. 1942 saw the additions of Ingham (May), Wickenby (September) and Kirmington (October). As in 5 Group this meant a reshuffle among the squadrons and the 1 Group Order of Battle in December 1942 was:

Wickenby
12 Squadron (Lancaster)
Grimsby
100 Squadron (Lancaster)
Elsham Wolds
103 Squadron (Lancaster)
Kirmington
142 and 150 Squadrons (Wellington III)
Ingham
300 Squadron (Wellington III)
Hemswell
301 and 305 Squadrons (Wellington IV)
Blyton
199 Squadron (Wellington III)

At all of these busy stations the ground-crews toiled to keep the bombers flying and more and more women of the Women's Auxiliary Air Force (WAAFs) were joining the fray. Pip Brimson was born in Lincoln but had moved away by the time war broke out; she joined the WAAF and arrived at Waddington in September 1941 as one of the first WAAF trainee ground radio-operators. Pip remained at Waddington until it closed for runway construction in 1943 and worked in the watch office (as the control tower was then called), and so was in a position to observe the flying activities, intially those of 44 Squadron (callsign 'Maypole') and 207 Squadron (callsign 'Lighthouse'), whilst Waddington's callsign was 'Jetty'. Not long after she arrived, Waddington was bombed; an event she described in a letter to the author:

'We were in the middle of landing ops, when an air raid warning Red was sounded, and bombs began dropping almost immediately. Lights were dowsed and our own aircraft had to circle in the darkness. We realised it was just one intruder dropping a stick of bombs across the airfield, but the explosions were getting nearer, until an almighty "Crump" was very close, and the Watch Office shook. I was not the only one to believe the next bomb was for us. My mind was quite blank, as I continued logging anxious conversation coming over the R/T but – the next one never came and the enemy aircraft departed. Immediately the airfield sprang to life – runway lights were relit, the Control Officer did a rapid inspection of the damage and reported the runways fit for use. There was a large crater between the Watch Office and No. 3 Hangar though!'

Pip met Sergeant Ron Atkinson, a wireless operator/air gunner of 44 Squadron but, like many wartime romances, it was destined to be brief; after only a couple of months Pip was on duty when 44 Squadron returned from a raid on Le Havre, but Ron's Hampden was not among them, having been shot down. Tragedy was never far away in the wartime RAF; one night Pip received a 'Darky' call (the code for aircraft in trouble):

Sally Whelan and Pip Brimson on night duty in Waddington's watch office, 1942, wearing civilian blouses especially donned for the photograph. The Women's Auxiliary Air Force played an increasing part in the work of the RAF throughout the war. Pip Brimson

King George VI visited Digby on 2nd November 1939, and is here inspecting the pilots of 611 (West Lancashire) Squadron, RAuxAF; behind lie the unit's Spitfires. RAF Digby via David Curry

' "May we land, may we land, one engine U/S" – the airfield lights and Chance Light were switched on and I gave permission to pancake. The voice I had heard sounded so young and so scared, and I waited anxiously. It seemed as if the aircraft was going round again, and I called to ask what the trouble was, on the Control Officer's instructions. There was a pause, and the pilot's mike was switched on – a few unintelligible words came over, then silence in spite of another call from me. This was followed by a dreadful, tearing, stomach-heaving crash – and a sheet of flame beyond the end of the runway. The Control Officer rushed out with all the other services... He returned, saying it was a 'Wimpey' from an OTU, and that they had apparently attempted a turn and been dragged down by the weight of the duff engine. There were no survivors. I was shocked... my voice had been the last human sound in that young pilot's ears – and somehow that related me to him. It haunted me, and I dreamed of it when I went back to my billet and bed.'

A strange footnote to Lincolnshire's early bomber operations is that, on 9th May 1943, a Ju 88R-1, the latest type of Ju 88 night fighter, landed at RAF Dyce (now Aberdeen Airport) in Scotland. The aircraft was flown by a German fighter pilot called Heinrich Schmitt who was, surprisingly, a British agent. The full story is told in *The Great Coup* (Robert Hill; Arlington Books, 1978). After the war Schmitt was interviewed for a German newspaper and claimed that he had landed a Dornier Do 217 at 'RAF Lincoln' on the night of 20th May 1941 to deliver a package to a waiting RAF officer. He claimed that this landing was official, on behalf of the Luftwaffe, and that other German pilots also landed in Britain, by arrangement, carrying peace proposals. The author has met one person who claims to have witnessed this event who was on guard duty at Coningsby and saw the Dornier land at dawn on 20th May.

Fighter Operations
As the RAF mobilised for war in August 1939, 504 (County of Nottingham) Squadron, AuxAF, took up its war station at Digby, joining 46 and 73 Squadrons. All three squad-

rons were equipped with Hurricane Is. Digby's first sortie was conducted on 3rd September by 46 Squadron, the order being to intercept an approaching raid which never materialised. Sister unit 73 Squadron was selected to form part of the fighter wing of the Advanced Air Striking Force which was being sent to France to provide air cover for the British Expeditionary Force and it left Digby for Cherbourg in September, one of the departing pilots being Flying Officer 'Cobber' Kain, a New Zealander who became the RAF's first 'Ace' of World War Two by shooting down 17 enemy aircraft during 73 Squadron's nine months in France. In October, 504 Squadron also left, for Debden in Essex, and the two units were replaced by 611 (West Lancashire) Squadron, AuxAF, equipped with Spitfire Is, and 229 Squadron, which formed at Digby on 6th October as a long-range and night fighter squadron with Blenheim Ifs.

The Spitfires of 611 Squadron made Digby's first enemy contact on 21st September but no results were obtained. The first action took place on 21st October when 46 Squadron, flying from North Coates, was on convoy patrol off the East Coast and intercepted a formation of Heinkel He 115 seaplanes which were possibly laying mines. This was the first attack of the war by Hurricanes on German aircraft and 46 Squadron claimed three destroyed and one damaged. 'Widge' Gleed, later to shoot down nine enemy aircraft before being killed in North Africa in 1943, was a pilot with 46 Squadron at this time when his flight was relieved by 'B' Flight on patrol. He had just landed when the Operations Room at Digby told 'B' Flight that 12 enemy aircraft were about 20 miles east of their convoy. In his book *Arise to Conquer* (Gollancz, 1942), Gleed recalled what happened when 'B' Flight returned to the scene:

'We crowded round their planes as they switched their engines off. "What happened, sir?" Pat asked [the Squadron CO, Squadron Leader Barwell].

"Twelve Heinkel 115s, big torpedo-carrying float-

planes. I saw them coming round into the sun, and went into line astern. Then into echelon for number three attack. They never saw us coming. The one I attacked caught fire and crashed. I chased another one which was trying to run for it. I saw him drop his torpedo, then I caught him. Two of the crew baled out. Then the plane went straight in. I steep-turned and saw the two floats bob up, and a large patch of oil. I'm damned if I could see where the blokes who baled out landed. Well, Billie, that was easy wasn't it?"

"It was just perfect, sir; if only we'd had the squadron, none of them would have got away. I gave mine a long burst; he fired back and hit my wing, then dived straight in."

'We all stared at Billie's right wing; it had two bullet holes in it. One had made quite a large hole coming out of the top of the wing.'

Apart from these occasional excitements all three squadrons flew fairly uneventful convoy patrols (nicknamed 'Kipper' patrols by the bored pilots) over the North Sea. Shortly after the action described above, Squadron Leader Kenneth Cross (commander of the V-Force in the 1960s) took command of 46 Squadron. In *Straight and Level* (Grub Street, 1993), he chronicled operational life on the squadron during the war:

'A few days after I arrived, we were inspected by the King accompanied by the Chief of the Air Staff, Sir Cyril Newall, and Leigh-Mallory. The King spent a good deal of time talking to the pilots and his visit greatly encouraged everyone.'

Cross took 46 Squadron over to North Coates at dawn each day, where it was closer to the likely scene of action:

'Sitting in the crew room all day in flying kit, I was able to get to know my pilots well. There were 19 of them – 13 officers and 6 sergeants – and a splendid lot they

were, mostly in their early twenties and only two married. As pilots they were very experienced, most having several hundred hours on Hurricanes alone.'

In early 1940 the threat from German night bombers gave rise to an order that one Flight of 46 Squadron should operate at night. Cross remembers the response to the order:

'These instructions were thoroughly unpopular with everyone in the squadron since the Hurricane was quite unsuitable for night fighting... Despite practising hard, our success on night interception was virtually nil... flying a single-seat Hurricane in blacked-out winter conditions meant flying almost entirely on instruments with one's head in the cockpit... Even taking off from a grass airfield with its glim lamp flarepath was a hazardous business. It had to be done visually because the bumpy surface made the flying instruments jump about so much that they were useless as a reference until the wheels left the ground. Most pilots managed somehow but one, Terry Scott, lost control on take-off, crashed and was killed.'

The squadron moved briefly to Acklington, from November to January 1940, while 229 Squadron re-equipped with Hurricane Is in March 1940, the one Spitfire and two Hurricane units operating routinely until the Germans invaded Norway in May. 46 Squadron then joined the Anglo-French force sent to repel the Germans but the campaign was short and the survivors – including those of 46 Squadron – were withdrawn by sea. The squadron's pilots performed a great feat of airmanship by landing their valuable fighters on the flight-deck of the aircraft carrier HMS *Glorious*. Tragically it was to no avail as the vessel was intercepted and sunk by the *Scharnhorst* and *Gneisenau*, only two members of the squadron being rescued, although some ground personnel on

another ship returned safely to Digby, where 46 Squadron worked up to operational standards once again.

As is evident from the lack of action near Lincolnshire, Digby was regarded as a 'quiet' sector by Fighter Command. In the summer of 1940, when the Command's squadrons in southern England began to be drawn into air battles over the Channel convoys, they were rotated to quieter areas to give them a breather. 1940 therefore saw a succession of fighter squadrons staying at Digby for only a month or so – 111 Squadron (Hurricane Is); 222 Squadron (Spitfire Is); 56 Squadron (Hurricane Is); 79 Squadron (Hurricane Is); 151 Squadron (Hurricane Is); and 402 Squadron (Hurricane Is).

The Battle of Britain largely passed Digby by; in fact, from 1st July to 31st October 1940 – the period commonly thought of as the Battle of Britain – 611 Squadron claimed one Junkers Ju 88, a Dornier Do 215 (2nd July) and three Dornier Do 17s (21st August), and 151 Squadron one Ju 88 (30th September). However, such was the fear of invasion in the summer that between June and September, dawn and dusk patrols were flown by Lysanders; 4 Squadron (Linton-on-Ouse) flew North Coates–Skegness–the Wash and return, while 16 Squadron (Cambridge) covered Sutton Bridge–Wells–Lowestoft.

The end of 1940 saw three units in residence: 46 Squadron, having seen action in the south, was back in its ancestral home, in company with 29 Squadron, a night fighter

Engine fitters of 402 (RCAF) Squadron check the R-R Merlin of one of the unit's Hawker Hurricane IIbs at Digby, c1941.
Public Archives of Canada

unit with Blenheim Ifs, and 402 (RCAF) Squadron with Hurricanes. This was the first of many Canadian units to serve at Digby and was the second Canadian fighter squadron to form in Britain. Its officers arrived on 11th December 1940, the Hurricanes on the 13th, and it became operational in early 1941. On its formation it was actually known as 2 Squadron RCAF but it was decided that all Commonwealth and Allied units would receive RAF squadron numbers to avoid confusion (e.g., with 2 Squadron RAF), and on 1st March 2 Squadron RCAF became 402 (RCAF) Squadron, RAF. The squadron's Hurricane Is worked up to operational efficiency and in May 1941 moved to Wellingore, which had become a satellite of Digby during 1940. A month later the Canadians moved south and began to fly sweeps over France.

While at Digby 402 (RCAF) Squadron had been joined by another Canadian unit, 1 Squadron RCAF, which replaced 46 Squadron when it finally left Digby in February 1941, and which had followed a completely different path from its sister squadron. Having seen action in the south of the country during the Battle of Britain it moved to Scotland for a 'rest'. At Digby it was retitled 401 (RCAF) Squadron and remained there until October when it flew down to Biggin Hill. One of 401's pilots was Hugh Godefroy who had trained on Hurricanes at 56 OTU, Sutton Bridge; he was billeted in the village with a widow during the winter of 1940–41 and remembered the arduous early morning conditions in his autobiography *Lucky Thirteen* (Croom Helm, 1983):

'I cannot say that I enjoyed the one-and-a- half-mile walk [to the aerodrome] before breakfast. As I plodded my way to the station, my shoes became wet from the morning dew. I always seemed to be facing a damp, penetrating wind off the Fens.'

Godefroy's training course included Poles, Czechs, Free French and Americans, and after 35 hours he was passed out as 'operational' and posted to 401. The squadron sometimes operated from Wellingore when Digby was too congested, as Godefroy recalls:

'We found it took a certain amount of ingenuity to be comfortable in a tent in the dampness of the Lincolnshire countryside. However, more casual forms of dress were allowed and complete freedom from the bull that was inescapable on permanent 12 Group stations like Digby. We were issued with collapsible camp beds, heavy canvas sleeping bags and canvas wash basins mounted on wooden tripods. Hot water was available in pails from the Mess, and we washed and shaved over our canvas wash basins under the apple trees… One flight of six pilots stayed in Dispersal from first light to noon when the other flight took over to finish at dusk. The sun rose about 4:15 in the morning and set about 11 o'clock at night.'

If on first readiness the procedure was to

'…put our helmets over the stick. Having plugged in the cord to the radio and the tube to the oxygen outlet, we hung our parachutes over the leading edge of the port wing with the straps hanging down'. The Hurricanes were expected to be airborne in a minute and a half if required.

Wellingore was also used for night operations as there was less to hit than at Digby if the flare path attracted German aircraft. Godefroy relates one such attack:

'Squadron Leader Bon Corbett had been shot down one time in flames, and burnt rather badly about the eyes. It had been rumoured Bon did not have particularly good eyesight to start with, and the fire had not improved it. It was traditional in the RAF to tolerate the idiosyncracies of anyone who had more guts than sense. One night Bon was circling Wellingore, having finished a fruitless search for bombers over Manchester. Upon his request to land, the flarepath was turned on. What Bon did not know at the time was that a Junkers 88 was also in the circuit. On his final approach Bon called for the Chance Light with the Ju 88 in shooting distance behind him. The '88 pilot held his fire for Bon to become nicely silhouetted against the beam of the Chance Light but had not reckoned with Bon's night landing technique. As usual on his first attempt, Bon bounced 30ft into the air and went round again. The '88 pilot, frustrated at finding that his target had disappeared before his very eyes, opened up with cannon fire. The only casualty was the poor litle erk who was manning the Chance Light. He ran so fast for cover that he broke his leg. Oblivious to all these goings on, Bon serenely completed his circuit and bounced his way into a successful landing.'

Digby was a Sector Station, which meant that it controlled its own squadrons and those at Wellingore and Coleby Grange. The Operations Room was transferred early in the war to Blankney Hall, in case of bombs on Digby, and information on enemy aircraft was fed to it from the Chain Home radar station at Stenigot and from visual sightings by the Lincolnshire posts of the Observer Corps.

Although the day fighter squadrons did not see much action the Luftwaffe had begun its night raids and, while Hurricanes and Spitfires did occasionally operate at night as related above, night fighting was the responsibility of the Blenheim Ifs of 29 Squadron. To this squadron, in October 1940, came Flight Lieutenant Guy Gibson, late of 83 Squadron at Scampton, posted in as a Flight Commander. 'On the aerodrome not a soul was in sight. The aircraft were covered up and the windsock hung water-logged and motionless from one of the hangars.' *Enemy Coast Ahead* (Crecy, 2003).

Gibson, despite his long sojourn in Lincolnshire, seemingly never appreciated the county's finer points 'At Digby, Lincolnshire is at its worst – a vast area of flatness, spreading out towards the East fenlands of the Wash. Hardly a tree breaks the horizon, hardly a bird sings.' *Enemy Coast Ahead* (Crecy, 2003).

At this time 29 Squadron was converting to the new and potent Bristol Beaufighter If,

one of the first units to so equip, and was operating from Wellingore which was codenamed WC1. In between learning to fly the 'Beau' and his new 'trade', Gibson married, the couple living at the 'Lion and Royal' at Navenby. The squadron became operational and on 13th March opened its score on Beaufighters when a Ju 88 was sent down by the CO near Louth. The same night Bob Braham, who finished the war as the RAF's top night fighter ace (with 29 kills), achieved his second victory, a Do17. Braham recalled the kill in *Scramble* (J R D Braham; Muller, 1961):

'Ross [the radar operator] and I were scrambled and vectored towards the coast near Skegness… The GCI controller directed us towards the enemy, keeping up a running commentary… then Ross came through over the intercom. "Contact 4,000 yards and 20 degrees above. Turn gently port." This was it. I pressed the transmitter and shouted "Contact" to the GCI controller. [The radar op. guided Braham towards the enemy aircraft until]… Yes, there he was, a black object moving ahead of me and above, still too far to make out what sort of aircraft he was… Now I could clearly make out the enemy and identified him as a Dornier… I had to get in closer to make certain of this. The Dornier had just crossed the coast near Skegness and might be heading for one of the Midland cities to dump his load of destruction… I eased gently back on the control column, allowing a little deflection and pressed the firing button. The four cannons roared for a second then stopped. "Damn it, they've jammed" I shouted. [Ross cleared the blockage and Braham, who was now chasing the Dornier out to sea, got in a second burst which exploded it.] The GCI operators were as bucked as we were over our success. Back at the airfield the news had gone ahead of us and we stepped out of the aeroplane to be surrounded by air and groundcrew.'

The night following these two victories Gibson shot down a Heinkel He111 over the North Sea. The squadron was definitely in business, but in April it was posted to West Malling in Kent. By this time the German night fighters and bombers were striking back and, as Gibson put it: 'After a while the aerodromes of Lincolnshire were in the front line. We had to change the flare path, amidst exploding bombs, on many occasions'. *Enemy Coast Ahead* (Crecy, 2003).

(Wellingore was attacked ten times and because of such attacks in the early part of the war, many airfields had decoy sites which, at night, were lit to resemble an airfield and thus attract German bombs. Some even had dummy aircraft to attract daytime attacks, and details of these decoys can be found in the Appendix.)

During 1941 three more Canadian squadrons formed up at Digby and its satellites. The first of the three was 409 Squadron, the second Canadian night fighter unit, which started life on elderly Boulton Paul Defiant Is in June, then moved to Coleby Grange the following month. It converted to Beaufighter IIfs in the summer of 1941 and the new and powerful aircraft took its toll of the crews, including the life of its CO, Squadron Leader

> I've topped the wind-swept heights with easy grace
> Where never lark, nor even eagle flew –
> And while with silent, lifting mind I've trod
> The high, untrespassed sanctity of space,
> Put out my hand and touched the face of God.

The poem gained renewed fame when used by President Ronald Reagan after the *Challenger* space shuttle disaster in January 1986.

In August 1941 Digby got its first Canadian CO, Group Captain Campbell – hardly surprising as all three of the Sector's squadrons were now RCAF. However, an RAF unit did replace 411 and 412 Squadrons, namely 92 Squadron, the highest-scoring squadron in the Battle of Britain; it was posted to Digby as non-operational and in February 1942 left a Lincolnshire winter for the warmer climes of the Western Desert, one of its pilots being Neville Duke who described Digby as *being* 'full of red tape and bullshit'; surprising, as Canadians were famed for their disregard of such things.

Another unit to have gained fame during the Battle of Britain, claiming over 100 aircraft destroyed up to October 1940, was 609 (West Riding) Squadron, which arrived with its Spitfire Vbs in November 1941. At Digby, because of its high turnover of pilots, it was nicknamed 609 Operational Training Unit, but it returned south in March 1942 shortly before re-equipping with Hawker Typhoon Is, a type which brought the squadron initial trials and tribulations before eventual fame.

A tragic event during 609 Squadron's stay was the loss, in a collision with another Spitfire, of the Belgian ace Jean Offenberg. Offenberg joined the Royal Belgian Air Force in 1939 and shot down a Do 17 before his country was overrun by the Germans. After several adventures he reached England, via Algeria, and joined the RAF; serving with 145 and 609 Squadrons he scored seven victories, five probables and 6 and a half damaged (the half was shared!).

Offenberg wasn't keen when it was announced that 609 Squadron was to be posted to Digby for a respite following its hectic time at Biggin Hill in late 1940, as he recalled in The *Lonely Warrior* (Souvenir Press, 1956): 'It was Gilroy who announced the great news: "We're being moved the day after tomorrow. The squadron's posted to Digby".' At first Offenberg hardly dared credit this because the station in question was so far away from their present scene of activity:

Petersen; but on 1st November a Dornier Do 217 was destroyed. A quiet time followed until in March a Heinkel He 111 was shot down, and during the summer several victories were claimed including five during July alone.

The next Canadian unit to form at Digby was 411 Squadron, also formed in June, together with 412 (Falcon) Squadron, both flying Spitfire IIAs. The latter unit received its first two Spitfires on 7th July, all the pilots then carrying out training with five more Spits delivered on the 9th. However the number was reduced by one the next day when Sergeant Ellis overshot on landing and hit an air raid shelter. On 17th July Flying Officer Neal of 401 Squadron, on leave with friends at Digby, volunteered to help, did not lock his undercarriage down, and wrote off another Spitfire. The first fatality occurred on 2nd August when Sergeants Smith and MacLean, practising air combat over Silk Willoughby, collided, Smith's aircraft losing its tail; MacLean made it back to Digby and was given seven days' leave to recover from shock.

After working up, these units took part in sweeps over Europe, being temporarily

based at airfields in the south for these operations. November 1941 saw 411 Squadron move to Hornchurch but it returned to Digby for brief periods during 1942. As for 412 Squadron, it made the short flight to Wellingore in October 1941 and stayed there for the winter, with occasional forays south for a bit of action, taking its final leave of Lincolnshire in May 1942. Another 412 Squadron pilot, killed in a collision with a Cranwell Airspeed Oxford over Roxholm, was a young Anglo-American, Pilot Officer John Gillespie Magee, who is buried in Scopwick Burial Ground. Magee was not an 'ace' or a well known pilot but he will be remembered for one of the best-known aviation poems of World War Two:

High Flight

Oh! I have slipped the surly bonds of earth
And danced the skies on laughter-silvered wings;
Sunward I've climbed, and joined the tumbling mirth
of sun-split clouds – and done a hundred things
You have not dreamed of – wheeled and soared and swung
High in the sunlit silence. Hov'ring there
I've chased the shouting wind along, and flung My eager
craft thro' footless halls of air.

Up, up the long, delirious, burning blue

'But Digby's in Group 12 isn't it? There won't be any fighting there. They might just as well have sent us to Australia or the Belgian Congo. [But move they did.]

'Digby possessed neither the comfort or reputation of Biggin Hill... If the countryside had changed, if other squadrons like warrior tribes camped with them round the airfield, the 609 was self-contained and the pilots were closer than they had ever been before... So they grew used to their misfortune in the icy winds that blew in from the North Sea...

'Sunday 23rd November: Mass at the camp. One Section of 609 had to escort a few coasters sailing south; we met them off the Wash, some minutes flight from base. I shall eventually believe that the War is still going on up here.

'From time to time the Luftwaffe sends a few bombers into the Digby Sector, but very rarely, and since the weather is against this type of exercise I shall have little chance of meeting any Nazi aircraft.'

Offenberg experienced one of the problems that was increasingly to plague pilots based in eastern England:

'Returning to our point of departure I caught sight of the flare path lights at Digby. As soon as I touched down I found to my amazement that I was on a strange airfield and that the landmarks were new to me. And yet when I called Digby they had given me permission to land. Where the hell was I? How incredibly stupid. A few moments later a British squadron commander explained the mystery, and laughed at my discomfiture. I was at Wellingore, five miles from my own base, and I had mistaken the two fields.'

For the remainder of 1942 day fighter squadrons rotated through Digby, on rest periods from the succession of sweeps over Europe or as their last UK station before an overseas posting. These included 601 (County of London) Squadron which arrived in March to train on Spitfire Vbs after an unhappy period on Bell Airacobra Is, an American fighter which just did not come up to the requirements of fighter operations in Northwest Europe. The squadron then took its Spitfires to Malta.

Another unit to form up on Spitfire Vs at Digby was 421 (RCAF) Squadron, in April, while 54 Squadron stayed briefly during June before shipping out to Australia and 242 Squadron arrived in September to prepare for a move to Algeria. A new fighter type made its first appearance in Lincolnshire when 198 Squadron formed up on Typhoon Is in December. One unit which was to stay at Digby for a longer period was 288 (Army

Co-operation) Squadron, which formed in November 1941 for the purpose of training Army and RAF Regiment anti-aircraft gunners in the area, and alternated between Digby, Wellingore and Coleby Grange. So, in December 1942 Digby housed 198 Squadron, 288 Squadron was at Wellingore and 409 (RCAF) Squadron (Beaufighters) was at Coleby Grange. In September 1942 Digby had become officially an RCAF station.

Whilst Digby was the county's first fighter station, the more northerly area of its Sector was taken over by a new airfield, Kirton-in-Lindsey, which had been planned pre-war and had opened in May 1940. Its role was very similar to that of Digby and its squadrons came up from the battles in the south for a rest, to train new pilots and to fly convoy patrols off the east coast. During 1940 there arrived, 253, 71 and 85 Squadrons with

The headstone of John Gillespie Magee's grave, in Scopwick burial ground, where lie many other airmen killed whilst flying from Digby and its satellites. Lincolnshire Library Service

The unsung groundcrews; a party from 401 (RCAF) Squadron carry out a 60 hour inspection on Spitfire Vb 'S for Sugar' in Wellingore's blister hangar, late 1941. Although the Squadron had Canadian aircrew, many of the groundcrew would have been British. R Jones via P H T Green

Hurricane Is; 65, 222 and 616 Squadrons with Spitfire Is and 74 Squadron with Spitfire IIAs; and 264 Squadron, equipped with Defiant Is, which proved to be easy meat for the Luftwaffe fighters and resulted in the unit's withdrawal from daylight operations. However, as a night fighter the Defiant was not so vulnerable and so it was assigned to 307 (Polish) and 255 Squadrons at Kirton.

During this period only one kill was recorded, by 616 Squadron on 16th September, but this is not to say there was a complete lack of action; Squadron Leader Peter Townsend, (romantically linked with Princess Margaret after the war), was CO of 85 Squadron at Kirton from October to November 1940, and recalled one alarming incident in *Duel of Eagles* (Weidenfeld & Nicholson, 1970):

'...I was nearly killed by enemy fire – not, I hasten to add, in some heroic combat, but while chatting quietly on the ground at Caistor, our satellite field, with Jim Marshall, one of our flight-commanders... As we chatted Jim suddenly dived at me, dragging me to *he* ground with him on top of me. I went down wondering what on earth had incited this aptparently unprovoked offence of striking a senior officer when I caught sight of a Heinkel streaking just above the hedge less than a hundred yards away, the rear gunner pouring forth tracer which zipped just above our heads.'

Jim Marshall took off and shot down the Heinkel but in the meantime it had bombed Kirton, demolishing 85 Squadron's offices, fortunately without injury to any personnel.

Worthy of a special mention is 71 (Eagle) Squadron whose Hurricane Is arrived at Kirton from Church Fenton in Yorkshire in November 1940. This was the first of three all-American piloted RAF fighter squadrons (though the groundcrews were RAF), the aircrew being made up of Americans who, though officially still neutral, had made their way to the UK during 1940 and volunteered to join the RAF. The squadron's first opera-

tional patrol was on 5th February 1941, but its combat record started in April, after a move to Suffolk. On America's entry into the war the three Eagle squadrons became part of the US Army Air Force's 4th Fighter Group.

Roger Hall, himself a Lincolnshire man, gave his impression of forming a new squadron and of night fighters in *Clouds of Fear* (R Hall; Bailey Bros & Swinfen, 1975):

'The aerodrome to which I had been posted was in my home county of Lincolnshire... The countryside round the airfield was flat and at the time I arrived was covered with snow. The squadron had been formed only a week before and, therefore, its entire complement was new, that is, they had all come from other squadrons or straight from OTUs. At all events we were new to each other. In the RAF, however, people had the habit of remaining strangers at the most an hour or so and at least ten minutes, particularly if they met in the bar.

During the next few days the entire personnel of the squadron arrived, and we started to sort ourselves out and begin training. Our CO, Smithy, gave us a brief lecture on what our work would entail. We would be given three months' training to acquire and perfect the art of night interception and night combat after which we should go south to operate against German night bombers. We were to spend the first month learning to handle the Defiant during the daylight hours so that we should accustom ourselves to its flying characteristics... We started to fly these machines the day following our arrival.

The Lincolnshire countryside lay beneath a mantle of snow and the whole panorama gave the impression of something inexpressibly bleak and melancholy. I flew over my home cautiously for I was far from happy with the strange aircraft. It seemed heavy and cumbersome compared to the Spitfire... Above us, as we flew, was a sky laden with snow clouds with their bases little more than a thousand feet. In these conditions, the aerodrome was difficult to find, for roads and other landmarks were all covered with snow. Lincoln Cathedral provided a good landmark, for it stood serenely on the top of a fairly high hill dominating the City. There were a lot of other RAF stations close to ours, mostly bomber stations, but all constructed to the same set pattern, and as they all presented from the air the same configuration of buildings it was easy to become confused.'

After getting used to the Defiant, and flying at night, 255 Squadron began its first sorties against German bombers raiding Sheffield and Hull. Flight Lieutenant Hall was ordered to orbit above the mouth of the Humber:

'We hurried to our machine which stood silently among the others in the dispersal area, looking like something quite sinister in its matt-black night camouflage... I opened the throttle of the heavy machine and at once it began to move. I steered it by alternate application of the wheel brakes towards the "Chance lights" which were situated at the take-off end of the flare path... the flare path was lit only by a row of goose-neck flares at intervals of some 50 yards or so along the whole length of the grass runway.'

Once airborne, Hall and his gunner had orbited for half an hour when:

'... I caught sight, from the corner of my eye, of a Heinkel 111 gliding silently and apparently furtively towards the coast... In a fever of excitement I switched on the 'intercom' and shouted to Fitz, "There it is Fitz- below us – see it?" and switched over to receive. Fitz said "No – haven't seen anything yet." While I was speaking to him I put the aircraft into a steep dive towards the Heinkel, for I was afraid I was going to lose sight of it in the darkness... Our aircraft shuddered slightly as Fitz opened up on the bomber with the four turret guns pointing directly backwards and firing up at the bomber's cockpit from a range of little more than than 20 yards. I looked over my shoulder as he fired and saw the great Heinkel sitting gracefully like a bird of prey above us as though quite stationary. I could see our bullets hitting the centre section from underneath and the shots were like small dancing sparks creeping forwards up to the cockpit of the enemy machine.'

After two more attacks the Heinkel exploded, 255 Squadron's first victory.

The year 1942 saw the departure of 616, 71 and 255 Squadrons from Kirton, the last to Hibaldstow, a newly opened airfield which was a satellite of Kirton and which thereafter took over the night fighter role, leaving the day fighters at Kirton. 616 Squadron was replaced by 65 Squadron, and 452 (RAAF) Squadron – the first Australian fighter squadron in the UK – formed up on Spitfires in April and flew convoy patrols until it moved south in July. Similar duties were performed by the Hurricanes of 121 Squadron, the second Eagle squadron, which formed up at Kirton in May. A Ju 88 was damaged on 8th August

Below: *Although something of a stop-gap, the Boulton-Paul Defiant was a reasonably successful night-fighter, until the Beaufighter took over. This example, possibly N3340, was one of 255 Squadron's, as flown by Roger Hall, and is pictured at Kirton-in-Lindsey in 1941. During the night of 8th/9th May 1941, 255 Defiants, and its CO's Hurricane, shot down six German bombers over East Yorkshire, a night-fighter squadron record which stands to this day.* P H T Green

Opposite page:

Hawker Hurricane I V7608 of 71 (Eagle) Squadron, at Kirton-in-Lindsey in early 1941. 71 was the first Eagle Squadron, the pilots of which were American volunteers who came to the UK before the USA entered World War Two. As with the Canadian squadrons most of the ground crew were British. The Squadrons transferred to the USAAF in 1942.

The concept of the Havoc-Turbinlite/Hurricane night-fighting combination was not successful and only 538/253 Squadrons at Hibaldstow shot down a Luftwaffe bomber whilst so equipped. AH470 is a Havoc II of 538 Squadron, 1942, and the searchlight in the nose can be clearly seen, as can the aerials of its AI-IV radar on nose and fuselage side. P H T Green

'Attention!' Raising the Stars and Stripes at USAAF Station 345, Goxhill, with the ubiqitous jeeps and bikes much in evidence. P H T Green

and 121 Squadron joined the West Malling Wing for occasional sweeps. Its first aircraft destroyed was unfortunately an RAF Blenheim, and the squadron converted to Spitfires before moving to North Weald in December. Another unit to reform at Kirton was 136 Squadron, with Hurricanes in August 1941, and Kirton was its only British base, as it spent the rest of the war in the Far East, where it became the top-scoring fighter squadron, disbanding there in 1945. Two pre-war AuxAF units, 616 and 611 Squadrons, served at Kirton into the new year and 133 Squadron, the third and last Eagle Squadron, paid a visit to its sister unit's birthplace.

1942 was a year of differing nationalities at Kirton, 486 Squadron (Hurricane IIbs) becoming the first Royal New Zealand AF Squadron to serve in Lincolnshire, joining the Poles of 306 and 303 Squadrons (Spitfire Vbs) and the Australians of 457 Squadron (Spitfire Vbs). The RAF was represented by one of its most famous pre-war squadrons, 43 'The Fighting Cocks', and in June a little piece of history was made when the 1st Fighter Group USAAF, equipped with Lockheed P-38 Lightnings, arrived to gain operational experience with the RAF. By mid-1942, 457 Squadron had returned to Australia from Kirton to help defend its

country against the Japanese but 303 Squadron was soon in action, shooting down three Ju 88s while on east coast convoy patrols. It was also detached to Redhill in Surrey for the Dieppe landings and scored nine kills for the loss of one pilot. By December 1942, 303 Squadron was the only resident unit at Kirton, 43 Squadron having used Kirton as a stopping-off base before sailing for Gibraltar and the Allied landings in North Africa as part of Operation 'Torch'.

Hibaldstow, having opened in May 1941, saw 255 Squadron trading in its Defiant Is for Beaufighter IIfs, but the conversion gave rise to several accidents. Declared operational in September, the squadron moved to Coltishall in Norfolk, being replaced by 253 Squadron with Hurricane IIs. This was, rather unusually, a single-seater squadron which operated largely at night, working with the Douglas Havoc Turbinlites of 538 Squadron. This new night fighting tactic required the Havocs, large twin-engined aircraft fitted with radar and a high-powered searchlight in the nose, to track down enemy aircraft and illuminate them with the searchlight for the Hurricanes to shoot down, the Havoc Turbinlite itself having no room for armament. It was largely unsuccessful, owing to dazzle problems and also the fact that the enemy were warned by the

searchlight; and it soon became apparent that the night fighter Beaufighters and Mosquitoes, armed and with radar, could do the job much more efficiently. However, the partnership between 253 and 538 Squadrons resulted in the shooting down of an He 111 on 1st May 1942 and also a probable and two damaged before 538 Squadron disbanded in January 1943, 253 Squadron having been posted to Northwest Africa in September 1942 and replaced by 532 Squadron, another Havoc-equipped unit. This too disbanded, a month after 538 Squadron, marking the end of Hibaldstow's operational period; the unlucky Heinkel was the only kill claimed by a Turbinlite squadron.

An unusual event took place when the new airfield at Goxhill opened in June 1942; it had originally been earmarked as a 1 Group bomber station and then as a fighter base in the Kirton-in-Lindsey Sector. In fact it became a station of the USAAF's 8th Air Force, well away from the 'Mighty Eighth's' other bases in East Anglia and was used initially to acclimatise newly arrived Fighter Groups to English weather and to operational flying. These Fighter Groups brought unfamiliar sights to Lincolnshire skies, namely the P-38 Lightning and Republic P-47 Thunderbolt, as well as Spitfires carrying American markings. Why Goxhill was chosen by the USAAF is a mystery but to the GIs arriving there in the winter of 1942–43, with the cold east wind blowing off the Humber, it must have seemed like the end of the world!

Coastal Command

North Coates had been evacuated by 1 Air Observer's School on the outbreak of hostilities, and for the first few months of the war housed only ground units, presumably because of fear of invasion or, possibly, because of Coastal Command's lack of flying squadrons (although, as related earlier, it was used as a Forward Operating Base by Digby's fighters). The ground units included 2 Recruit Training Pool and also 1 Ground Defence School, which trained airmen in the arts of airfield defence and had a few aircraft on strength.

However, operational flying returned in February 1940 with the arrival of two of

North Coates can be rather bleak, and looks to be so in this shot, as a 235 Squadron Bristol Blenheim IVf sits amid the thawing snow in March 1940. Under the fuselage can be seen the gun pack, containing four Browning machine guns, which distinguished this variant of the Blenheim. P H T Green

Muscle power; 18" torpedos destined for 22 Squadron's Beauforts at North Coates, 1940. Behind one of the Beauforts can be seen a Fairey Swordfish of 812 Squadron also based at North Coates at this time.
B Stafford via P H T Green

The Lockheed Hudson was Coastal Command's unsung workhorse from 1939 to 1942, and this trio of Mark Vs from 59 Squadron, North Coates, is flying near its base, May 1942. Just visible above the far aircraft is a large mast which may be that of Humberston Chain Home Low radar station. 59 Squadron, via P H T Green

Coastal Command's long-range fighter squadrons, 235 and 236, both equipped with fighter versions of the Blenheim I and IV. These two units patrolled far out over the North Sea and were joined by a similarly equipped unit, 248 Squadron, in March; by May all had departed to help out Fighter Command in the south.

North Coates now assumed the role it was to carry out for the rest of the war, attacking enemy shipping, and it fell to 22 Squadron to open the proceedings. The squadron was reformed in the torpedo-bomber role in 1934 and had been the first squadron to replace its elderly Vildebeest biplanes with the brand new Bristol Beaufort I. In April the Beauforts touched down at North Coates and the crews continued to train on them. In August three crews from 22 Squadron were chosen to form 431 Flight, equipped with another new type, the American Martin Maryland I, leaving for Malta, via Thorney Island, in September, where it eventually became 69 Squadron and performed valuable recconnaissance work over the Mediterranean.

Back at North Coates, 22 Squadron was joined in May 1940 by 812 Squadron, Fleet Air Arm, whose Fairey Swordfish biplanes appeared very antiquated compared with the Beauforts but were much more reliable as the Beaufort did suffer teething problems with its Bristol Taurus VI engines. (Set against this, though, was the Beaufort's ability to carry every weapon then in the RAF's inventory, up to the 2,000 lb bomb.) The two squadrons operated across the North Sea, bombing German ports and shipping.

In early April 1941 22 Squadron sent a detachment to St Eval in Cornwall and from there on the 6th it attacked the German battlecruiser *Gneisenau* in Brest harbour; during this operation Flying Officer Keith Campbell was awarded a posthumous VC for pressing home his attack against intense anti-aircraft fire, his torpedo hitting the stern of the ship and putting it out of action for eight months. The squadron was replaced in May by a sister unit, 86 Squadron, in the process of trading-in its Blenheim IVs for Beaufort Is, while 812 Squadron was relieved by another Fleet Air Arm Swordfish squadron, 816. These were the only front-line Fleet Air Arm squadrons to serve in Lincolnshire.

In June 1941 the Hudson IIIs and IVs of another Canadian unit, 407 Squadron, came to the county and joined 86 Squadron on highly dangerous anti-shipping operations off the German and Dutch coasts. These were conducted at sea level with no room for error and 407 Squadron aircrew became expert in the role, damaging 150,000 tons of enemy shipping during its eight months at North Coates. The new AOC Coastal Command, Sir Philip Joubert, had put a stop to the bombing raids on German ports, leaving these to Bomber Command, while Coastal Command concentrated on shipping.

October 1941 saw two non-operational units arrive to share the airfield, necessitating the opening of a relief airfield at Donna Nook (though it was never to be the official home of any flying units but took North Coates' overspill). The Lysanders of 6 Anti-Aircraft Co-operation Unit (AACU) towed targets with which to give practice to the Army's anti-aircraft gunners in the region, whilst 278 Squadron, based at Matlask in Norfolk, flew a detachment of Ansons, Lysander IIIAs and Supermarine Walrus amphibians on air-sea rescue duties along the Lincolnshire and Yorkshire coasts, working closely with 22 Motor Launch Unit at Grimsby.

The Blenheims and Hudsons of 86 and 407 Squadrons left North Coates in February 1942 and were replaced by the Hudson Vs of 53 and 59 Squadrons, joined from time to time by Beaufort detachments from other squadrons. Together, the two types continued to attack shipping, the Beaufort operations being eventually taken over by 415 (RCAF) Sqn, which operated a familiar aircraft in an unfamiliar role as the Hampden, now quickly being replaced as a bomber, was converted into a quite successful torpedo- bomber. Designated the Hampden TB.1, these aircraft carried a single Mk XII each in a deepened bomb-bay. Amongst the non-operational units, 6 AACU was replaced by a 7 AACU detachment.

By mid-1942 the anti-shipping strike units had proved their worth against the enemy shipping which skirted the north German and Low Countries' coasts; for example, 407, 53 and 59 Squadrons between them sank 13 ships between July 1941 and August 1942.

A new concept was now to be tried, the Strike Wing, and North Coates was selected to house the first of these. Three Beaufighter squadrons (143, 236 and 254) assembled there during the autumn of 1942, each being assigned a particular role within the Strike Wing, which would operate as an entity; 143 Squadron's cannon and machine gun armed Beaufighter IIfs were to concentrate on suppressing fire from the escort ships; 236 Squadron's similarly armed Beaufighter VIcs also carried bombs for the same task, while 254 Squadron's Beaufighter VIcs (nicknamed 'Torbeaus') would use their torpedoes to attack the merchant ships. On 20th November, 236 and 254 Squadrons mounted the Strike Wing's first operation, against a convoy of 12–16 ships heading for Rotterdam. A combination of circumstances led to the loss of three aircraft for only three hits on the ships, an inauspicious start especially as four other Beaufighters were seriously damaged. The C-in-C immediately withdrew the Strike Wing from operations to undertake further training.

Training

Most of Lincolnshire's training units were withdrawn westwards on the outbreak of war, but four Flying Training Command stations remained in the county. Before detailing their activities it is neccessary to outline the RAF flying training system during this period: pilots started their flying training at Elementary Flying Training Schools (EFTS) where they learnt the basics of flying, including their first 'solos', generally on de Havilland Tiger Moths or Miles Magisters. On satisfactory completion of this stage they moved on to advanced training at Service Flying Training Schools (SFTS); depending on their ability, choice and the needs of the RAF at the time, they went to single-engine SFTS, flying Masters or Harvards, or twin-engine SFTS flying Oxfords.

From 1940 onwards most of the EFTSs and SFTSs were located abroad, particularly in Canada, where the students could fly safe from attack and from the dreaded 'black-out' during night flying. British airfields were thus freed for operational flying. However, this did have disadvantages as the newly trained pilots, arriving back in the UK, had great difficulty in adjusting to the crowded skies and the inclement weather, leading to the establishment, from mid-1942, of (Pilot's) Advanced Flying Units ([P]AFU) to which they were sent for acclimatisation, flying the same types of aircraft. After this stage the student moved from Flying Training Command to his operational Command, where he joined an Operational Training Unit (OTU). Here he flew, as far as possible, the type of aircraft he would eventually fly on operations, learning air fighting tactics, gunnery, bombing, etc, and for multi-crewed aircraft he would team up with his crew. In Bomber Command this meant his navigator, who had come through Air Observer School (again often abroad), renamed (Observer)

Advanced Flying Unit ([O] AFU) in 1942; wireless operator (from Radio School); bomb-aimer (AOS and Bombing and Gunnery School); and gunners (from Air Gunnery School).

Nearly all bomber OTUs flew the Wellington and all of the airmen arriving on a particular course were put into a hangar and left to sort themselves into crews, this seeming to work very well. From OTU, until 1942, crews went straight to their squadrons but, with the advent of the four-engined heavy bombers, a further training stage was introduced, the Heavy Conversion Unit (HCU), where another crew member, the flight engineer was added and the crew learnt to handle these sophisticated aircraft. As Lancasters were always in short supply, Lancaster crews usually flew Halifax or Stirlings at HCU. Day fighter pilots went from a Hurricane or Spitfire OTU to a squadron, while night-fighter pilots crewed up with a radar operator at their OTU. There was a similar pattern for Coastal Command crews and, later in the war, Transport Command. Pilots selected to become instructors went to Flying Instructor Schools (FIS).

Lincolnshire's part in this programme took several forms. Cranwell had always been a large camp and World War Two saw it filled to overflowing. The RAF College, on 3rd September 1939, was renamed the RAF College SFTS and carried out the same training as the other SFTSs, equipped with Oxfords. By the spring of 1941, again in common with other SFTSs, RAFC SFTS was using a fantastic number of aircraft by today's standards – 150 Oxfords – necessitating relief airfields at Fulbeck and Barkston. Ron Waite arrived at Cranwell during the hot summer of 1941 and after three hours of dual on the Oxford was ready for his first 'solo', which was performed from Barkston Heath. It was to be an eventful flight, as Ron recounted in *Death or Decoration* (R Waite; Newton Publications, 1992):

'...the temporary airfield looked only slightly larger than an ordinary farm field... In one corner, I saw the black Nissen hut which served as a Flight Office. In the opposite corner, I could see what appeared to be a small, ruined red brick building... As I was approaching the ground, suddenly, a large dark shadow swept across my aeroplane. A wave of apprehension froze my blood... I could only afford a brief glimpse backwards, and to my horror, I saw another Oxford heading straight towards me and barely 20 yards behind... A second later, a shuddering crash behind me shook my aircraft violently, making it uncontrollable. The ground rushed up to meet me. The crash was now inevitable, so I pulled the control column back to bring the nose up and lessen the impact. There was a terrific jolt and sound of splintering wood as the plane struck the ground and slithered across the grass – minus the undercarriage.'

Ron was shaken but unhurt, though the pilot of the other Oxford was seriously injured; such were the hazards of training in crowded skies without radios. Nor was the

SFTS the only occupant – 1 E&W School became 1 Signals School, then 1 Radio School, training both air and ground radio operators and equipped with Westland Wallaces, Vickers Valentias, de Havilland DH.86bs and Miles Mentors early in the war, before standardizing on Percival Proctors. In September 1940, 2 FIS formed with 38 Oxfords and 18 Tutors, becoming 2 Central Flying School (CFS) in November and leaving Cranwell in the summer of 1941. The RAF Hospital, at Cranwell since 1922, was moved from this noisy and crowded environment to Rauceby Hospital, which grew to house 1,000 beds at its peak, plus a Burns Unit where the famous Sir Archibald MacIndoe sometimes operated.

A rather unusual addition to Cranwell's occupants was 3 (Coastal) OTU, which arrived in August 1941 equipped mainly with Armstrong Whitworth Whitleys, a type new to the county, and some Wellingtons. This OTU trained Coastal Command crews in operational techniques after converting them to the Whitley; bombing and gunnery training was carried out and a feature of the course were the long cross-country flights, including one to Rockall which involved 980 miles of flying. It was a 3 OTU Whitley which caused the most serious war damage to the College when it hit the roof in fog, killing three crew and one student in the building. Otherwise, although aircraft were attacked in the circuit by intruders, Cranwell escaped lightly.

A change of role in January 1942 resulted in half of the SFTS Oxfords being replaced by Masters which enabled the school then, unusually, to run both single- and twin-engine courses. Ground units at Cranwell during this period were HQ 21 Group Training Command, the School of Clerks, Accounting (to 1941), the Equipment Training School (to June 1941) and a Supplies Depot.

Despite the undoubted value of Cranwell's training role during World War Two, perhaps its most important contribution to the history of the RAF and its future took place in May 1941 when, on the 11th, a small, partially dismantled aircraft arrived by road, followed later by a team of engineers from Leicestershire, led by one of Cranwell's 'Old Boys', Wing Commander Frank Whittle, who recalled those historic days in May in *Jet* (F Whittle; Muller, 1953):

'I had not flown since June 1939, so I took the opportunity to borrow an Avro Tutor from 2 CFS. I was very pleased to feel that I felt completely at home... On the morning of the next day, the 15th May, the weather was quite unfit for test flying, and so I returned to Lutterworth. But when I returned the weather was improving. I hurried back to Cranwell in the evening, by which time the weather had improved to the point where it was suitable for flight. It was by no means ideal, but there was some blue sky and the cloud base had lifted considerably. While the E.28 taxied to the extreme eastern end of the runway, a group of us went by car to a point about 400 yards along the runway. Sayer [Gerry Sayer,

In 1938, when this photo was taken, the Airspeed Oxford advanced twin-engined trainer was a new aircraft, and these pilots from the RAF College must have noticed a great difference from the biplanes they would have flown previously. L4586 was one of the first batch of Oxfords, a type which saw much service in Lincolnshire. RAF Cranwell via P H T Green

test pilot] was in position at about 7.40pm. He ran the engine up to 16,500rpm. against the brakes. He then released the brakes and the aircraft quickly gathered speed and lifted smoothly from the runway after a run of about 600 yards. It continued to the west in a flat climb for several miles and disappeared from view behind cloud banks.'

This was the first flight by the Gloster/Whittle E.28/39, Britain's first jet-powered aircraft, and was completely successful. Cranwell was chosen because of its comparative closeness to Whittle's Power-jets factory at Lutterworth, and for its long runway and clear approaches. It was also a particularly appropriate choice because it was at Cranwell, as a Cadet, that Frank Whittle had written the thesis which first turned his thoughts to the jet engine. Seventeen trial flights were made from Cranwell under stringent security arrangements but the RAF personnel did, of course, notice this strange aircraft, as Whittle noted:

'One officer at least was greatly disturbed by what he had seen. He sat in the Officer's Mess with a puzzled frown. When asked what was troubling him, he replied that he had seen a strange aeroplane "Going like a bat out of hell" and there was something odd about it, but he couldn't think what it was. After a pause, he said "My God! chaps, I must be going round the bend – it hadn't got a propeller!" '

The E.28/39 was later fitted with a developed engine and its flights were then carried out from a newly built airfield at Edgehill in Warwickshire. As a footnote, Sir Frank went to live in the USA after the war, feeling he had been shabbily treated by the Government, but he subsequently paid several visits to Cranwell and after his death his ashes were flown to the station, in September 1998, in a Meteor, escorted by his son, Ian, in a Vampire, and there scattered.

Sutton Bridge had been evacuated by 3 ATS on the outbreak of war and briefly gained an operational role with the arrival of 64 Squadron's Blenheim If fighters during August 1939. It also saw the formation in October of two fighter squadrons, 264 and 266, the former destined to be the first squadron to operate the Defiant I. However, teething troubles delayed delivery of the aircraft until after the squadron had moved to Martlesham Heath in December; it was to suffer heavy losses during the Battle of Britain.

It was also a while before 266 Squadron received any aircraft, December seeing the delivery of Battles to give flying practice before Spitfire Is arrived in January 1940. The squadron worked up on these before following 264 Squadron to Martlesham Heath in March. Sutton Bridge reverted to training when 6 OTU was formed, with Hurricanes, in March. The OTU trained newly qualified pilots to fly and fight with the Hurricane and in November 1940, in common with the other fighter OTUs, had '50' added to its number, thus becoming 56 OTU. This OTU played an important part in helping to replace the heavy fighter pilot losses in the first years of the war, though it had quite a high accident rate of its own, and moved to Scotland in March 1942. The replacement unit was the Central Gunnery School, which operated a variety of fighters and bombers on which to train air gunnery instructors, and to run specialised gunnery courses. Jack Bushby was sent on a course from 83 Squadron at Scampton, an experience he recounted in *Gunner's Moon* (J Bushby; Ian Allan, 1972):

'Royal Air Force, Sutton Bridge, at first sight gave the impression that, in its remote corner of the fen country, no one had yet broken the news to it that the war had started nearly three years before. A smallish grass air-feld, it lay to one side of the ruler-straight River Nene running right through the fens and carrying the drainage water out to be lost among the sandbanks of the Wash. A small, untidy village straggled on the other bank, and the two were connected by a bridge. On a convenient open space, in the middle of the village, temporary accommodation huts had been erected and it was but a few minutes walk from these across the bridge to the airfield offices and hangars. These latter housed the antique Wellington and Hampden which formed the aircraft of the Central Gunnery School; whilst in another hangar stood about half a dozen Spitfires... The course itself went deep into the theory of aerial gunnery and the mechanics of guns, turrets and the mysteries of ballistics. There was plenty of flying in the Hampden and Wellington, putting theory into practice, not only at live targets but also conducting fierce mock battles against attacking Spitfires from the fighter end of the school, using camera guns...However, the principal exercises laid on for our delight were those known as Full Scale Tactical Formation Defence. Now these were grand occasions when the entire school strength of three Hampdens and three Wellingtons would become airborne in an imposing circus which flew majestically over the flat fen country at some point along its route to be attacked by the Spitfires.'

Grantham started the war equipped with Ansons, Harts and Audaxes, and was brought up to a personnel strength of 927 during September 1939. By November the

An unmarked Fairey Battle Trainer of 12 SFTS runs up at Grantham, 1941; the houses on the airfield's northern boundary can be seen in the distance. 12 SFTS's situation near to the East Coast saw it lose two Battles to Luftwaffe intruders. Mrs Descelles via P H T Green

SFTS was operating 105 aircraft, flying 2,800 day hours and 100 at night during that month; this number of aircraft was the norm for an SFTS, and to this total could be added the Tutor, Oxford and Magister of 5 Group Communications Flight, used to ferry the 'St Vincents' officers around the 5 Group airfields, and further afield as required. By July, Battles had replaced the 12 SFTS biplanes and it was operating 64 Ansons and 48 Battles, Harlaxton having re-opened as a relief landing ground. New equipment also arrived for 5 Group Communications Flight in the form of Proctors, to add to its miscellany of impressed civil aircraft, such as the de Havilland Puss Moth.

In the autumn of 1940 the SFTS was warned to prepare for a move to Canada but this was cancelled in October and training in earnest was renewed. April 1941 saw one of the school's Battles shot down over Harlaxton by an enemy intruder, an act repeated on 18th May, whilst on 11th October an Oxford collided, intentionally or otherwise, with a German night raider over the town, which at this time was one of the most heavily bombed in the country. It is likely that 12 SFTS had the unfortunate record of losing more aircraft shot down than any other training unit.

The Oxfords had begun to arrive in April and fully replaced the Ansons by October, and the school now had the role of training pilots intended for night fighter training at 51 OTU, located at Cranfield in Bedfordshire. The OTU flew Blenheims and these formed the Advanced Training Squadron of 12 SFTS, the pupils doing their initial flying on the Oxfords. High spirits among the pupils sometimes led to them breaking the rules, and in October 1942 one Sergeant Allen was reduced to the ranks and given 21 days' detention for low flying; this may sound harsh but the RAF lost too many young pilots in this way to be lenient. Personnel at Grantham and Harlaxton now totalled 2,593. A similar training establishment, 15 (P) AFU with Oxfords, lodged at Kirmington from March to October 1942.

Manby continued to house 1 AAS and early development of the new 20mm can-non – a weapon built by BMARC at Grantham and fitted to all RAF fighters later in the war – took place. Flying and testing were sometimes interrupted by the Luftwaffe, and the airfield's defences shot down a Ju 88 in December 1940. In mid-1940, 2 Ground Armament School formed to train the armourers and bomb-disposal squads but this unit left for Lancashire in November 1941.

The original Battles of 1 AAS were beginning to be replaced by Blenheims and Wellingtons and the increase in activity saw Manby using Caistor as a satellite from December 1942, this airfield having been used by Kirton-in-Lindsey's fighters up to then. Jack Bushby arrived at Manby for Air Gunner training in 1941:

'[Manby had] efficient administration and a strict discipline, to give it the time honoured soubriquet, bags of bull. It was the home of air armament and contained not only a Gunnery School but also ran specialist courses for Armament Officers and sundry other explosive activities. There were 3,000 officers and airmen and everyone thought, lived and breathed armament... We were marched down to the Stores there to be issued with a small triangular piece of white linen to slip into the front of our side caps, thus to signify aircrew under training. "Aircrew under training" indeed! Just wait until the the girls in Louth got a load of this. In truth the young ladies of that sleepy market town had seen so many sprog airmen come and go over the last year that they were now completely immune and blase to any glamorous connotation...We sat in ground rig training turrets and twirled, rotated, elevated and depressed until we were dizzy... We spent hours on a cold windswept part of the coastal sand dunes firing at cardboard Me 109s a half mile away... In its instruction, as in its discipline, Manby was thorough. There were other gunnery schools but Manby was the original and the best and it was soon made plain to 32 Course how lucky it was to be there.' (IBID)

Non-flying Units

Lincolnshire, being one of the counties closest to the enemy and eminently suited to the building of airfields, housed very few non-flying RAF establishments, these being concentrated further north and west. However, those that were located in the county played important roles, whilst perhaps not seeming as glamorous to the reader as those of the flying units.

Stenigot Chain Home radar station (or Air Ministry Experimental Station as it was at known at the time) opened, as part of the world's first radar chain, in 1938, its four 360ft steel transmitting towers and four 240ft wooden receiving towers dominating the county from their position atop the Wolds. With the amount of flying over Lincolnshire they were a danger to aircraft in bad visibilty and it is recorded that on a foggy 4th August 1941 a very fortunate Blenheim flew *between* the towers! The radar systems were progressively improved throughout the war, Stenigot's normal range being 100 miles out from the coast, plus a height finding ability. Occasionally, good conditions increased its capability and in June 1942 one of our high-flying reconnaissance aircraft was plotted over Bremen, 340 miles distant. The responsibility of becoming a GEE navigational aid transmitting station was added in 1941–42, by which time the personnel numbered 143; the towers could, of course, be plainly seen by German aircraft so Stenigot was defended by 363 Anti-Aircraft Squadron of the RAF Regiment with three Bofors guns.

The Chain Home radars had long range but could only pick up aircraft flying above 10,000ft, leaving aircraft at lower levels to be picked up visually by the Royal Observer Corps; Chain Home's other disadvantage was that its beams searched only seawards. A complimentary system, Chain Home Low, came into use during 1941 and this could scan 360 degrees with its rotating aerial, also picking up low-flying aircraft though with a much shorter range. Three Chain Home Low stations opened in Lincolnshire: Humberston (December 1941), Ingoldmells (1942) and Skendleby (1941). Both of the latter were also Royal Artillery Coastal Defence gunnery radars, watching for ships and jointly manned by 545th Coast Defence Regiment, but Ingoldmells seems to have been wrongly sited and operated for training and as a reserve only from February 1943.

The Chain Home Low stations were quite small, Skendleby having only 37 personnel and Humberston 47. This larger number at Humberston was because it became, in May 1942, a Ground-Controlled Interception (GCI) radar in addition to its Chain Home Low role, operating for Kirton-in-Lindsey Sector. The GCI was a further development which, although of shorter range, enabled the Controller watching the radar screen to talk directly by radio to the pilots intercepting enemy aircraft, whereas the information from the Chain Home and Chain Home Low stations was reported to the Sector Operations Room which then passed it on to the fighters.

Chain Home and Chain Home Low still had an important role because of their longer ranges. Orby, the GCI for Digby Sector, had opened, as one of the first such radars, in March 1941, while Wittering Sector's GCI opened at Langtoft in the south of Lincolnshire, also in 1941. Radar was, of course, extremely secret but Vernon Price worked for William Wright (Lincoln) Ltd as an apprentice bricklayer in 1941 and started his career helping to build the GCI at Langtoft, as he recalled in a letter to the author:

'When working on the roof of the radar room one had to seek permission. This being given resulted in the interior shutters being placed over the windows by the staff to prevent us seeing inside. Come lunch time, everything was left unattended, even the entrance door remained unlocked!'

So much for secrecy. Mr Price also remembers that when the station became operational the barbed-wire perimeter fence had to be removed as it affected the radar picture. When Langtoft was completed he moved on to Coningsby to build WAAF quarters – a reminder of the work of the civilian contractors and of 'Works and Bricks', the Air Ministry Works Directorate (AMWD). The wartime RAF establishments initially came under No. 5 Works Area HQ at 10, Upgate, Louth but moved to Eastgate House as its responsibilities and staff grew. Louth controlled four Section Offices, at Louth, Lincoln, Grantham and Newton (Nottinghamshire), and the personnel totalled about 120 technical and administrative staff, while small numbers of staff were attached to each station. The camp at Honington railway station was an AMWD depot.

As World War Two progressed more and more advances were made in radar and radio as new technology was used, and countered, by both sides. Almost the first example of this was as a result of the discovery that the German bombers were flying along radio beams to their British targets, a cross-beam cutting the first at the target itself to indicate when the bombs should be released. The first such beam was discovered by radio in an Anson flying just south of Spalding on 21st June 1940 and, immediately, countermeasures had to be devised. The most obvious was to 'bend' the beam, thus diverting the bombers to drop their bombs in open country, but there was no time to perfect this. Instead, powerful radio stations were established which transmitted Morse dashes on the German beam frequencies, (the beams worked on mixtures of dashes and dots), so that the constant dashes confused the bomber crews. The radio stations established to carry out these duties were, of course, most secret and

were given the code name 'Aspirin'; one of these opened at Holton-le-Moor in December 1940.

Another technique was to to pick up and repeat the German signals so that the operator in his aircraft could not tell which was the genuine signal and which was not; stations able to do this were codenamed 'Meacon' (Masking Beacon) and one of these opened at Louth in March 1941, its transmitters being sited at South Elkington and receivers at Legbourne, in a field opposite the school, later moving to Gayton Top. The 'Aspirin' station moved to Louth from Holton-le-Moor in June 1941 and Louth continued to perform this vital work.

As the war progressed Louth radio station took on a new role, in April 1942, as a 'Splasher' station, this time aiding our own and Allied aircraft, especially the USAAF bombers. The 'Splasher' stations operated on four frequencies, each with the same callsign, and as our aircraft called up for bearings they could very quickly change frequency if one was jammed by the Germans. Louth was 'Splasher 4'. These camps consisted of several wooden huts and the radio masts, as did that at Mere, near Branston, which housed No. 2 Direction Finding Station.

The only RAF high-speed launch ASR unit based in LIncolnshire was 22 Motor Launch Unit (MLU), the next south being at Wells in Norfolk. Helping to bridge this large gap was, of course, Skegness lifeboat, and Royal Navy rescue launches from Immingham. 22 MLU arrived at Grimsby in June 1940 and the crews were billeted in Abbey Road in the town, the launches being berthed in the Royal Docks. Both aircraft and launch units did extremely important work, not least in helping the morale of aircrew operating over the cold North Sea, who knew that they now had a fighting chance of rescue if forced to ditch.

As an example, Whitley V T4266 'GE-O' of 58 Squadron ditched 90 miles off the Humber estuary on 18th April 1941, exploding shortly after the crew took to their dinghy (which had overturned); they clung to this for two days, first being sighted by another Whitley, which lost them, and then by a Hudson on the second day, which dropped supplies and flame floats. A Hampden then dropped Lindholme gear and, after 64 hours afloat, the weary crew were picked up by a Grimsby high-speed launch.

Also at Grimsby Docks was No.2 Area HQ of the Air Department's Moorings and Salvage Branch, which was civilian-manned and operated three vessels to maintain the coastal bombing ranges' buoys and targets.

Four of these 360ft high masts once towered above the Wolds at Stenigot Chain Home radar station during World War Two; now only this one remains, still used by the RAF but not as a radar station, and a rare structure in the 21st Century. Author

To keep the bombers flying during World War Two four things were required: aircrews, groundcrews, bombs and fuel. Aircrew training has already been covered, whilst groundcrew training in the county is discussed later. Fuel depots at Torksey and Stow Park supplied fuel for most of the Lincolnshire stations. The bombs, ammunition and oxygen were the responsibility of three depots in the county.

93 Maintenance Unit opened in August 1939 on a site adjacent to Swinderby railway station and on the outbreak of war it was heavily camouflaged, including its roads; it began to issue bombs to Hemswell, Waddington and Scampton, having 132 airmen on strength by July 1940. When Swinderby airfield opened the 93 MU site was renamed Norton Disney, although this village was several miles away, raising the issue of why the RAF sometimes chose a particular name. Whatever, Norton Disney continued to supply 5 Group with its explosives.

In March 1942, 100 MU opened at South Witham, with three officers and 90 men under canvas, five Nissen huts soon being erected. Some idea of the physical work involved at these depots can be judged by the fact that in July 1942, 3,769 tons of ammunition were brought in by rail and lorry, whilst 1,724 tons were issued to the airfields. There was some excitement in November when a Halifax crashed and burnt a mere 35 yards from a high explosives storage area! The third depot opened in January 1943 and is covered later.

The first taste of RAF life for airmen (and women) was recruit training and many recruit centres were established to cope with the great increase occasioned by the

war. At Skegness, 11 Recruits Centre opened in February 1941, with an establishment of 1,134. Surprising as it may now seem, there was no camp as such for these airmen because they were billeted in the numerous boarding houses and hotels which the resort had to offer. (Butlins at Ingoldmells already housed HMS *Royal Arthur*, a Royal Navy recruits' camp, so that Skegness must have been swamped with light and dark blue uniforms.)

Station HQ was in the Seacroft Hotel, sick quarters in Seacroft Boys' School, the guardroom on the corner of Somersby Grove and a rifle range on Seacroft Esplanade; so overcrowded did the available accommodation become that No. 2 Wing moved to Boston. Meals were taken in a school hall, to which the airmen marched, and the training included PT, drill, bayonet, grenade throwing, firing practice and the dreaded assault course, lasting in all about six weeks. The Centre was commanded by Group Captain Insall, who had won the VC in the RFC in World War One. Even at this early stage in their RAF careers the recruits were faced with death, three being killed in a bombing raid on 15th September 1942 and another nine on 24th October.

At the beginning of the war, 1 Ground Defence School at North Coates had trained airmen in airfield defence, and they were organised into 'Defence Squadrons'. However, as the war went on a better system was needed, not least to free the soldiers who were guarding the airfields for other duties. In December 1941 the RAF Regiment was formed, to be responsible for the defence of RAF airfields and other stations from air and ground attack. The RAF Regiment Depot was established at Belton Park, Grantham (the site of a massive World War One Army camp), and there was a Battle Training School at Anderby Creek. RAF Regiment squadrons were based on many Lincolnshire airfields for the rest of the war.

The Observer Corps (it gained the prefix 'Royal' in 1941 in recognition of its work during the Battle of Britain) was a civilian organisation formed in 1925 to 'spot' enemy aircraft and provide the defences with their whereabouts. It was operationally part of Fighter Command and, from the outbreak of war, stood watch 24 hours a day, seven days a week, despite most of its members having a full-time job.

Observer posts were placed at about five-mile intervals around the country, reporting hostile and friendly aircraft movements to back up the radar system. In Lincolnshire these posts reported by landline telephone to the Operations Room of 11 Lincoln Group which was, from 1936, located in a room at the top of Lincoln General Post Office on Guildhall Street, moving in 1940 to St Peter's Chambers in Silver Street, where there was room for offices and rest rooms. The increasing work and decreasing manpower led to the recruitment of Women Observers from 1941, and these soon became the majority in the operations room.

High Speed Launch 142, of 22 Motor Launch Unit, at its berth in Grimsby Dock Basin c1942. HSL 142 was 63ft long and its Class was nicknamed 'The Whalebacks', for obvious reasons. L Chapman via Graham Chaters

Chapter Four

World War Two –
The Later Years 1943-1945

The Bomber's War

After three and a half years of war Bomber Command was developing into a mighty force and its new aircraft, weapons and navigation aids were all contributing to greater effectiveness: The first thousand bomber raid had been carried out against Cologne in May 1942; Lancasters and Halifaxes were coming from the factories in large numbers (the faithful Hampdens conducted their last bomber operation in September 1942), fitted with the new GEE and H2S target finding equipment; 8 (Pathfinder Force) Group had been formed and some of its Mosquitoes were equipped with Oboe, another new target finder; and last, but not least, Arthur Harris was now C-in-C.

Bomber Command's role was also made clear by the Casablanca Conference Directive of January 1943. Together with the US 8th Air Force, it was to be used

'...for the progressive destruction and dislocation of the German military, industrial and economic system, and the undermining of the morale of the German people to the point where their capacity for armed resistance is fatally weakened'.

The Command gathered its resources for this task. In March 1943 Lincolnshire's bomber stations were:

1 Group

Wickenby	12 Sqn	Lancasters
Grimsby	100 Sqn	Lancasters
Elsham Wolds	103 Sqn	Lancasters
Kirmington	166 Sqn	Wellingtons
Ingham	199 Sqn	Wellingtons
Hemswell	300, 301, 305 Sqns	Wellingtons

Total: 57 Lancasters and 80 Wellingtons

5 Group

Waddington	9, 44 Sqns	Lancasters
Fiskerton	49 Sqn	Lancasters
Skellingthorpe	50 Sqn	Lancasters
Scampton	57 Sqn	Lancasters
Woodhall Spa	97 Sqn	Lancasters

Total: 105 Lancasters

In March 1943 Guy Gibson returned to Lincolnshire to command a new, top-secret unit, known as 'X' Squadron, at Scampton. A few days later the Air Ministry allocated it a number, 617. The story of its raid on the Ruhr dams in May 1943 is well known and will not be repeated here; suffice to say it caught the public imagination and 617 Squadron became known as 'The Dambusters', a name which the squadron retains to this day.

Originally intended to be used only for the Dams raid, 617 Squadron carried on after it, although Gibson left for a well deserved rest, the exploit having earned him Scampton's third VC. Morale in the squadron at this time was not good, as no further operations were carried out until July 1943 when it raided Italy, flying on to North Africa, with another raid on the way back. August saw the squadron move to Coningsby with its brand-new runways, while Scampton's other unit, 57 Squadron, moved to the new airfield at East Kirkby, thus permitting Scampton to close so that it too could have hard runways built. However, although the station had no flying units based on it, it was still the HQ 52 Base and controlled its satellites at Dunholme Lodge and Fiskerton.

The Base system was a new organisation introduced to simplify the chain of command and increase operational efficiency; commanded by an air commodore, the first digit of the Base number denoted its Group and the second the individual Base, each of which comprised the HQ airfield and one or two satellites, the HQ controlling operations. The HQ airfield also housed the Base Major Servicing Unit. During its non-flying period Scampton was home to the Aircrew Commando School, which moved in from Morton Hall near Swinderby (leaving the Hall to become HQ, 5 Group, itself moving from St Vincent's, Grantham). The Aircrew Commando School served to physically toughen newly arrived aircrew, and to train them in survival and evasion should they be shot down.

New bomber airfields were opening almost monthly during 1943: on 14th April Bardney received the Lancasters of 9 Squadron, which had taken off from Waddington the previous evening for a raid on Spezia, Italy. The groundcrew left Waddington at 21:00 hours and the aircraft landed back at Bardney at 06:30 hours; such was the pace of the bombing offensive. Dunholme Lodge opened in May and 44 Squadron arrived from Waddington which then, like Scampton, got its concrete runways. The personnel of 44 Squadron used up the stock of the Sergeants' Mess at an enormous party the night before the move! This may account for the sight enjoyed by Pip Brimson the next day when 44's final two Lancasters, flown by Canadian Cliff Schneider and a Flight Lieutenant Pilgrim, took off, formed into line abreast and

'...flew directly at the Watch Office at naught feet, only at the last minute climbing away, one to port, the other almost vertically. We had stared mesmerised, and a great gasp went up at this final display. It was a magnificent beat-up and a great flourish of farewell!'

Over on the Wolds, June saw the Lancasters of 101 Squadron fly into Ludford Magna, its home for the remainder of the war. Ludford soon rejoiced in the nickname 'Mudford Magna' because here, as at all other war construction airfields, mud was omnipresent after wet weather. Its near neighbour, Kelstern, opened in October and its unit, 625 Squadron, like 617 Squadron, was completely new, without the traditions and service of squadrons such as 44, 100 and 101. This made no difference at all to the performance and morale of the personnel and 625, with its motto 'We Avenge', operated Lancasters throughout its brief history and, after the war, was the first squadron to erect a memorial to its fallen members, on the site of its airfield. (This started a trend which has seen memorials put up at virtually every airfield in the county.)

The end of one 625 Squadron crew was witnessed by Russell Margerison, who recounted the tragic event in his book Boys at War (Ross Anderson Publications, 1986):

'On this beautifully clear night we were flying down wind at some 400ft, parallel to the welcoming lane of runway lights as S-Sugar, containing Cosgrove's jubilant crew [Russell's skipper and Cosgrove always raced to be first back], banked slightly in the funnel lights on her landing approach. With wheels and flaps down she was almost there, then to my utter amazement a pair of navigation lights appeared directly behind 'Sugar'.

'I pointlessly shouted into my switched-off intercom, "Look out, look..." My involuntary warning was never finished, for streams of cannon shells were being pumped into the Lanc from a terrifyingly close range. Red and white sparks danced along the fuselage, the machine shuddered violently, like a dog which had just emerged from water, and in she went, with feeble flames never having the chance to envelop her. No explosion occurred. It was all over in seconds. Frighteningly final.'

The Luftwaffe Ju88 had followed the bombers home, a not-infrequent occurrence.

At the southern end of the Wolds Spilsby had opened in September 1943, housing 207 Squadron, while Metheringham (106 Squadron) and North Killingholme (550 Squadron) joined the order of battle before the year's end. The construction of these new airfields all over the UK did, of course, involve great loss of agricultural land and demolition of farms and buildings, causing hardship to the people concerned; more details of how this occurred can be found in the book *Airfield Heyday* (P Berry; Berry, 1989). Suffice it to say that a Lincolnshire bomber airfield cost some £785,000 to build, had 2.5 miles of drains, 35,000 yards of tarmac, 11 miles of roads, 5 miles of water mains and 3.5 miles of sewers, with 4 million bricks being used.

Despite the fact that all RAF bomber squadrons were extremely cosmopolitan, being composed of British, Commonwealth and Allied personnel, the Commonwealth air forces did form their own squadrons as already related, numbered in the 400 series, the 300 series being used by Allied countries. Some Canadian squadrons had already served in Lincolnshire, but with the formation of 6 (Canadian) Group in Yorkshire, the bomber units moved there. The Australian units were not of sufficient number to form their own Group, many Australians having returned home to fight against the Japanese threatening their own country; however, they did form three Lan-

caster squadrons, all of which were operating from Lincolnshire by 1944 (there was also a Halifax squadron in 4 Group). In *Strike and Return* (Brokensha Pty Ltd, Australia), P Firkins recalls his time on 460 (RAAF) Squadron, which moved with its Wellington IVs from Molesworth to Breighton in Yorkshire in January 1942:

'After having been at Breighton for over a year the squadron had really become a part of that normally peaceful section in the East Riding of Yorkshire... The people of Breighton looked upon them as their protégé, and were grieved at their losses and tolerant of their pranks... On 14 May the transfer to Binbrook officially took place. The aircrews and maintenance personnel flew over in Lancasters, whilst the main body were transported by Horsa gliders.'

This was a quick method of moving and provided much needed training for the Army glider pilots and their tow tugs; no doubt the RAF personnel were not too keen!

'Binbrook, their new home, was situated on the top of the highest point of the Lincolnshire countryside, and it proved bitterly cold in winter for, apart from the snow, it caught the full blast of the winds whipping in from the North Sea. However, despite the comparatively harsh climatic conditions, Binbrook being a peacetime station provided many comforts which were certainly not available at Breighton. The crews were billeted in what were peacetime married quarters, and both the offi-

'Mudford Magna' shows how it got its nickname in this view of a 101 Squadron Lancaster, 'G for George', ready to go; judging by the state of the ground and the groundcrew's apparel this is winter atop the Wolds. Note the FIDO pipes running parallel to the runway. 101 Squadron

cers' and sergeants' messes had the reputation of providing the best meals available at any RAF station in England.

'The squadron settled comfortably into the life at Binbrook, the favourite pub being the "Marquis of Granby"... "Smokey Joe's", an old hut about half-way between the station and village, had been converted into a restaurant of sorts, and used to dish out tea and baked beans on toast during the idle moments of day or night.'

The squadron was soon back on 'ops', the first being two days after the move and the second a raid on Dortmund, when Bomber Command dropped, for the first time, over 2,000 tons of bombs on a target. Two Australian crews were lost from the 22 taking part. The squadron was to lose 48 more crews of seven men each during the rest of 1943, from 67 operations.

Not all of the action took place in the air however – bomb explosions on airfields were fortunately rare but did take place, causing much damage and shaking the local communities (the reason why airfield bomb stores were situated on the opposite side of the airfield to the living quarters and any villages!) At Binbrook, in July 1943, an electrical short-circuit caused the entire bomb-load of one Lancaster III (DV172) to fall to the ground, causing the incendiaries to ignite, as P Firkins remembers:

'Two of the ground staff were inside the bomber at the time and they leapt out and tried to roll the 4,000lb ('Cookie') bomb away, but found it was hopeless and ran for safety. They had gone about 400 yards when the 'Cookie' together with two 1,000lb bombs exploded, scattering the incendiaries among the other aircraft and knocking the two escaping airmen to the ground. The Lancaster standing in the next dispersal point [R5745] burst into flames and about two minutes later its bomb-load exploded.'

Thanks to brave work by ground staff, further explosions were averted, and in half-an-hour the danger had passed; 17 Lancasters later took off for Cologne. Binbrook's CO, Group Captain Hughie Edwards VC, later

'...swore that whilst going from one bomber to another in his staff car, he was doing about 50 and was passed by an RAF erk running from the danger area!'

A sideline on this incident is provided by ex-WAAF Maud Baxter in a letter to the author:

'I was on duty that evening in the Sergeants' Mess. We were preparing the ops meal when, on looking out of the window, I noticed aircrews and other personnel running helter-skelter down the hill past the Mess, at the same time calling to us to join them as a big "cookie" was about to blow up and would flatten the place. I turned to our Flight Sergeant and said "Should we run?" He replied "Certainly not, we've the meal to prepare and we are staying here to get on with it." I thought how foolish when most probably there would be no Mess to return to. But, as always, we obeyed orders and got on with the job. We were told to open all windows and doors to let the blast through. We felt it alright and heard other minor explosions.

'Some time later, the crews drifted slowly back, looking rather sheepish, I thought, eventually coming in for their meal which, incidentally, was served on time. We cooks were quite proud to think we had stayed at our posts. But, believe me, I think we were all a bit scared and, if it had not been for the Flight Sergeant, we would have run too.'

Accidents on take-off also happened and, fully laden with fuel and bombs as the aircraft were, usually proved fatal. Flight Lieutenant B A Knyvett of 460 Squadron took off on the first operation of his second tour (all crews had to do a tour of 30 operations, second tours were usually voluntary) on 2nd January 1944; as P Firkins recalls, Knyvett's Lancaster III (JB738 'AR-T')

'...crashed immediately after take-off, apparently as a

result of some technical defect, because he was never in control of the aircraft during the short time it was airborne. He pleaded over the radio telephone with Group Captain Edwards, watching from the control tower, to advise him what to do, but before he had a chance to reply the lurching bomber, fully laden with bombs and petrol, crashed after doing half a circuit and killed the whole crew. A WAAF, also standing in the control tower, was carried away hysterical after hearing the screams of the doomed crew over the R/T just as they crashed'.

Such was the price bomber crews sometimes paid and, because of these dangers, they played hard and often drank hard. Every squadron had its favourite local pub, such as the 'Marquis of Granby', Binbrook, the 'White Hart', Lissington, 'The George', Langworth, the 'Horse and Jockey', Waddington, the 'Abbey Lodge', Kirkstead, the 'Golf Hotel', Woodhall Spa, 'The Ship' and the 'Callow Park', Skegness, the 'Shades', Spilsby, 'Peacock and Royal', Boston, 'Houghton Arms', Timberland, and many others. In Lincoln the 'Saracen's Head' and 'Ye Olde Crowne' were the haunts of all the Lincolnshire squadrons. Parties were held at the slightest excuse, as when 460 had one in the dance hall on the pier at Cleethorpes, as P Firkins recalls:

'Almost 1,000 people attended, and it was paid for by the aircrews as a gesture to the ground staff... As the evening wore on and became more rowdy, one intrepid type decided to dive off the end of the pier but overlooked the fact that the tide was at low ebb, with the result that he landed with a sickening thud on his head in the sand. His pulse rate is reported to have dropped to an alarming 34 for some time, but he lived, and a relieved MO said he didn't think this could happen to any other squadron.'

1943 passed into 1944, the bombing offensive continued, and the Lincolnshire

This explosion is not that at Binbrook but one that took place at East Kirkby on 17th April 1945 which, in fact was much more serious, destroying six of 57 Squadron's Lancasters, seriously damaging a hangar and other buildings, and killing three RAF men and one Pioneer Corps soldier, with 14 seriously injured. S F Porteous

squadrons flew every night that the weather permitted. Most of the squadrons flew the normal 'Main Force' raids, loaded with HE bombs and incendiaries, but there was the odd squadron which had 'special duties' (not those normally connected with this phrase, which entailed dropping agents and supplies to occupied Europe, but those outside the 'Main Force' raids). One such unit was 617 Squadron, Arthur Harris having decided that

'We'll make 'em a special duties squadron. They needn't do ordinary ops, but whenever the Army or Navy want a dam or a ship or something clouted we'll put 617 on to it'.

Sir Ralph Cochrane, AOC 5 Group, carried this a stage further and got the squadron training with the new Stabilizing Automatic Bomb Sight, from 20,000ft. The bomb load was to be the 10-tonner, designed by Sir Barnes Wallis, which only the Lancaster could carry. The squadron, now commanded by Leonard Cheshire, trained over Wainfleet Range; in January 1944 they moved from Coningsby to the tree-surrounded Woodhall Spa and all the time were evolving new techniques, culminating in low-level marking by Cheshire himself; this was used very successfully when 12 Lancasters flattened the Gnome-Rhone aircraft engine factory at Limoges (using normal bomb loads) without damaging the surrounding French housing.

In April 1944 four Mosquito VIs were loaned to 617 Squadron for target marking, being much more manoeuvrable than the heavy Lancaster, and proved so successful that Air-Marshal Harris transferred an entire squadron of these aircraft, 627, plus 57 and 83 Squadrons with Lancasters from 8 Pathfinder Group to be the target markers for 5 Group, based at Woodhall Spa. This was much resented by the crews of these three squadrons, who had volunteered to join 8 Group and regarded 5 Group as 'Cochrane's Private Air Force'. Be that as it may, later still Cheshire was to use a Mustang to mark for 617 Squadron on daylight raids on French targets, which was also a success and led to 54 Base, Coningsby, 'borrowing' a P-38 Lightning from the US 8th Air Force, later replaced by the two-seat version of the P-38, commonly called a 'Droop Snoot'. These aircraft were never officially taken on charge by the RAF but operated from Coningsby until October 1944.

One pilot who sometimes flew the P-38s was Wing Commander Guy Gibson VC DSO DFC, once CO of 617 and now a staff-officer at 54 Base and forbidden by the RAF's 'top brass' to fly on any further operations subsequent to the Dams Raid – much to his chagrin. Gibson also flew, non-operationally, the Mosquitoes of Woodhall Spa-based 627 Squadron and, having directly appealed to 'Bomber' Harris, was given permission to fly one of these as Master Bomber for a raid on the towns of Rheydt and Mönchengladbach; this was to be positively his last operation and it took place on 19th September 1944. As his navigator Gibson took Squadron Leader J B Warwick DFC, a staff-navigator at 54 Base, and the raid was a success, Gibson congratulating the Lancaster crews before he too turned for home – but over Holland disaster struck and Mosquito XX (KB267 'AZ-E'), for reasons still unknown, plunged into the ground, killing both men; so perished one of Lincolnshire's best-known airman.

An unusual task for 617 Squadron was to fly, together with a Stirling squadron, extremely accurate, slowly advancing orbits across the English Channel on the evening of D-Day minus 1, throwing out 'Window' to simulate, on enemy radar, an invasion force moving at 12 knots towards Calais, a spoof

which was completely successful. Shortly afterwards 617 Squadron took a more active part in the invasion by dropping the first 12,000lb 'Tallboy' bombs on the Saumur railway tunnel, cutting a vital reinforcement link to the German army in Normandy. In September the first raid was made on the Tirpitz, anchored in a Norwegian fjord and posing a severe threat to the Royal Navy. The squadron operated from a base in Russia for this and a second and third attack were needed before the German battleship capsized after being hit directly (and surrounded by other hits) by the Tallboys.

March 1945 saw the first use of Barnes Wallis's even bigger bomb, the 22,000lb 'Grand Slam', when 617 Squadron dropped it on the Bielefeld Viaduct. The bombsight was extremely accurate; after the war Flying Officer Muhl's crew dropped a Tallboy on the U-boat pens at Bremen, to test its penetrating power. A black 20ft square was painted on the top of the pens and the bomb (not fused) hit almost in the middle.

The other squadron which used Tallboys, and operated with 617 Squadron on all three raids against the Tirpitz, was 9 Squadron at Bardney; the squadron was selected for the Tirpitz raids because of the accuracy of its practice bombing on the ranges, and also bombed dams, bridges and viaducts. On 1st

101 Squadron's Lancasters carried special electronic equipment to make life difficult for the German air defence system and 'W for Whiskey' has the distinctive ABC aerials above its fuselage, with another just visible below the nose. This equipment was obviously very secret at the time (and for a long while after the war) so it is no wonder that the taker of this photograph was hiding in a hut when he took it!
101 Squadron

January 1945, it was ordered to mount a fourth attack on the quickly repaired Dortmund–Ems Canal. Two of the ten Lancaster Is (NG252 'WS-R' and PD368 'WS-A') crashed on take-off from Bardney and one aircraft which had just bombed the target (PD377 'WS-U') was hit by flak. Flight Sergeant G Thompson, the wireless operator, rescued the mid-upper gunner from his burning turret and then, although badly burned and frostbitten, pulled the rear gunner from his turret which was also on fire. The Captain, Flying Officer R F H Denton, crash-landed the bomber in liberated Europe near Heesch, but Thompson died three weeks later; he received a posthumous VC. These raids, together with the Dams operation, were the most accurate of World War Two.

The third 'special' squadron was 101 at Ludford Magna which, from October 1943, undertook what is now known as electronic countermeasures. All of its Lancasters carried Airborne Cigar (ABC) radios, which could search out the frequencies used by the German night-finders and then transmit noises which effectively jammed any enemy broadcast. The 'special operator', the eighth crew member carried by 101's Lancasters, was German-speaking and could, if required, give out misleading directions to the German pilots in their own language. All of this was carried out on top of normal bombing ops and, because the Germans could sometimes home onto the Lancasters' radio transmissions, 101 Squadron suffered above average losses. Some of the 'special' wireless operators were in fact German-born and thus took a double risk when flying over Germany.

The night-bombing offensive took a heavy toll of the crews, especially in late 1943 and the first few months of 1944, until the offensive was switched to tactical targets prior to D-Day. Binbrook-based 460 (RAAF) Squadron, for example, lost 39 crews from January to June 1944, but only 44 during the remainder of the war. Martin Middlebrook's excellent book The Nuremburg Raid paints an authentic picture of one of Bomber Command's costliest operations, on the night of 30th March 1944; in all, 96 aircraft failed to return out of the total of 779 despatched. The effort of the Lincolnshire squadrons was as follows:

9 Sqn, Bardney: 16 sent, 1 missing
12 Sqn, Wickenby: 14 sent, 2 missing
44 Sqn, Dunholme Lodge: 16 sent, 2 missing
49 Sqn, Fiskerton: 16 sent, 2 missing
50 Sqn, Skellingthorpe: 19 sent, 3 missing,
    1 crashed on take off
57 Sqn, East Kirkby: 18 sent, 1 missing
61 Sqn, Coningsby: 14 sent, 2 missing
100 Sqn, Grimsby: 18 sent, all returned
101 Sqn, Ludford Magna: 26 sent, 7 missing
103 Sqn, Elsham Wolds: 16 sent, 2 missing
106 Sqn, Metheringham: 17 sent, 3 missing
166 Sqn, Kirmington: 20 sent, 4 missing
207 Sqn, Spilsby: 18 sent, 2 missing
460 Sqn, Binbrook: 24 sent, 3 missing
463 Sqn, Waddington: 18 sent, all returned
467 Sqn, Waddington: 17 sent, 2 missing
550 Sqn, North Killingholme: 17 sent,
    2 missing
576 Sqn, Elsham Wolds: 16 sent, 1 missing
619 Sqn, Coningsby: 16 sent, 1 missing
625 Sqn, Kelstern: 13 sent, 1 missing
626 Sqn, Wickenby: 16 sent, all returned
630 Sqn, East Kirkby: 16 sent, 3 missing

This one night, admittedly with abnormally high casualties, meant 45 empty dispersals and the staggering figure of 317 empty beds in the Lincolnshire officers' and sergeants' messes (248 were killed, 63 taken prisoner and six evaded capture and eventually returned home; in addition, 12 wounded airmen were in aircraft which got back to base. 101 Squadron alone lost 56 men). What was a normal figure for that night was the number of aircraft despatched, the Lincolnshire squadrons sending a total of 281 Lancasters to Nuremburg. The sound of 1,124 Merlins at take-off power must have made sleep impossible for many county residents – and this was a nightly occurrence. An evocative picture of a typical squadron take-off is given by Jack Currie in Lancaster Target (J Currie; New English Library, 1977), just after he arrived at Wickenby to join 12 Squadron:

'Lancaster PH-C for Charlie was lurching slowly out of dispersal, marshalled by an airman walking backwards, beckoning hands above his head. As the bomber swung on to the taxiway, the marshaller turned and ran for the grass, out of the aircraft's path. He stood, holding up his thumbs, as Charlie lumbered past, and then bent over, clasping his cap to his head, as the slipstream of four propellers washed over him. The Lancaster moved warily along the taxiway, rudders swinging, brakes squealing, and as it passed me I saw the mid-upper gunner's face behind his gun barrels. I put up a thumb and saw his gloved hand wave in reply. Now all around the darkening airfield the bombers were moving, making the amber taxying lamps twinkle as they passed between them, forming two processions, one from either side of the main runway, converging on the steady red light that marked the airfield controller's caravan...

'A green light flashed from the caravan – the leading aircraft moved on to the runway, straightened into wind, paused while the engines cleared their throats, and drove, uncertainly at first and then with gathering momentum, into headlong chase for flight. As it lifted, the next Lancaster was already rolling forward, and then another, until three aircraft moved within my field of vision. The first was slowly climbing to the left, its navigation lights just visible above the tree line, the second running tail up for take-off, and the third swinging on to the runway by the caravan. The air was filled with heavy noise, which mounted to a peak as each successive bomber passed my vantage point. I put my fingers to my ears, and wondered how much noise the night could hold.'

November 1943 saw Waddington reopen, resplendent with its new runways, and into it flew 467 (RAAF) Squadron from Bottesford; later in the month the squadron's 'C' Flight split away to become 463 (RAAF) Squadron, Lincolnshire's third Australian Lancaster squadron. From its Nissen huts at Dunholme 44 Squadron noted with some envy that the Aussies had moved into its former luxurious accommodation and suggested that this was because '...if the Aussies were sent to the quagmires of Dunholme they would give more trouble than the Germans!' (44 Sqn ORB) However, 44 Squadron was joined in the 'quagmire' by 619 Squadron in April 1944; it was now becoming more common for airfields to house two squadrons as new units joined Bomber Command. Scampton re-opened in October 1944 with 153 Squadron, which had just disbanded in North Africa as a Beaufighter VIf night-fighter unit. Still operating at night, but now with Lancasters, it had reformed at Kirmington and moved almost immediately to Scampton where it stayed until disbanded again, at the end of the war.

Strangely, two airfields ceased to operate bombers during 1944; Ingham, which did not have hard runways, had housed the two Polish squadrons (300 and 305) but could not operate Lancasters, so 300 Squadron moved across to Faldingworth in March. When the two squadrons had moved to Ingham, in June 1943, it was recorded that (Destiny Can Wait: Heinemann; 1949):

'The airfield itself left much to be desired. There were no runways and the grassy area was muddy, pot-holed and bumpy all the year round – in the middle of the airfield there was a farmstead in a grove of tall but sturdy trees... any pilot who managed its peculiarities could be confident of landing safely in the middle of, say, Romney Marshes or Epping Forest... On 1st March 1944, some kindly soul in HQ Bomber Command did his good deed for the day and transferred 300 Squadron from Ingham to RAF Station, Faldingworth. Faldingworth became, by May, a fully Polish manned station, with 854 personnel, 194 of which were Polish WAAFs, and 163 aircrew.'

Until that time some of the groundcrew had been RAF and WAAF, the latter being very popular with the Poles! Wally Phillips , in a letter to the author in 1981, remembers that his then girlfriend (and later wife) Margaret, wangled a posting to Faldingworth to be near to Wally at Wickenby: 'Margaret would be the first to point out that service on a Polish squadron means that even today, at the age of 57, she can still run a six-minute mile!'

After 300 Squadron left, Ingham took in 1687 Bomber Defence Training Flight, the Spitfires and Hurricanes of which executed mock attacks on the bombers, giving them practice in evading these. Dunholme, although it had runways, was found to cause problems when Scampton re-opened, being so close that the circuits overlapped, and so it closed for operations in November and was then used by General Aircraft Ltd as a modification base for their large Hamilcar gliders, used in the Rhine crossing in March 1945.

For most of the Lincolnshire-based squadrons the last operation of the war was, rather appropriately, against Hitler's mountain retreat at Berchtesgaden on 25th April in which 359 Lancasters took part, with only two losses. After this they were kept busy ferrying back PoWs from Germany and Italy, whilst another mercy operation was the dropping of 6,700 tons of food to the starving Dutch population, this taking place before hostilities ceased but with the agreement of the Germans. Taking the groundcrew to look at the damage they had helped to cause was another task. In April 1945 the Lincolnshire squadron line-up was as follows:

Squadron	Base	No. of Lancasters
1 Group		
12	Wickenby	23
100	Elsham Wolds	21
101	Ludford Magna	45
103	Elsham Wolds	21
150	Hemswell	21
153	Scampton	19
166	Kirmington	33
170	Hemswell	20
300	Faldingworth	21
460	Binbrook	37
550	North Killingholme	30
576	Fiskerton	31
625	Scampton	19
626	Wickenby	22
5 Group		
9	Bardney	19
44	Spilsby	22
49	Fulbeck	20
50	Skellingthorpe	23
57	East Kirkby	15
61	Skellingthorpe	22
106	Metheringham	21
189	Bardney	22
207	Spilsby	21
227	Strubby	21
463	Waddington	19
467	Waddington	21
619	Strubby	21
630	East Kirkby	21
617	Woodhall Spa	25
		+1 Mosquito

Polish airmen flew their bombers from Lincolnshire throughout the war; here, at Ingham in mid-war, a 300 Squadron Wellington III sits on its dispersal, with its groundcrew taking a well-deserved break. The Wellington equipped most of the north Lincolnshire airfields, 1940-43, and 300 had them longer than most, until April 1944.
R Stadtmuller via Mike Ingham

In addition, three Pathfinder squadrons had been loaned to 5 Group, these being 83 Squadron at Coningsby (21 Lancasters), 97 Squadron at Coningsby (23 Lancasters) and 627 Squadron at Woodhall Spa (27 Mosquitoes – the only non-Lancaster squadron in the two Groups). It can be seen that all 1 and 5 Group squadrons were now Lincolnshire-based, and even before the war had ended Grimsby and Kelstern had closed for operations, while Strubby and Fulbeck had been taken over by Bomber Command. Lincolnshire could, in fact, offer a total of 721 Lancasters and 27 Mosquitoes for operations.

When the war in Europe ended in May 1945, several squadrons were earmarked for the Tiger Force, the RAF's contribution to the strategic bombing of Japan, and at Swinderby 13 Aircraft Modification Unit was formed to modify the Lancasters which would equip this force – this work entailed fitting improved navigation aids and extra fuel tanks as well as other changes required for operations in a tropical climate. However, the two atomic bombs dropped on Japan in August 1945 removed the necessity for the Tiger Force Lancasters and Bomber Command was now at peace. The bombers' war had lasted from the first day of World War Two almost to the last and by the end of hostilities they were a formidable weapon. Many criticisms have since been levelled at the strategic bombing offensive, which failed to reduce Germany's production of war materials by as much as had been expected; one can only wonder what it would have been if Bomber Command had not disrupted it. In any case, the raids forced the Germans to concentrate on fighter production, not the bombers which could have caused havoc in this country. They had to convert anti-tank guns for anti-aircraft duties and they had to keep the Luftwaffe largely for the defence of Germany rather than air support for their armies on the Western and Eastern Fronts.

RAF Bomber Command suffered heavy losses, 1 and 5 Groups (together with the nearby HCUs) losing 22,000 aircrew, the names of whom are recorded in two large books kept in Lincoln Cathedral – an appropriate location as the three towers of the Cathedral, sometimes the only landmark showing above fog and mist, welcomed the returning crews, for whom it became a symbol. Since the 1970s many ex-airmen have returned to Lincolnshire to visit their old airfields at which, as already related, many

memorials have been erected to honour those who did not come back. One who did survive was Wally Phillips, once an air-gunner with 12 Squadron at Wickenby, who wrote to the author:

'My recollections mainly are that in six years of service with the RAF, including a couple of years with the Desert Air Force, the last two years, with Bomber Command, were the most frightening of my life, and attempts at recollection end in bad dreams... I go back to Lincolnshire not only to see wartime friends but because, for some reason I cannot explain, I have to go back, if only for a few hours.'

Undoubtedly there are, for many, echoes of their youth in Lincolnshire, the county in which they experienced the terror (and also the joy) which few of us have had to experience since; but for all too many airmen Lincolnshire was their last view of Britain and they did not live beyond youth. Perhaps the best tribute to the bomber crews is paid in *Royal Air Force 1939-45* (D Richards and H St G Saunders; HMSO, 1954. Reproduced by permission of the Controller of HMSO):

'Those who held the controls of the bomber in their firm young hands truly deserve a crown of bays. Night after night in darkness bathed in silver or veiled with clouds, undeterred by the "fury of the guns and the new inventions of death" they rode the skies above Germany, and paid without flinching the terrible price which war demands. In the select company of those who have laid down their lives to save the lives of others these British airman who died bombing Germany must hold high rank. The assault, which they maintained with unswerving vigour and energy, was so well sustained, so nourished, and became so effective that the total casualties suffered by the British army in the 11 months which elapsed between its landing upon the shores of Normandy and the unconditional surrender of Germany upon the heath at Lüneburg were less than the losses incurred in one month by their fathers in the Battle of the Somme.'

During World War Two VCs were awarded to seven Lincolnshire-based airmen: Flight Lieutenant Roderick Learoyd, 49 Squadron, Scampton, August 1940; Sergeant John Hannah, 83 Squadron, Scampton, September 1940; Squadron Leader John Nettleton, 44 Squadron,

A photo to represent and honour all of Bomber Command's Lincolnshire-based aircrew. This 207 Squadron crew at Spilsby, c1944, had not long returned from a raid and the strain still shows; 'Grandpop' Millward, the flight engineer (second from right) was, at 33, old by aircrew standards. On the night of 21st/22nd June 1944, their Lancaster, ME827, was shot down over Holland during a raid on Wesseling and only Warrant Officer Young, the navigator (third from left) survived to become a prisoner-of-war. 36 other Lancasters (including four others from 207 Sqn), one Mosquito and two Fortress IIs were also lost that night.
Terry Millward

Waddington, April 1942; Flying Officer Leslie Manser, 50 Squadron, Skellingthorpe, May 1942 (posthumous); Wing Commander Guy Gibson, 617 Squadron, Scampton, May 1943; Flight Sergeant George Thompson, 9 Squadron, Bardney, January 1945 (posthumous); and Sergeant Cyril Jackson, 106 Squadron, Metheringham, April 1944.

The groundcrews too should not be forgotten; whilst their jobs were undoubtedly 'safer' than those of front-line soldiers and sailors, Air-Marshal Harris paid them this tribute:

'Some 8,000 men and women were killed at home in training, in handling vast quantities of bombs under the most dangerous conditions, in driving and dispatch riding in the black-out on urgent duty and by deaths from what were called natural causes. These deaths from natural causes included the deaths of many fit young people who to all intents and purposes died from the effects of extraordinary exposure, since many contracted illnesses by working all hours of the day and night in a state of exhaustion in the bitter wet, cold and miseries of six war winters. It may be imagined what it is like to work in the open, rain, blow or snow, in daylight and through darkness, hour after hour, 20 feet up in the air on the aircraft engines and airframes'.
(Ibid)

Many groundcrew, by the end of the war, were WAAFs who, like the airmen, enjoyed the brief times they could spend off their stations; however, on these occasions they were still subject to RAF rules and regulations (some quite petty!) and the people of Lincoln were not averse to helping the girls against authority, as Sally McIntosh (nee Whelan) remembers:

'My friend Madeleine and I wanted to go to a dance in Lincoln and I believe it was at a dance hall called the "Montana" – and it so happened that, though in midsummer, it was a cold pouring afternoon. This suited us as we intended to go (as we usually did) with civvy dresses under our greatcoats. Madeleine cycled over from Branston [Mere W/T station], which was then an all-WAAF unit, and we caught the bus from Waddo – with what passed for civvy shoes and stockings in our bags. Of course, we had to fasten our greatcoats up to the collar to hide the fact that we were not wearing a collar and tie, and also take small steps so that the dresses did not show through the vent at the back of our greatcoats. All went well until we got to Lincoln – then, lo and behold, the sun came out in all its heat and glory and the rain disappeared! And there we were, hot and perspiring with coats buttoned up to the collar. We went into a Toc H Club for a cup of tea, and although sweltering, dared not even undo the top button. We were at a table with a lot of soldiers, who were most concerned and asked had we got a cold – weren't we feeling well? And our faces were getting redder and redder with the heat.

'The time finally came for us to go to the dance and with relief we shed our coats, put on shoes and stockings, touched-up our faces – and had a marvellous time. When we came out, about 10.30 (22.30!), it was still light and we were in our greatcoats again. On our way to the bus station we passed two WAAF Service Police standing on a corner. As we passed, one of them said "Have you got a pass?", Neither of us had, and we did not answer. Then a more pressing, "WAAF, have you got a pass?" With our mincing little steps, to hide our dresses, we began to walk quickly, still not answering. Then, as we realised they were following us, the mincing steps became a run. We turned the corner

This anonymous Lancaster, at Fiskerton in 1943, must have been newly delivered to 49 Squadron, as it is completely devoid of any unit markings. It seems to be an early production aircraft, having the row of fuselage windows which were later deleted on the production lines. New, or reconditioned, aircraft were flown into all the airfields to replace losses, usually flown by civilian male and female pilots of the Air Transport Auxiliary.
J Allan via P H T Green

where the buses were and found that the SPs had also broken into a run.

'There were some homes with doors opening directly on to the street just by the bus terminus, and in one open doorway a woman stood, enjoying the last of the fine evening. In panic and desperation we pushed her and ourselves in and banged the door! After getting our breath back we apologised and explained. Fortunately for us, she was a humane and kindly woman, and after a while, we all began laughing at the situation – somewhat hysterically – she as well. After a further interval, she went out to have a look round for us and said, on her return, that there were two WAAF SPs going round the queue at the Waddo stop. She was a sweet person. A little later still she went out again to reconnoitre. This time, the SPs had gone. We thanked her profusely – and eventually got a bus back to camp and got in safely – though late!'

In this chapter so far I have described the salient features of Bomber Command's war as it affected Lincolnshire, but what was life like on an average bomber airfield? Fiskerton lies half a mile across the fields from my home and I walk across its expanse regularly; it was the base of two Lancaster squadrons and existed, as a flying station, from January 1943 to September 1945. Initially it was the home of 49 Squadron and was, from May 1943, a sub-station of 52 Base, Scampton. There is not enough space in this book to give a full history of station or squadron (readers who wish to learn more detail are recommended to consult Beware the Dog at War by John Ward), but some of the facts concerning Fiskerton can be presented. Operations first, as they were why the airfield existed; for example, in August 1943 49 Squadron's ops were as follows:

2nd Aug 15 a/c to Hamburg; 1 rtn early, rest safe.
9th Aug 17 a/c to Mannheim; 1 rtn early, ED719 'EA-K' FTR (7 PoW).
10th Aug 12 a/c to Nuremburg; ED625 'EA-B' FTR (5 killed, 2 PoW).
12th Aug 13 a/c to Milan; all safe.
14th Aug 6 a/c to Milan; 1 rtn early, rest safe.
15th Aug 8 a/c to Milan; LM337 'EA-V' FTR (5 killed, EC).
17th Aug 12 a/c to Peenemünde; 'L', 'O', 'S' and 'U' FTR.
22nd Aug 9 a/c to Leverkusen; all safe.
23rd Aug 9 a/c to Berlin; all safe.
27th Aug 12 a/c to Nuremburg; all safe.
30th Aug 15 a/c to Mönchengladbach; all safe.
31st Aug 16 a/c to Berlin; 1 rtn early, rest safe.

Aircraft 'returned early' because of some sort of mechanical failure or, occasionally, a sick crew member. On 10th September the airfield was closed for runway resurfacing and ops were carried out from Dunholme Lodge but Fiskerton reopened on 24th October and the aircraft came home. Just over a month later, on 26th November, saw aircraft 'C' crash in the circuit on return from Berlin, killing the crew.

With winter setting in there were normally fewer operations because of the weather so in January 1944 49 Squadron's ops were fewer in number:

1st Jan 15 a/c to Berlin; all safe.
2nd Jan 12 a/c to Berlin; 1 rtn early, JB231 'EA-N' (7 killed) and JB727 'EA-S' (7 PoW) FTR.
5th Jan 6 a/c to minelaying; all safe.
5th Jan 5 a/c to Stettin; all safe.
14th Jan 9 a/c to Brunswick; JB295 'EA-R' FTR (5 killed, 2 PoW).
20th Jan 12 a/c to Berlin; all safe.
21st Jan 10 a/c to Magdeburg; all safe.
21st Jan 2 a/c to spoof on Berlin; 1 rtn early, other safe.
27th Jan 13 a/c to Berlin; 2 rtn early, JB360 'EA-M' FTR (3 killed, 4 PoW).

A message was received from Sir Arthur Harris, C-in-C RAF Bomber Command, to all groundcrew:

'On January 20, 1,030 a/c were serviceable out of I. E. strength of 1,038. When work has to be done under such trying conditions this record is almost incredible. My thanks and congratulations to all concerned in this great achievement. You are, after the crews, playing the leading part in getting on with this war.'

The summer months of 1944 were devoted, against the wishes of Harris, to supporting D-Day and the Battle of Normandy and the targets switched from Germany to such tactical targets as 'construction works, St Leu D'Esserent', 'railway junction, Nevers', 'enemy positions, Caen', 'marshalling yards, Givors', 'battle area Cohaques' and so on, all bombed by 49 Squadron in July 1944; only two raids on Germany were made that month.

So the ops carried on. Fiskerton housed 1,150 airmen and women; what of their daily life? In January 1944 33 airmen and 3 WAAFs were 'Mentioned in Despatches' and, in February, a station newsroom was opened in the NAAFI to enable personnel to keep up to date with the outside world. It was recorded that the RAF Central Library was providing books for serious study regarding post-war careers back in 'civvy street'. The maintenance crews, during January, checked-in six new Lancasters and carried out six engine changes and 17 minor checks. Flying control reported that the Fog Intensive Dispersal Operation (FIDO) was 'lit' on 16th January after being told that 10 USAAF C-47s were diverting from Fulbeck due to fog; they didn't land 'due to bad navigation and disregarding of diversion instructions'. An eleventh aircraft, en route to Fulbeck from Liverpool, did land safely, though visibility off the airfield was only ten yards and a crosswind made the FIDO difficult to control; eventually, an arch of approximately 100ft was cleared over the runway.

On the medical side the MO reported 90 patients at Station Sick Quarters from 28th November to the end of January. He also reported that the present Station Sick Quarters was 'deplorable' and that new quarters, under construction for six months, were urgently needed. On 11th February the whole station, except WAAFs, had an FFI inspection – all passed! Snow and frost caused the Motor Transport Section many difficulties, as vehicles froze-up at dispersals and the servicing areas were open to the weather. The taxiway lighting also had weather problems and constantly failed owing to water in the 'electrics'.

Cookhouse menus are not recorded in Fiskerton's Operational Record Book but the Air Ministry sent a signal saying that explosives had been found in a consignment of Spanish onions and instructing that 'all stocks are to be placed outside, at least 50 yards from any buildings'. Owing to the

distance between dispersals, offices, workshops and living accommodation, bicycles were standard and indispensable RAF equipment; 11th February saw 50 new WAAF bicycles arrive, so that 'all personnel on Technical Site now have one'. Such transport was probably in high demand on 20th February when Lancaster "R" [ND498] burst a tyre on take-off, caught fire, and eventually blew up, fortunately without casualties. John Chaloner, one of its crew recalls the incident in The Other Battle (P Hinchcliffe; Airlife, 1996):

'We'd got about halfway down [the runway], and the port inner set on fire. And we went at right angles to the runway, to port, and I thought, "This is it, for sure!" – we'd got a full load of fuel and 16,000lb of bombs on board – "There's going to be one big bang any minute now!" And the wheels folded up, and we came down – well, we'd never got airborne really. We swung off the runway. I was standing behind the pilot for take-off, and it seemed as if we were frozen, waiting for the damned explosion. We pulled down the pilot's clear-view window at the side, and Ernie went out first, and I followed headfirst behind him. We thought we were going to hit the inner engine, which was on fire... We'd come to a grinding halt, and we were expecting the explosion at any time and we just ran like crazy towards the air traffic control building.'

Some of the other 49 Squadron Lancasters could not take off that night and those already airborne were diverted, on their return, to Dunholme; it was reported that wreckage from the explosion fell at Sudbrooke, some two miles away, but the runway was repaired by the 25th.

March saw a Sister of Princess Mary's RAF Nursing Service talk to the WAAFs on hygiene, and to compliment them on 'the cleanest accommodation in 5 Group'. The runway was blocked again when a 101 Squadron Lancaster crashed on it. Flying Control reported the incident thus:

'Ludford a/c landed without instruction with FIDO and blocked r/w. Representation made to Ludford's Flying Control urging them to brief crews more thoroughly. Further, it has been suggested to them to illuminate the top of Stenigot wireless pylons with Sodium Flares to form a navigation aid in fog.'

It is not recorded whether this took place.
In April, Lancasters returning from one operation carried a dead rear gunner, killed by a night-fighter, and a bomb aimer killed by flak. The peritrack was reported to be in very bad condition, while heavy rain put a large number of the station's telephones out of action – 'the new exchange building is extremely badly built'. Sports on the station included football, Canadian softball, tennis and squash, and an exchange visit with the USAAF at Langar was arranged. June saw 49 Squadron's (and Fiskerton's) worst night of the war when on the 21st no fewer than 20 Lancasters raided an oil plant at Wesseling; three Lancaster Is (LL900 'EA-T', ME675

'EA-R' and ME808 'EA-D') and three Lancaster IIIs (ND683 'EA-K', ND695 'EA-B' and NE128 'EA-J') from 49 Squadron failed to return, including those of the CO, Wing Commander M Crocker DFC & Bar, and a Flight Commander, Squadron Leader L E Cox. A total of 37 aircrew were killed, as was Mr K Stevenson, a BBC correspondent aboard LL900. The squadron was stood down for a few nights.

The taxiway was still breaking up and 130 bays of concrete had been replaced; 'each area dug up revealed the poorness of the original work'. It did not stop ten USAAF Consolidated B-24 Liberators from North Pickenham, Norfolk, being diverted on 22nd July; and during the month, 49 Squadron dropped 1,006 tons of bombs.

Fiskerton airfield and its related sites; the technical site contained the various workshops and offices, communal sites had messing and recreational facilities, and other sites were living accommodation – it can be seen why bicycles were necessary! Many of the sites were used as temporary civilian accommodation for several years after World War Two. RAF Museum

A major change took place on 17th October when 49 Squadron left for Fulbeck, taking most of the personnel with it; from 18th to 30th October Fiskerton was placed on 'Care and Maintenance', with only 33 officers and 116 airmen on strength, at the same time transferring from 5 Group to 1 Group. The final day of October saw 576 Squadron fly in from Elsham Wolds; on 2nd November it flew its first op from Fiskerton to Düsseldorf, and lost Lancaster I LM122 'UL-X2' and Lancaster III NE115 'UL-B2'.

On 1st November 150 Squadron had formed at the station but it transferred to Hemswell on the 22nd. January 1945 saw the disbandment of 1514 Beam Approach Flight, which had been resident since January 1944. Station personnel during the early months of 1945 included 13 Australians and three Canadians. The end of the war now looked likely, the WAAFs having lectures on 'mothercraft', and on 23rd April the last bombing operation took place, against the SS Barracks at Berchtesgaden, 23 aircraft of 576 Squadron taking part. After this the squadron flew supplies to Dutch civilians and 'for the first time in its history, the squadron was received by enthusiastic crowds throughout the target area'.

The groundcrews were flown over German cities to show them the results of their efforts on the Lancasters, and many sorties were flown to Germany and Italy to repatriate PoWs and demobbed personnel. Ammunition was taken to Theddlethorpe Range to be exploded, and the station began to run down. Then on 19th September 1945, 576 Squadron ceased flying and the airfield was closed for flying on the 21st. During October the Lancasters were flown away to MUs to be scrapped, and from 15th December the airfield went on to 'Care and Maintenance'; so ended the flying career of a typical Lincolnshire bomber station which, after a period when it was used to store bombs and equipment, was returned to agriculture and of which little now remains. One building which has survived is that which housed the Sergeants' and Officers' Messes, taken over by Lindsey County Council as the local primary school (which my daughter attended in the early 1970s). Airfield ghost stories are legion but I include this one because I know and respect the people involved; Tony Holland started to teach at Fiskerton Church of England Primary in 1967:

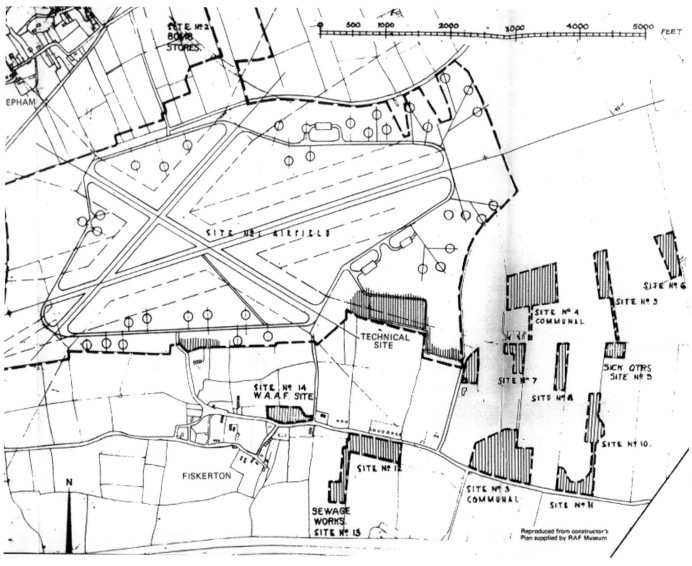

'Many staff were frightened of the atmosphere in the school! One teacher described it as being unfriendly. Most staff either did not or would not be on their own. 'I had a strange experience one Christmas. I am not a person who is frightened easily, nor was I frightened to be in the school by myself, and I did not worry about going into school on my own one very dull December afternoon. I was fixing the stage lights, so all electricity was off. I was hammering a bank of lights into the roof when I heard a strange knocking. I thought it was an echo, but it was not the same rhythm, and when it carried on knocking for some seconds after I had stopped, I went home!

'Josh Williams (an ex-RAF pilot) was at Fiskerton as well at that time. When I mentioned it to him, he did not laugh but told me of a similar experience. He was at school on his own one summer evening. He heard footsteps down the corridor outside his room; when he went to open the door no-one was there, nor had anyone time to go back down the corridor. We told the Headmaster, Mr Curtis, of these experiences and he told us of doors opening and closing for no apparent reason and firmly closed doors opening.'

Both episodes happened in the old Sergeants' Mess. On a lighter note, whilst Tony was at the school (which moved to new buildings in 1973), a former squadron leader from 49 Squadron visited the site and told a story which might ring a bell with old 'Fiskerton-ites'. On the mantelpiece of the Officer's Mess was kept an old Maori rain god statue which was kept wet at all times in the hope that it would produce non-flying weather. It was a rule that the first pint of beer of the evening always went over the rain god!

Bomber Support

As the number of Bomber Command airfields increased during the war, together with the increase in bomb loads carried by the squadrons' aircraft, so the workload on the ammunition MUs increased and to meet the demand a third unit, 233 MU, opened atop the Wolds at Market Stainton in January 1943, joining Norton Disney and South Witham in supplying 1 and 5 Groups with their explosives. Market Stainton had 267 airmen on strength and during December 1943, for example, they unloaded 1,632 railtrucks and 218 lorries, and sent 543 trucks and 481 lorries laden with munitions out to the airfields. Storage space was at a pre-

This rather bizarre photo was taken during a Press visit to Skellingthorpe c1944, and seems to show 50 Squadron aircrews undertaking a fighter-style 'Scramble'; whatever the reason it seems to be giving the airmen plenty of amusement and for the reader a good view of a T2 hangar, long since demolished, and plenty of detail of a Lancaster nose.
Via John Lintin

mium and 233 MU made use of 60 miles of grass verges in surrounding country lanes, while a railhead was established at Brocklesby to speed supplies to the north Lincolnshire RAF stations. After much discussion with the local authorities, a chemical weapons (ie, mustard gas bombs) storage site was opened at Hemingby and similar sites were established at Norton Disney and South Witham, in case the increasingly desperate Nazis resorted to using such weapons themselves. The first 'Tallboys' arrived at 233 MU in April 1944 and the unit strength was expanded by the addition of a party of Italian co-operators who made 'most

Essential in keeping the bombers flying were, of course, petrol and oil. These Scammell tankers (with Bedfords behind) are filling up at the Stow Park Fuel Distribution Depot, which held 8,000 tons in its underground tanks. This was supplied by rail from Misterton Reserve Fuel Depot (80,000 tons) in Nottinghamshire, which was itself supplied by pipeline from Stanlow refinery in Cheshire. The tankers shown held some 3,000 gallons each and for an average operation by one Lancaster squadron, each Lanc carrying 2,000 gallons, 14 of these tankers would have to deliver a full load to the airfield.
Information from Steve Vessey,
photo from G Taylor

effective tradesmen and labourers'. 'Grand Slams' started to arrive near the war's end and extra storage was obtained at the already disused airfields at Caistor and Goxhill; rail traffic arrived via Donington-on-Bain, Hallington and Withcall stations.

At South Witham an extra HE store was established on Stretton Road and the personnel strength had risen to 211 by May 1944, when 340 railtrucks and 303 lorries delivered to the unit and 565 lorries and 427 trucks were despatched. One can only imagine the effect this number of lorries had on the surrounding roads! A V1, air-launched from out over the North Sea, crashed and exploded nearby on 13th October 1944 and 'Tallboys' started to arrive in February 1945. The carriage of so many loads of high explosive around Lincolnshire was not so dangerous as it at first sounds as the bombs were unfused and therefore, at least in theory, safe. They were treated in a fairly cavalier fashion, rather like beer barrels, and Douglas Cowley, a young civilian lorry driver, remembers one rolling from the back of his lorry as he climbed Canwick Hill in Lincoln! On another occasion Squadron Leader Mick Maguire, 9 Squadron's Armaments Officer, had to deliver a 'Tallboy' to a 9 Squadron Lancaster which had diverted to Waddington the previous evening owing to fog at its Bardney base and was scheduled for the raid that night. Mick recalls the saga:

'There was no reason why we should not transport the big bomb over the dozen or so miles to Waddington. After all, the roads of Lincolnshire were full of bomb convoys in those days, but this one was going to look different... So our small convoy of one motor cycle and a David Brown tractor hauling a big H-type trolley loaded with a gleaming wet "Tallboy" and draped with sundry armourers, slipped through a dark and fog-bound Bardney village to Potterhanworth. There we parked by the pub and went in for half a pint of mild – to the consternation of an elderly local who came in, eyes popping and shouting about a ruddy great rocket parked outside. We departed in a hurry and came into Waddington through the back entrance.'

Mick found his stray Lancaster but was surprised to find it surrounded by HQ Base staff eager for a glimpse of their first 'Tallboy'. He intercepted and warned his team of armourers who, rising to the occasion, 'completed their safety checks and did a very slick bombing-up operation in twenty minutes, with Corporal Spencer adding the last dramatic flourish by checking the lower bomb fin and bomb door clearance with a cigarette card, before leading the team out into the glare of the floodlights to take a cheeky bow to the audience'.
(9 Squadron Archives, via Roger Audis)

Another Maintenance Unit, which provided non-explosive stores to most of the Lincolnshire stations, was 209 MU based at Broughton which formed as an Equipment Park on 16th April 1943, changing its name to Brigg in October to avoid confusion (perhaps with the airfield at Church Broughton, Derbyshire?). It was situated in the woods north of the village and parented by Elsham

Wolds. Airmen's huts were completed in May and 209 MU began to work in earnest, its motor transport clocking up 3,000 miles delivering supplies during that month, rising to 10,600 miles by August. A record issue of 1,800 items was recorded in one December week of 1943, the personnel performing this work numbering about 80, 35 of whom were 'very pretty WAAFs' according to Roy Raynor of Cookham Dean who remembers his time at Brigg as

'some of the happiest times of my long association with the RAF... the main headquarters off the camp was the "Dog and Rat Inn" which occupied the site of the present pub of the same name – beer was drawn from the wood'. (Letter to the author)

In February 1944 heavy snow cut the camp off and in order to ensure delivery of its urgently needed equipment the RAF and Lindsey CC cleared the road to Appleby station. Increased demand by the summer of 1944 saw the July deliveries at 18,241 miles, but when the war ended the MU quickly ran down and was disbanded on 15th February 1946. Some concrete hut bases remain in the woods as a reminder of this unglamorous but essential unit.

Bomber Training

The training of the bomber crews has already been described and, although Lincolnshire was mainly operational bombing country, some Heavy Conversion Units did begin to form on the county's most westerly airfields. May 1942 saw the formation, at Swinderby, of the first Lancaster conversion unit, 1654 HCU, operating eight Lancasters and eight Manchesters and moving to the satellite at Wigsley, just in Nottinghamshire, a month later. In October the Conversion Flights of 61, 97, 106 and 207 Squadrons came together to form 1660 HCU, again at Swinderby, while January saw 1661 HCU established at Winthorpe near Newark, also a satellite of Swinderby. Sergeant Trevor Muhl, the bomb aimer of a crew converting to Lancasters, recalls taking off from Winthorpe at 1430 hours on New Year's Eve 1942 for a two-hour cross-country trip. The weather was poor and, once airborne, the GEE navigational aid and radio both failed. Navigation suffered and the crew found themselves over the sea; turning back for land they identified Boston and set course for base. Low cloud now obscured the ground, it was getting dark, and owing to the radio failure there was no way of checking if the barometric pressure had changed, affecting the reading on their altimeter. Thinking they were at 2,000 feet the crew suddenly saw, in front of them, a weathercock which they missed by application of full throttle and a frantic pull back on the stick. The weathercock was attached to St Wulfram's Church in Grantham and their trailing aerial was found later in a house at Great Gonerby; it was a very shaken (and lucky) crew which landed at Wittering at 1900 hours, to find that they had been ordered to set the aircraft flying out to sea and abandon it – but, of course, the radio message never reached them.

Swinderby then became HQ 51 Base, controlling the other two stations, each of which had its major servicing hangar at Swinderby, the base's role being to co-ordinate and standardise the training of Lancaster crews for 5 Group. Initially the aircraft were Halifaxes, Manchesters and Lancasters but a reorganisation in 1943 which established No.5 Lancaster Finishing School at Syerston in Nottinghamshire, saw the HCUs re-equip with the Short Stirling, thus freeing precious Lancasters for the operational squadrons. Crews obtained four-engine experience on

the Stirling before moving on to Syerston for a short conversion to the Lancaster and then to a squadron. One instructor, Flight Lieutenant Clarke, recalls one such flight in *There Shall Be Wings* (M Arthur, 1993; reproduced by permission of Hodder & Stoughton Ltd):

'We were doing three-engine overshoots one day, on a short runway, and there was a steady wind, which slows you down. I was up with a pupil pilot, and he was doing very well, and we came in on a normal approach, to practise a three-engine landing. As we got to about a hundred yards short of the runway, I looked out and, hey ho, saw the windsock hanging limp.

'Flying Control should have told me about that, but I suppose they thought I'd been at it too many years to come unstuck. On three engines you can't initiate an overshoot; when you are committed to a landing you must make it, because you've got your wheels and flaps down, and you've got too much drag – you'd never get out of it. I said, "OK, I've got her" and landed the thing. We were a bit high, so I'd not got anything to play with. Directly we touched down and run a couple of hundred yards, I said, "Normally you wouldn't do this, but I've got no option, because we're short of runway, so we're going for the corner of the field."

'I knew that the corner of the field had no ditch, because it was the junction of the Lincoln-Newark road and the Swinderby-Morton Hall road. It all happens so quickly, you can't really describe it – all the time you're rattling along, bumping and galumphing over the grass. By the time I'd got to the Lincoln-Newark road, I was almost parallel to it. So as I turned on it I felt I was literally rolling up the runway again. Except that it wasn't the bloody runway – it was the Lincoln-Newark road! Squeezing brakes hard I pulled up outside a little pub, The Half-Way House, right on the road, with about half a dozen cars up the back of me, and half a dozen in front.'

In July 1944, 51 Base flew its highest monthly hours. All leave was cancelled to provide the urgently needed replacement crews for 5 Group. The Base now came under the command of No.7 (Operational Training) Group and so changed its title to 75 Base. In December 1944 Lancasters, now more plentiful, started to replace the Stirlings; this change meant that airmen used to dodging under the turning props of the tall-undercarriaged Stirling had to change their habits very quickly! 75 Base disbanded just before the war ended.

In the north of the county a similar organisation existed to supply 1 Group with its crews. In this case Lindholme in Yorkshire was No.11 Base HQ, and its two satellites were Blyton (1662 HCU) and Sandtoft (1667 HCU), both of which opened in February 1943 equipped with Halifaxes. As with all HCUs the aircraft were those discarded by the squadrons which, not unnaturally, had first priority for new machines. The combination of inexperienced crews and old aircraft gave rise to a high accident rate and 69 Halifaxes were lost flying from these two airfields. Not for nothing was Sandtoft referred

The different members of a bomber crew first got together at a bomber Operational Training Unit, all of which were equipped with Wellingtons by 1943; this Mark X belonged to 11 OTU, based at Westcott, Buckinghamshire, and was visiting Digby in the winter of 1944. By this time in the war OTUs were at last receiving reasonably new aircraft and MF560 seems to be in pristine condition. From OTU the crews moved on to HCUs like those in Lincolnshire. RAF Digby via David Curry

to as 'Prangtoft'! At Blyton, Russell Margerison remembers that the NCO in charge of sick quarters from September 1943 to September 1944 attended 120 crashes but, on a lighter note,

'Across the drome, well inside the boundary fence, lay an old farmhouse in which lived two elderly ladies. Each day they baked pies of every variety and literally filled a massive white wood table with them... No charge was made but a plate was provided if one should wish to pay'. (*Boys at War.* Ibid)

Lindholme became 71 Base under the reorganization and re-equipped with Lancs, disbanding in 1945. The last Lincolnshire wartime station to open, Sturgate in 1944, became a relief landing ground for Blyton. As in 75 Base, the HCUs had disbanded by the end of 1945. 7 Group had its HQ at St Vincent's, Grantham, the HQ covering all aspects of the Group's work; for example Ron Waite was posted there in 1945 as Flying Accidents Officer, and had to calculate the accident rate per flying hour for each unit. An unduly high accident rate meant that the unit concerned was visited by his CO or himself to ascertain the causes and advise a remedy, flying in an aircraft from the Group's communications flight at Grantham.

Operational crews too had to train, and bombing was carried out on the various ranges on the coast (Donna Nook, Theddlethorpe, Wainfleet, Holbeach) and the smaller ranges inland (Alkborough, Manton Common, Lea Marsh, Roman Hole (near Thoreswamy), Fenton, Bassingham Fen, Leverton, and Grimsthorpe Park). They also had to hone their bad weather landing skills and for this purpose Beam Approach Training Flights were established, using various aircraft types until standardizing on the Oxford by 1943. 6 Blind Approach Training Flt formed at Waddington in January 1941, became 1506 Beam Approach TF in October and moved subsequently to Fulbeck (February to August 1943) and then Skellingthorpe where it disbanded in October. 14 Blind Approach TF formed at Coningsby, became 1514 BATF, and moved to Woodhall Spa whilst runways were laid at Coningsby, returning there in August 1943 but moving to Fiskerton in January 1944 where it disbanded a year later. 1518 BATF formed at Scampton in November 1941 before moving out of the county in June 1943 and 1520 BATF moved into Sturgate in September 1944, remaining until disbandment in May 1945. Finally, 1546 BATF formed at Faldingworth in May 1944, disbanding in January 1945. Gunnery training was the responsibility of the Target Towing/Gunnery Flights, the last digit of their number signifying their Group; thus No1 Group Target Towing Flt formed at Goxhill with Lysanders in September 1941, moving to Binbrook and being retitled 1481 (Target Towing and Gunnery) Flt in November; from here it moved successively to Blyton, Lindholme (Yorks), back to Binbrook and then Ingham, its aircraft changing to Whitleys, Defiants, Martinets, Wellingtons and Hurricanes. It disbanded in December 1944. 5 Group Target Towing Flt moved into Coningsby, from Driffield, in February 1941 with Battles and became 1485 (Target Towing and Gunnery) Flt, with Lysanders, in January 1942, moving on to Dunholme Lodge, Fulbeck, Skellingthorpe and Syerston, its aircraft approximating to those used by 1481 Flt. Fighter evasion was practised against the Bomber (Defence) Training Flights, with 1687 BDTF forming at Ingham in February 1944, with Hurricanes and Spitfires, moving to Scampton and Hemswell before disbanding in October 1946; 5 Group was catered for by 1690 BDTF, using similar aircraft and based at Scampton and Metheringham until June 1945.

Fighter Operations

By the beginning of 1943 the risk from a daylight attack by the Luftwaffe was negligible and, consequently, the fighter squadrons at Kirton-in-Lindsey used it as a rest and training station. The Spitfires of 303 Sqn were replaced by those of another Polish unit, 302, in February and this veteran squadron was replaced, in turn, by a 'younger' Polish unit, 317. When 317 Sqn moved to Suffolk in April the station changed its role to the formal training of fighter pilots, becoming 53 Operational Training Unit equipped with Spitfires. Hibaldstow, having lost its two Turbinlite squadrons, became Kirton's satellite and it was here that ACW Margaret Horton had an inadvertent flight in 1945 sitting on the rear fuselage of a Spitfire (necessary to keep the tail down when running up the engine and during taxying in rough weather); unfortunately the pilot then took off before she had a chance to get off but he managed to fly a circuit and land without injury to either of them. Another Hibaldstow pilot had a lucky escape when, on taking off at night, he swerved off the runway and inadvertently flew through a blister hangar, passing over the top of two parked Martinets and losing both wings before emerging virtually unscathed from the wingless fuselage. 53 OTU, by 1944, had three Squadrons; A Sqn at Hibaldstow taught newly 'winged' pilots from (P) AFUs how to fly the Spitfire, and B Sqn, also at Hibaldstow, then taught them how to use it in combat. The students then moved to C Sqn, at Kirton, and learnt the techniques of ground attack as part of a large formation, reflecting the role of Spitfires at that stage of World War Two. 53 OTU left the two stations in May 1945.

In the meantime RCAF Digby acted as a working-up and training base for the Canadian fighter squadrons although RAF squadrons also used it, including 19 and 167, both with Spitfires. Digby also kept its contact with the Belgians, begun with 609 Sqn; both Belgian fighter squadrons, 349 and 350, were based there during the summer of 1943. However, it was a RCAF station and so the Canadians were the main users, 1943 seeing 411, 402 and 416 pass through, all returning twice during the year between operations over France. 438 Sqn formed at Digby in November with Hurricanes, receiving Typhoons after moving to Hampshire. The pattern continued during 1944 when a complete Canadian Spitfire wing of three squadrons, 441, 442 and 443, formed in February, later moving south to take part in pre-D-Day ops. One further nationality was added to Digby's list when, in August, 310 (Czech) Sqn flew in for a rest from the tactical air offensive now raging. When 310 left Digby took on a non-operational role with 116 Sqn (Oxfords) and 527 and 528 with Blenheims performing the unglamorous but vital tasks of radar calibration and other, miscellaneous, duties. In May 1945 some former inhabitants returned from the Continent, namely 441 and 442 Sqns now with Mustangs, and these proved to be Digby's last fighter units, the station returning to RAF control that month.

Wellingore, still a satellite of Digby, also mainly housed RCAF units, although 349 (Belgian) Sqn flew from it. Lincolnshire's first Mustang squadron was 613 which used it for tactical reconnaissance and stayed at Wellingore from April to May 1943. 439 Sqn, a sister unit to 438 at the parent station, formed with Hurricanes in early 1944 and Wellingore's last squadron was 402 which left in March 1944, after which the airfield was used by Digby's calibration units and trainers from Cranwell.

Although the day bomber menace had almost gone by 1943, that of the night bomber was still very real as was the threat of Luftwaffe intruders operating against the returning Lancasters. With Hibaldstow closed as a night fighter base, Lincolnshire's night defences rested with Coleby Grange, from which station 409 Sqn's Beaufighters had departed in February 1943, being replaced by another RCAF Squadron, 410, equipped with the best night fighter of all, the Mosquito. Like the day fighter squadrons, 410 was not solely a defensive unit although this was its primary task; on its move to Coleby, the Squadron looked forward to its first 'Ranger' operation, which entailed individual Mosquitos flying over occupied Europe shooting down aircraft and strafing road and railway transport. In one such attack, on 28th March, the crew claimed one tug, two barges, six goods vans, two locomotives and two military buses! Three Ranger sorties were carried out each night, weather permitting, but in the defensive role a Dornier 217 was destroyed through its own evasive action on 18th March.

27th September 1943, saw Flight Lieutenant Cybulski, RCAF, and Flying Officer Ladbrook, RAF, airborne at 2012 hours for a 'Ranger' over Holland; they had turned back

towards base when Ladbrook got a radar contact which, when visually identified, proved to be a Dornier 217. So close was the Mosquito that when Cybulski gave the enemy aircraft a three-second burst of cannon it immediately exploded leaving him no alternative but to fly through the fireball, which temporarily blinded him and severely damaged the Mosquito, causing it to go into a dive. Ladbrook took over until Cybulski recovered and they flew the 250 miles back to Coleby on one engine, with both of Cybulski's feet on the opposite rudder to counteract the swing. When they landed back at Coleby they had been airborne for 4 hours and 41 minutes and the Mosquito was found to have had all of its paint burnt off, plus the fabric covering of the rudder. 410 left for West Malling in October and was replaced by 264 Sqn, also with Mosquitos; they were replaced in turn by the Beaufighters of 68 Sqn, in February 1944, and the final night cover came from 307 (Polish) Sqn and its Mosquitos, from March to May when Coleby's operational role came to an end. Coleby Grange's squadrons operated mainly under the control of Orby GCI but Orby was not retained after the war and closed in August 1945.

Coastal Command

The North Coates Strike Wing trained hard after its setback in November 1942 and in the following April three squadrons, 143, 236 and 254, all with Beaufighters, became operational once more while, in June, the rocket-armed Beau became available. Jack White joined 236 Sqn as a 'sprog' navigator

on 31st March with his pilot Myles Scargill, and they trained for four weeks in formation flying, cannon firing and attacks with dummy bombs before being considered ready for operations. Their first sortie was rather disastrous as the Wing was sent to attack the *Prinz Eugen* and *Nürnberg* which were reported to be sailing off the Norwegian coast; the report was wrong and the wing lost five aircraft to Focke-Wulf 190s from Stavanger. On 17th May the crew took part in a convoy attack off Texel and their Beau was hit twice, damaging the rudder and aileron controls so that Myles had to force-land at Donna Nook, North Coates' satellite. Air Chief-Marshall Sir Neil Wheeler, one of the Strike Wing COs, remembers that Donna Nook was used a lot for night flying and emergency landings

'We were always very sensitive to blocking the only runway at North Coates. Moreover, we did not want to attract enemy attention at night to NC where we all lived!' (Letter to the author)

Myles Scargill broke his ankle a few days after the Texel operation and Jack White was crewed up with the new Wing Commander Flying, Wing Commander W Davis:

'I flew with him for two months until Myles was fit again, a hectic time but a fine experience for a new navigator as we led the Wing on several occasions. I first flew with him on 16th May on a short exercise logged as "Air-to-air cannon firing". When we landed he remarked on the noise the cannons made. I asked him whether this was the first time he had fired cannons and he replied: "It's the first time I've flown a Beaufighter!"'.

A very unhappy looking de Havilland Mosquito NFII of 410 (RCAF) Squadron, after its return to Coleby Grange in the hands of Flight Lieutenant Cybulski and Flying Officer Ladbrook. Despite the damage DZ757 was repaired and survived until scrapped in 1945.

On 22nd June the Wing first used its rockets operationally, the 60lb variety, when 236 and 143 attacked a convoy off Scheveningen, with 254 using torpedoes, but the results were disappointing as the heavy warheads upset the trajectory of the missile; later they were replaced by 25lb armour-piercing warheads which were much more effective. 18th July saw Jack White airborne with Wing Commander Davis, as Wing Leader, for an abortive strike against a convoy which, although at sea when first sighted, had entered Den Helder port by the time the Wing arrived; returning to base they learned that the convoy was again at sea and set off for a second time but the Germans were expecting them and two Beaufighters were lost to Me109s. The Wing Commander's aircraft was hit and the starboard engine put out of action.

'Davis appeared to make no problem of it and flew back on one engine making what seemed to me to be a perfect single-engined landing at Coltishall'. (Letter to the author)

For such attacks the Wing was usually composed of up to 12 torpedo aircraft whose targets were the merchant ships,

This remarkable sequence shows a very lucky escape by the pilot of Spitfire Vc AR515, of 53 OTU at Hibaldstow, on 2nd November 1944. The first photo gives the pilot's view (had it not been night time!) as he veered off the runway towards the blister hangar. 2. The hangar in close-up, showing the space above the parked Martinet target tugs through which the Spitfire went. 3. The damage to the Martinet EM477, which was a write-off. 4. A wing removed by the Gas Cleaning Post behind the hangar. 5. And the pilot walked away! AR515 had survived since 1942 and seen action with five squadrons. *Bob Poynton via Pat Horton*

A sight like this would not have been at all welcome to German sailors. It is a Beaufighter X of 236 Squadron, North Coates Strike Wing, carrying eight rocket projectiles under its wings and these, together with the four 20mm cannon under the nose, could wreak havoc on enemy shipping. LZ293 crashed in Cornwall on 11th August 1944. J H White

The attack by North Coates Wing on convoy 453, 2nd August 1944; two plumes of smoke indicate damaged ships. AC-M Sir Neil Wheeler

while up to 16 rocket and 8 cannon armed Beaus took on the escorts. These tactics paid off and by the end of 1943 13 enemy ships, totalling 34,000 tons, had been sunk; this success led to the formation of a second Strike Wing at Leuchars in Scotland.

236 Sqn now re-equipped with the definitive version of the Beaufighter, the Mark 10, and the first operation with these aircraft took place on 2nd August:

'A reconnaissance Beaufighter of 254 Squadron, flown by Sqn Leader F T Gardiner, spotted a large enemy convoy off the island of Terschelling, at 06.23 hours. Two

minutes later, the German gunners saw the Beaufighter and opened fire, their heavy flak being wide of the mark but their light flak passing uncomfortably close. Gardiner flew back to North Coates, bearing photographs that were rapidly developed. The convoy was number 453, consisting of three columns. They were carrying iron ore. Four M-Class minesweepers sailed in front, whilst seven flak ships and a harbour-defence vessel provided close escort on the flanks. An R-Boat tender called the *Alders* guarded the rear. The Commandant, an Oberleutnant Zur See Eggars, in Vp111, the leading flak-ship on the starboard flank. The convoy had left Cuxhaven at 11.00 hours on the previous morning, bound for Rotterdam. It was running late since the *Fortuna*, a German vessel of 2,700 tons had developed engine trouble. Eggers had been forced to reduce speed to three knots whilst repairs took place, although by the time Gardiner saw the convoy a speed of eight knots had been resumed. The German Commandant reported the Beaufighter and a "Schwarm" of four Me109s swept out to protect the vessels, being replaced at intervals. The Germans were on the alert.

'The North Coates Wing lost no time, by 10.30 hours twelve Torbeaus of 254 Squadron were in the air, with ten Beaufighters of 143 and fourteen of 236 Squadron providing anti-flak protection. Wheeler led the formation, the anti-flak aircraft being armed with 60lb rockets and the usual cannon. On this occasion their fighter escort consisted of no less than fifty-one long-range Spitfire Vs of 118, 402 (RCAF) and 611 Squadrons, led by the Wing Commander Flying at Coltishall, L V Chadburn. In all, eighty-seven aircraft headed for convoy number 453.

'Wheeler saw the enemy at 11.34 hours, off the

island of Texel. The Germans spotted the aircraft at the same time; they thought at first that they were friendly fighters, but were soon to be disillusioned. The Beaufighters and the convoy were converging on a reciprocal course, but Wheeler swung his formation out to sea, attacking from the west. Twenty-four Beaufighters dived down in a copy-book attack, through a curtain of fire towards the balloon carrying merchantmen and their escorts. The pilots had become more proficient with their tricky rockets. All four flak ships on the starboard of the convoy were hit as was NH04 the harbour defence vessel on the port flank. Seven seamen were killed and twenty-eight wounded, some seriously.

'Then the Torbeaus released their torpedoes. According to the Germans, four of these struck the seabed in the shallow waters, but two found their marks. The unlucky *Fortuna* was hit; weighted down with her cargo of iron-ore, she went to the bottom in thirty seconds, with her captain and five of his crew. The Vp1108 was hit and exploded, with the loss of thirteen of her crew. Meanwhile, the Spitfires pounced on four Me109s, who fought a desperate air battle against impossible odds. Unteroffizier Gotthard Obst was shot down and killed, whilst Feldwebel Werner Sadrina was wounded and baled out to safety...
'None of the Beaufighters were lost.'

I am indebted to Roy Conyers Nesbit for allowing me to reproduce this graphic account from his book The *Strike Wings* (Kimber 1984) which gives a detailed history of a hitherto neglected aspect of the RAF's World War Two operations.

Just after this, North Coates Wing was reduced to two squadrons when 143 left. Not all operations were carried out by as many aircraft as described above; for example 236 Sqn carried out a sweep from Nordeney to Schiermonnikoog on 28th January 1944 in which 11 aircraft took part, plus some of 254, escorted by three squadrons of Typhoons. Attacking a convoy they had came across, a 236 Sqn aircraft hit by flak disintegrated, hitting a 254 aircraft which had to ditch. German convoys were heavily defended and attacks often proved costly to the Wing such as one in April when aircraft 'Y' had a bullet through its starboard wing, 'S' a shell through the nose, injuring the pilot, 'P' its starboard engine cowling shot away and its port elevator and wing damaged, and 'R' a hole in its starboard wing and a shell in the radio, injuring the observer.

On 15th May the Wing struck at a convoy off Schiermonnikoog (an island in the Friesian chain) and, in one its most successful attacks, sank the one merchant vessel (an 8,000-tonner), one escort and one M Class minesweeper, leaving two other minesweepers on fire. 143 Sqn returned to the fold in February but left again, in May 1944, for Manston in Kent to cover the eastern approaches to the D-Day beaches; it returned for a brief period in September but then left to form part of a new Wing at Banff in Scotland. North Coates Wing finished the war with a bang as 236 and 254 Sqns sank 5 U-Boats during May 1945, by which time 254 had on strength some Mosquito Mk XVIII boasting a 6-pounder cannon specifically designed for use against U-Boats. The Wing disbanded in May/June 1945, its dangerous work highlighted by the fact that 484 aircrew had lost their lives in operations from North Coates, mainly in two-seater aircraft.

Unlike many Lincolnshire RAF stations, and despite its hazardous operations and bleak situation, North Coates seems to have been popular with its personnel. When 254 Sqn was detached to Predannack in Cornwall for a strike across the Channel in December 1943:

'...it was the possibility of being away from North Coates over Christmas that bothered the aircrews, especially the NCOs... The food in their messes was excellent by wartime standards, and they were looking forward to their turkey dinner and Christmas pudding. There were also the attractions of the friendly pubs of Grimsby, as well as the dance halls where local girls were by no means averse to the sight of men in RAF uniform'. (*The Strike Wings*)

Jack White remembers:

'There always seemed to be a keen wind blowing and the two winters I spent there were hard. However life on the station more than made up for the rigours of the climate. North Coates Officers' Mess was renowned throughout the Group for the quality of its catering and the bar equally so for its beer and conviviality. Off-duty excursions were made into Grimsby for evenings in the Officers' Club also frequented by the Navy from Immingham and occasionally the Army. Privately owned buses ran from North Coates to the centre of Grimsby from about 4.00pm each day with the last bus back around 11.00pm. Occasionally some of us would go out on "egg forays" among the friendly farms around North Coates and its satellite Donna Nook. Not strictly according to the book (ration) but a few obtained here and there subsequently shared out among one's friends'.

Let the last word on North Coates rest with Mr Jessup of Pudsey, a ground-electrician at the station, who can perhaps represent all the wartime groundcrew:

'There was the everyday slog of mud, rain and snow, snags etc, not very glamorous but there it is!'

Unlike North Coates, which operated as part of Coastal Command for five years, Lincolnshire's second Coastal airfield, Strubby, only came under the Command's control for six months. It opened in April 1944 to house an air-sea-rescue squadron, No280, which was the first to operate the Vickers Warwick aircraft, intended as a successor to the famous Wellington but superseded as a bomber by the Stirling, Halifax and Lancaster. However, the Warwick found a new role as a long-range search and rescue aircraft, equipped to drop airborne lifeboats or survival gear to ditched airmen. Strubby soon took on a more offensive role, as the success of the North Coates strike wing led to the formation of further Beaufighter antishipping units; the need to restrict the Germans' shipping reinforcements and supplies to France and Belgium saw the arrival of 144 and 404 (RCAF) Sqns to form the Strubby Strike Wing in July. They had already been in action over the Western Channel before and after D-Day and they operated in much the same way as the North Coates Wing until the decrease in enemy shipping off the Low Countries and northern Germany meant that North Coates could cope alone. 144 and 404 then departed for Dallachy, Scotland, to seek fresh targets near the Danish and Norwegian coasts, and Strubby transferred to Bomber Command.

Warwick ASR 1, HG 211, of 280 Squadron, up from Strubby in 1944, shows off the Airborne Lifeboat Mk II nestling in its bomb bay, ready to be dropped to any aircrew down in the drink. Air Britain via P H T Green

Flying Training

Cranwell started 1943 housing the RAF College FTS, operating Oxfords, Masters, Tiger Moths and Blenheims, while 3 (Coastal) OTU still soldiered on with the venerable Whitleys. No1 Radio School had Proctors, Dominies and Oxfords. Barkston remained the RLG until April when it closed for runways to be laid, whilst Fulbeck was already being used for other purposes, so Caistor and Wellingore were used as replacements. It was proving unsatisfactory to operate the Whitleys (replaced by Wellingtons in May) alongside the numerous smaller training aircraft so, in June, 3 OTU moved to Pembrokeshire. The RAFC SFTS trained some Turkish pilots during 1943 and in September the largest station parade ever held in the UK took place for Battle of Britain day, when 7,000 airmen and women, plus 3,000 civilians, took to the square! The title RAF College SFTS, apart from its length, was also something of an anachronism and in March 1944 it was brought into line with similar units and numbered 17 SFTS, its role remaining the same. Spitfires, Hurricanes and Harvards joined the unit during the year but in May 1945 it transferred to Grantham.

Earlier in the war Grantham/Spitalgate was still occupied by 12 SFTS (soon to be retitled 12 (P) AFU) with Harlaxton as its satellite, and by September 1943 was wholly equipped with various marks of Blenheim, students having already done their twin-engine conversion at other (P) AFUs; its role was to train night fighter pilots so 1536 BATF was an important lodger unit. Social life was quite full for the personnel – a live ENSA show called 'More heather breezes' was

The Miles Master was the RAF's first British single-engined advanced trainer monoplane, and it shared the training of fighter pilots with the American Harvard throughout the war. This Bristol Mercury engined Mark II, coded 38, was with the RAF College Service Flying Training School at Cranwell in 1943.
A S Thomas via P H T Green

recorded as 'quite good all round, but inclined to be blue' and there were also whist drives, a model aeroplane club at Harlaxton, and concerts by Aveling-Barford's concert party. For the sporting types there were badminton, squash and snooker and the station football team beat Ruston & Hornsby 15-0! By November 1943 the grass surfaces at both airfields began to break up owing to bad weather and the constant comings and goings of the Blenheims, so Balderton near Newark was used for three weeks; the airfields deteriorated further and many of the Blenheims flew away to Cheshire and Lancashire airfields. In early 1944 steel tracking was laid on the grass and the aircraft returned.

At about this time Richard Gentil arrived at 12 (P) AFU, having trained in Canada and then done an Oxford course at Shawbury, Shropshire. In his book Gentil records:

'Grantham was a large station, dating from peacetime, with good amenities. The Nissen hut area was enormous, and there was a large permanent staff'.

His course included Poles, Americans, Australians, Canadians, New Zealanders and South Africans, a microcosm of the wartime RAF. Although he was favourably impressed by the airfield his opinion of the town was not quite as good:

'It didn't take... long to realise that wartime Grantham was a ghastly place. It had ninety-three pubs – many of these being merely near-beer joints; just a single room with a licence to sell beer and cigarettes. All of them were packed every night either with aircrew or the nearby Army personnel... The "popsy" situation was also pretty dire, as the servicemen far outnumbered the local females'.

The actual course involved intensive day and night flying, parachute drill (with instructors from the locally-based Parachute Regiment), a spell in an oxygen tank to point out the dangers of oxygen starvation, swimming, dinghy and survival training, and so on. A trip was also arranged to the BMARC factory where the pilots saw the manufacture of the 20mm cannon they would shortly be using. Accidents still happened and eight members of the course were killed, but after three months at Grantham and about 600 flying hours for each pilot there were the celebrations before the survivors moved on to the Beaufighter OTU at Cranfield. By this time they had discovered the attractions of Nottingham and:

'the last Nottingham-Grantham train on Sunday night was known as the "Aircrew Express", and there has never been another train like it. It always left on time – 10.30 pm – but, as we were all boozed up to the eyeballs, negotiating the last half-hour from our respective hotels always took longer than expected... it was the habit of the boys to leave all the train windows down to enable those who arrived at the station at just moving off time to fly... right past the ticket barrier on to the platform... so that they could hurl themselves at the window and clamber in!' (*Trained to Intrude*: R Gentil; Bachmann & Turner, 1974)

Grantham came back into favour when Nottingham was placed out of bounds to US troops because of a VD epidemic, this fact quickly stopping British servicemen visiting the city too. In the summer of 1944 Oxfords came back on strength and there were 57 Blenheims, 30 Oxfords and three Ansons at the two airfields. February 1945 saw 12 (P) AFU move to Hixon and Cranage in the north-west Midlands.

Manby's war continued developing new ideas and training techniques until, in July 1944, No1 Air Armament School was renamed the Empire Air Armament School; this unit was to

'...ensure that our armament training throughout the British Commonwealth is kept at a high progressive standard'.

To this end Manby ran the following courses – the Post-Graduate Armament Course, Advanced Armament Course, Specialist Armament Course, Bombing Leaders' Course, Air Bombing Instructors' Course and the Senior NCOs' Armament Instructors' Course; its aircraft were mainly Wellingtons.

At Sutton Bridge the Central Gunnery School continued to operate courses for gunnery leaders and pilot gunnery instructors, but it left in February 1944 and, as the area was now considered safe from air attacks, was replaced by 7 (P) AFU, the HQ of which was at Peterborough; the Harvards and Oxfords of the unit made use of Sutton Bridge as a satellite but training was running down, particularly after the war ended, and 7 SFTS, as it became in December 1944, moved to Kirton-in-Lindsey in April 1946.

Non-Flying Units

The radar stations at Orby, Langtoft, Stenigot, Ingoldmells and Skendleby have already been covered, as have the ammunition MUs. Louth 'Splasher' station was joined from February 1944 by an American radio station at Skidbrook, the most northerly of a chain of air-sea-rescue fixer stations. The USAAF personnel at Skidbrook picked up distress calls on their radio receiver and the directional aerial of the set gave the bearing from which the call came,

HSL 2594 of 22 Marine Craft Unit berthed in Grimsby Dock basin c1943. This class of HSL was nicknamed the 'Hants and Dorset' after a famous bus company, because of its high superstructure. Launches were sometimes subject to air attack and 2594 has extra protection around her bridge. W Miller via Graham Chaters

this being telephoned to a central point at Saffron Walden, Essex, where it was plotted with the bearings from other fixer stations, the point where they crossed being the position of the aircraft; the ASR services were then sent out. Skidbrook closed at the end of the war. RAF Mere, close to Waddington, was a W/T station, meaning it communicated by Morse code, not voice, and had a much longer range. 11 Recruits Centre at Skegness continued to train recruits until it closed in October 1944.

The RAF Regiment Depot at Belton was very busy training the airmen whose job it was to protect RAF airfields and other establishments, at home and abroad, from ground or air attack; these airmen wore khaki battledress until 1949 and they trained under realistic conditions at the Battle Training Schools at Anderby Creek, Gibraltar Point and Swayfield; 1,850 were on strength at Belton in November 1944. Regiment squadrons were stationed at many of the Lincolnshire airfields during the war, before moving to France after D-Day and to the Far East. The airfields they protected sometimes needed to be repaired and this was the task of the RAF Airfield Construction Squadrons, one of which, 5002, trained at Grantham in 1944, possibly in connection with the break-up of the surface there.

22 Marine Craft Unit at Grimsby's Royal Dock Basin worked in concert with the Royal Navy rescue launches based at Immingham (where HSLs on 'crash alert'

were sometimes based if the tides at Grimsby were unfavourable) and the Warwicks of 280 Sqn from Strubby. It rescued many airmen throughout the war and had, in January 1945, eight launches and 145 personnel on strength. A typical example of the kind of work they performed was carried out by High Speed Launch 2578 on 29th December 1944:

'1705 hours, proceeded to position 53.26N, 00.32E. Man in dinghy. Two Beaufighters circling. At 1800 hours approx ten miles from position, flares were seen ahead. I acknowledged with rocket. On reaching position at 1835 hours the survivor was being taken from the water by HMS Croome L62. I went alongside at 1845, taking the survivor, Flight Sergeant Gregg, 236 Sqn North Coates, aboard. He was given dry clothing and his wounds treated. Flight Sergeant Gregg was suffering from shock but stated that he was certain navigator went down with aircraft. Moderate sea, heavy swell, fine and clear'.

By August 1945 the number of launches was down to three and personnel to 63, and on 16th December the Unit disbanded. The full story of 22 ASRMCU is being written by Graham Chaters of Grimsby and his records show that, between May 1942 and disbandment, the MCU carried out 162 searches, totalling 1264 hours at sea, during which it rescued 107 survivors and, less happily, found five bodies.

Also concerned with Allied aircraft and aircrew safety was the Royal Observer Corps and, by 1943, this was in fact its main work as the number of enemy raids decreased. In October 1943 the Lincoln Group Operations Room moved yet again, this time to St Martin's Hall on Beaumont Fee, Lincoln, where it remained for the rest of the war. Although there were now few enemy raids a notable exception was Operation Gisela on the night of 3rd March 1945 when Luftwaffe night fighters made a concerted effort to attack returning RAF bombers over eastern England, also indulging in some bombing, which killed and injured civilians in Gainsborough, Coningsby and Kirkstead. Waddington and Friskney also suffered casualties, in their case from crashing RAF bombers shot down by the Germans. In all, three Halifax and three Lancasters were lost over Lincolnshire that night. There was also a tragedy closer to home for the ROC; Observer Jack Kelway was driving along the Welton to Spridlington road at 3.05am to take his shift at Hackthorn post when a Junkers Ju88 saw the dimmed lights of his car and came in to attack, possibly thinking its target was an aircraft bound for Scampton. Cannon and machine guns were used but the 88 misjudged its height and hit a telegraph pole and wires at the Cold Hanworth lane junction, this sending it into Obs. Kelway's car and killing him and the crew instantly as the wreckage scattered over the fields (now Manor Oak Sports Fields, Welton). Jack Kelway has the dubious distinction of being the only member of the ROC to have been killed by enemy action whilst on duty in the UK. On 12th May 1945 the ROC was stood down, having been on watch from the first day of the war until the last.

The Americans and Parachute Operations
Goxhill, as part of the 8th USAAF, continued to receive newly arrived American fighter groups throughout 1943. Each was shipped as an entity from the States and at Goxhill trained on operational European techniques in a European climate! During 1943 came the 78th, 353rd and 356th Fighter Groups, all equipped with the P47 Thunderbolt and each stopping for several months. By the end of 1943 the build-up of groups was virtually complete and the need was for replacement pilots; thus, in December there came into being the 496th Fighter Training Group and this was responsible for the training of pilots destined for the Mustang and Lightning equipped fighter groups of the 8th and newly-arrived 9th Air Forces. A second FTG in Shropshire trained the P47 pilots and in August 1944 Lightning training was also transferred there, leaving the 496th solely with the P51 Mustang. Fighter training meant air-to-air gunnery so the 2nd and 3rd Gunnery and Target Towing Flights were also at Goxhill, equipped with Havocs, Lysanders, Masters and Vengeances. The 496th left Goxhill in February 1945.

The USAAF in Britain during World War Two is popularly thought of as the 8th Air Force's heavy bombers and escort fighters, but there was also the 9th Tactical Army Air Force, which moved from Italy in late 1943 to give air support to the US Army before, during and after the Invasion. Its Groups flew fighter-bombers, medium bombers and transports and it was the latter which came to Lincolnshire. The 9th Troop Carrier Command HQ moved into St Vincent's, Grantham, which meant that 5 Group HQ moved north to Morton Hall on 14th November 1943. Under the control of 9th TCC were 14 C47 Dakota-equipped Troop Carrier Groups, split into three Wings, one of which was situated in the West Country, close to the 101st US Airborne Division's area, one in Berkshire near the camps of the British 6th Airborne Div., and one in the East Midlands where the US 82nd Airborne Div. had its HQ in Leicester and its units in the surrounding area. The RAF's own transport force at this time was comparatively small and it was anticipated that the USAAF Dakotas would carry British paratroops in addition to their own. North Witham was the first airfield taken over by the Americans when, in September 1943, the 1st Tactical Air Depot was established; this unit was the equivalent of an RAF MU, preparing newly delivered Dakotas for issue to the groups and performing major maintenance unable to be done at Group level – it was thus a very busy unit and remained until 1945.

The first Troop Carrier Group to arrive was the 434th at Fulbeck in October 1943; it stayed only until December when it moved south to Aldermaston, a new airfield in Berkshire (and now the Atomic Weapons Establishment). Its place was taken by the 442nd TCG in March 1944 but this also was a temporary arrangement until Weston Zoyland, its airfield in Somerset, was vacated by the RAF in June. Barkston Heath and Folkingham, however, were chosen to be permanent bases under the 52nd Troop Carrier Wing, along with Saltby (Leics), Cottesmore (Rutland) and Spanhoe (Northants), and in February 1944 Barkston received the 61st TCG and Folkingham the 313th. Each group had some 70 C47s, divided between four squadrons, the 61st having the 14th, 15th, 53rd and 59th TCS, and the 313th the 29th, 47th, 48th and 49th. The task of the groups was to drop paratroops and to tow the Waco CG4 gliders, many of which were stored on the airfields; as they were vulnerable to bad weather four new hangars were erected at Barkston in which to place them under cover.

When the USA came into the war in December 1941 the British had been fighting for over two years and the Americans relied heavily on this experience until they had built up their own skills, some of their servicemen being attached to British units to learn the techniques. Herman Brooks was a 2nd Lieutenant in the US Army Signal Corps and was sent to the HQ of the fledgling 8th Air Force at High Wycombe in May 1942, to establish base communications; (at this time the US air forces were a corps of the Army). Not long after his arrival in England, Herman was sent to Waddington to observe the airborne communications equipment, and took the opportunity to visit Lincoln:

'I was walking up the street alone and I believe I was one of the first "Yanks" many of the people had ever seen. I was wearing my class A uniform with light coloured trousers and the children followed along pointing to my "pink pants". The people were wonderful and I spent the evening discussing America with groups of adults that came out of their homes to see me'.

By May 1943 Herman commanded the 1038th Signal Company at Bushey Park near London and he and his men were somewhat disappointed to be parted from the pleasures of the capital when the Company was attached to the 78th Service Group of the 9th Air Force at Barkston Heath. The task of the 1038th was:

'...to supply, install and maintain communications and navigational equipment in the C47 aircraft as well as the establishment and maintenance of a base communications system for the airfield... Initially, the majority of our Company returned to London on leave whenever possible and we knew very little of the Grantham community. However, as time progressed organised groups of young ladies started attending parties and dances on

This P-38J Lightning of the 55th Fighter Group, 8th US Army Air Force, is seen at Goxhill in 1944, possibly just before joining the resident 496th Fighter Training Group. It was certainly with the unit when it later crashed, killing its pilot, and one of its propeller blades now forms the centrepiece of Goxhill's memorial.
P H T Green

the base and we met many lovely people. Three of my enlisted men married local girls while we were stationed there. As I left Grantham for only a 30 day leave (in the States) I was supposed to return in April 1945. Consequently security regulations did not allow me to transport names, addresses, logs etc out of England but I was then reassigned to the West Coast of the United States and I now have no records, nor can I remember, the names of people I knew at the time. I certainly wish I could renew acquaintance with some of the people who were so kind to us'. (Letter to the author)

It was North Witham which became the first Lincolnshire USAAF base to mount an operation when, at 21.30 hours on 5th June 1944, the Pathfinder paratroops of the 82nd and 101st US Airborne Divisions took off in 11 C47s of the 9th Pathfinder Group, heading for turning points on the River Severn near Gloucester, at Tarrant Rushton, Dorset and at Portland Bill; they then crossed the Channel and dropped the Pathfinders on drop zones in the south of the Cotentin peninsula, to set up their British-designed Eureka beacons on to which the Rebecca sets in the main-force Dakotas homed, ensuring accurate drops. Of course, the beacons had to be in the right place to start with and the 9th Pathfinders' Group navigators dropped all of theirs' within a mile of

their designated zones. They landed at 00.15 on D-Day, the first Americans into France, just as their British counterparts landed near Caen. An hour later 13,000 men of the 82nd and 101st Divisions began to descend into France.

The 101st are outside the scope of this book but the 82nd's drop went as follows: Cottesmore and Spanhoe sent 118 aircraft of the 315th and 316th TCGs, dropping 2,090 men onto DZ 'O', north-west of St Mere Eglise, most being within two miles of their DZ. Saltby (72 C47s of the 314th TCG) and Folkingham (60 of the 313rd TCG) carried 2,183 men to DZ 'N' west of the River Merderet, but the two groups were scattered by flak, 39 aircraft being hit and four shot down, resulting in the paratroops being widely scattered. The 61st TCG at Barkston Heath got all of its 72 Dakotas off in vics of three at seven-second intervals, all leaving the airfield in the space of five minutes headed for DZ 'T' north of La Fiere, also the destination of the 442nd TCG Fulbeck. Both Groups ran into cloud over France, but the experienced 61st stayed together whilst the inexperienced 442nd scattered, losing 2 aircraft with 21 damaged against the 61st's seven damaged. The 1,936 paratroopers were thus widely scattered, some more

than 25 miles from the DZ! The 82nd fought in France for three weeks before returning to their camps, and lost 1,142 men killed with 840 missing.

In late 1943 the British 1st Airborne Division returned to the UK from Italy, as had the American 82nd Airborne, and it settled into camps in Lincolnshire and Leicestershire. Not enough aircraft were available to the Allies to include 1st Airborne in the Normandy landings, the 6th Airborne undertaking these but, after several false alarms, the 1st were earmarked for the next airborne operation, Market Garden, on Arnhem in September 1944. For the record, its component units and bases in Lincolnshire were as follows, and they flew to Arnhem from the airfields or areas, if out of Lincolnshire, given in brackets; those with the title 'Airlanding' flew in gliders.

Divisional HQ
Fulbeck Hall. (Barkston and Saltby);
1st Parachute Brigade HQ,
Syston Old Hall, (Barkston and Gloucestershire);
1st Parachute Battalion,
Grimsthorpe Castle and Bourne, (Barkston and Dorset);
2nd Parachute Battalion,
Stoke Rochford Hall and Grantham, (Saltby);
3rd Parachute Battalion,
Spalding, (Saltby);
1st Airlanding Anti-tank Battery RA,
Heckington and Helpringham, (Kent and Glos);
1st Parachute Squadron RE,
Donington, (Barkston);
16 Parachute Field Ambulance RAMC,
Culverthorpe, (Barkston and Saltby);
1st Airlanding Brigade HQ,
Woodhall Spa, (Oxon);
7th Battalion Kings Own Scottish Borderers
Woodhall Spa, (Glos);
1st Border Reg,
Woodhall Spa. (Glos and Oxon);
2nd South Staffordshires,
Woodhall Spa, (Kent and Oxon);
181 Airlanding Field Ambulance RAMC,
Stenigot House and Martin. (Glos);

A familiar sight over south Lincolnshire during 1943/44 were C-47 Dakotas towing Waco GC-4a Hadrian assault gliders, training for the assault on Europe; this formation was from the 61st Troop Carrier group, 9th Air Force, from Barkston Heath. Herman Brooks

Lt Herman Brooks, USAAF, in his office at Barkston Heath, 1944. Note the security posters on the wall. Herman Brooks

British paratroopers of 1st Airborne Division sample American coffee at Barkston Heath, probably before take-off for Arnhem, September 1944. In the background are the 61st TCG's C-47s. Herman Brooks

The War is over. This delightfully informal group are the Care and Maintenance party at RAF Goxhill in May 1945; the CO sits in the centre. LACW Nora Clark, 2nd row, third from left, described the unit as 'No1 RAF Paradise'! Nora Hanley

The cost. Typical of the many war graves in Lincolnshire churchyards and cemeteries are these at North Coates, wherein lie buried British, Canadian, Australian, New Zealand, American and German airmen. From 1943 airmen who were killed or died in the county and who were not taken to their home towns for burial, were interred in the RAF Regional Cemetery at Cambridge. Author

2nd Airlanding Anti-Tank Battery RA
  Harrowby, (Glos);
1st Airlanding Light Regiment RA
  Boston, (Glos);
1 Forward (Airborne) Observation Unit RA
  Harlaxton Hall, (Wilts);
1st Airborne Divisional Signals,
  Caythorpe.
9th (Airborne) Field Company RE,
  Tattershall and Coningsby, (Wilts);
1st Airborne Reconnaissance Squadron,
  Ruskington, (Barkston and Dorset);
250 (Airborne) Light Composite Company
  Longhills Hall, Branston and Lincoln,
  (Barkston, Saltby, Dorset);
1st (Airborne) Divisional Field Park RAOC,
  Grantham, (Barkston);
1st (Airborne) Divisional Workshops REME
  Sleaford, (Glos);
1st (Airborne) Divisional Provost Company
  CMP, Stubton Hall;
89th (Parachute) Field Security Section,
  Intelligence Corps, Wellingore;
Polish Independent Parachute Brigade HQ
  Rock House, Stamford;
Polish Medical Company,
  Stamford and Blatherwycke.

The British paratroopers were carried mainly by the 61st TCG, Barkston Heath,

314th TCG, Saltby and the 315th TCG, Spanhoe while the airfields in the south of England operated RAF Dakotas, Halifax, Stirlings and gliders. The 82nd American Airborne were carried by the 313rd TCG from Folkingham and Fulbeck. The story of the Arnhem operation has been told many times and when the surviving paratroops returned to their Lincolnshire camps, their reported losses resulted in many sad people in the surrounding villages. The soldiers had lived in close proximity to the locals; when the 1st (Airborne) Divisional Provost Company, Corps of Military Police, returned from Italy with the rest of the Division in December 1943, it was sent to Stubton

'Stubton Hall was a small family residence built in the Georgian style and standing in its own grounds. The Hall had been requisitioned by the War Office and a number of Nissen huts erected in the grounds to serve as billets, dining hall, stores etc. The Company officers lived in part of the Hall along with the owner and his family. Close by was the village Rectory which was the temporary war-time home of a bevy of attractive Land Army girls, much to the surprise and delight of the young Military Policemen. 'Dozens of towns and villages around the County of Lincolnshire were suddenly occupied by men wearing the Red Beret. Large country Halls and Mansions, stables, empty houses, farm

buildings, all were requisitioned to house thousands of troops'. (The Pegasus Patrol: J Turnbull; Turnbull, 1994)

In early 1945 the 313th and 61st TCGs moved across to the Continent, Barkston then being taken over by the 349th TCG, equipped with the C46 Commando; this type was rarely seen in Europe and had a reputation for catching fire easily – so much so that the 9th Troop Carrier Command banned them from operations. The 349th left Barkston Heath in April and as the HQ, 9th TCC, had left St Vincent's in November of the previous year, this marked the end of the American presence in the county.

The Reckoning

So the war in Europe ended. Lincolnshire had been the base for almost every type of air warfare – bombing, day and night fighter interception, anti-submarine patrol, shipping strike, flying training, armament training and transport. Forty-six airfields had been established, having the greatest impact on the landscape since the Enclosure Acts. A rough estimate is that some 30,000 acres of the county's land were claimed for use as airfields, about 1.5% of the total area; much of this was under concrete and remained so even when many airfields were disused, until the road building programmes of the 1970s and 1980s demanded much hardcore. The impact on the population must have been just as great; at a conservative estimate there must have been some 80,000 RAF personnel stationed in Lincolnshire, 1944-45. Before the war, it had been a rural county, largely unvisited except for the coastal holiday resorts; and yet its own young men (and later women) were suddenly taken away and replaced by other young men and women from all parts of Britain, the Commonwealth and other countries. This cannot have failed to affect the thinking and day-to-day lives of the local people, especially the younger women. As a small example, the RAF stations all had electricity, running water and flush toilets, amenities lacking in many rural homes just outside the airfield boundaries. Overall, the most noticeable effect must have been noise, from which there would have been little respite. Crashed aircraft were a common sight, sometimes claiming civilian lives and damaging property.

Despite all of this, Lincolnshire people generally made the RAF welcome, although the then LACW Vicki Muhl, stationed at Spilsby and Metheringham, recalls that WAAFs were rarely asked to people's homes, as the airmen were, and were not liked by the local girls who, not unnaturally, saw them as competition. WAAFs therefore usually left the camps in groups for company, though not for security – several ex-WAAFs have commented that they never felt threatened walking or cycling alone in towns or country lanes, unlike the present day. The Spilsby-based WAAFs and airmen frequented Skegness whenever possible, travelling by train from Firsby Station; when someone unhooked the guard's van one night, the LNER took the train off for a few days, proving that the 'Yellow Bellies' exercised control when necessary!

Not really low, Sir! A Lincoln B2 of 50 Sqn from Waddington inspects the Cathedral, some time in 1948. 50 Squadron

Chapter Five

Rundown and Resurgence
1946-1970

As had happened after World War One the coming of peace meant rapid demob for many airmen and women with subsequent disbandment of squadrons and closure of airfields; the immensity of the task can be judged by the fact that the RAF had 760,000 personnel on strength at the beginning of 1946, falling to 375,000 by 1947. The immediate post-war period saw a shuffle round of units as it was decided which to disband and which to retain, a problem also raised by the airfields where the obvious choices for retention were those of the pre-war Expansion period, with comfortable, pleasant, brick-built accommodation. In Lincolnshire only the following were still open for flying by 1946 — Binbrook, Coningsby, Cranwell, Digby, Elsham Wolds, Faldingworth, Hemswell, Kirton-in-Lindsey, Manby, Metheringham, North Coates, Scampton, Skellingthorpe, Spilsby, Sturgate, Sutton Bridge, Swinderby and Waddington. As far as the squadrons were concerned, the first to be disbanded were those formed during the war, with no other traditions or history – an exception to this rule was 617 Squadron, which was retained.

The Bombers

As was to be expected, most of the remaining Lincolnshire airfields housed bomber squadrons, as any potential enemy (and the USSR was already acknowledged as the threat) would be in northern Europe. Lancasters were still the main equipment but were steadily being replaced by a developed version, from the same manufacturer, appropriately named the Lincoln. Compared to the Lancaster it was larger, with a longer range, but with the same bombload and only 10mph faster; it did, however, have 20mm cannon and .5 machine guns instead of the Lanc's puny .303 machine guns. The first Lincolns went to 57 Sqn at East Kirkby in August 1945 and it fell to 57 to iron out the snags before Lincolns joined Tiger Force, the RAF bomber force intended for the war against Japan. This was overtaken by the Japanese surrender and so re-equipment became more leisurely but by 1950 the squadrons at Binbrook, Waddington and Hemswell had Lincolns and there were two Mosquito units at Coningsby. 5 Group had disbanded in December 1945 and the Lincolnshire bombers were now controlled by No1 Group, with HQ at Bawtry Hall, except for Coningsby which was part of 3 Group, Mildenhall.

The number of aircraft in each squadron had been drastically reduced, to eight, so that it was possible for several units to share one airfield – thus 9, 12, 101 and 617 Sqns were at Binbrook, 83 and 97 at Hemswell, 50, 57, 61 and 100 at Waddington and 109 and 139 at Coningsby. The bad winter of 1946/47 curtailed flying at all stations and Binbrook, high on the Wolds, was completely cut off for a time, with essential supplies being dropped from Transport Command Dakotas.

Some of the war-construction airfields lingered on for some time after the war; Elsham Wolds housed a Transport Command unit, unique for Lincolnshire to date, when 21 Heavy Glider Conversion Unit (HGCU) arrived in December 1945, and for a year its Albemarles, Dakotas and Halifaxes, towing Horsa gliders were a familiar sight over north Lincolnshire. When the HGCU left at the end of 1946 Elsham became non-operational. Metheringham lasted until February 1946 when its longtime resident, 106 Sqn, disbanded, while Faldingworth continued to operate as the home of 300 Sqn until that unit disbanded in October 1946. It was replaced by the Mosquito fighter-bombers of 305 (Polish) Sqn which returned from Germany, disbanding in January 1947, while the station itself closed in October 1948. Skellingthorpe became the home of 58 Maintenance Unit, which moved from its wartime location next to Castle Station, Newark, and was responsible for salvaging crashed and force-landed aircraft in the East Midlands; it left for Newton in April 1947. Spilsby ceased to operate Lancasters in October 1945 but not before it added another Commonwealth country to the list of Lincolnshire bomber squadrons, 75 (New Zealand) Sqn, which had arrived in July. Spilsby's proximity to the coastal armament ranges saw it operate briefly as No2 Armament Practice School, with short visits from fighter squadrons (one equipped with Lincolnshire's first jets, Meteor F3s), this unit leaving in November 1946. The county's newest airfield, Sturgate, also operated Lancasters until 50 and 61 Sqns left in January 1946.

The Berlin airlift highlighted the threat from the USSR and the RAF began to grow again, and to re-equip with new aircraft to replace the obsolescent wartime designs. The tension generated by the Airlift also saw the return of the Americans, by now called the United States Air Force, (having gained its independence from the Army and with its personnel wearing blue uniforms); 30 B29 Superfortresses of the 28th Bomber Wing flew into Scampton in July 1948, followed by the 301st BW in October, this stopping until February 1949 when, as tension eased, it returned to the States, leaving Scampton to the RAF. The 301st was actually split between Scampton and Waddington, where it had replaced the 307th BW. More sinister B29s were the four belonging to the 374th Reconnaissance Sqn, which arrived at Waddington in December 1948, for a stay of a few weeks, and were probably flying 'spy' missions over the USSR.

The B29s were a taste of things to come as Bomber Command's heavy bomber, the venerable Lincoln, was by now outclassed so, as a stopgap, the RAF ordered 87 B29s which it called the Washington B1. Washingtons equipped the 3 Group squadrons and in October 1950 149 Sqn flew its aircraft into Coningsby, followed during 1951 by 15 and 44 Sqns, displacing the two Mosquito units which moved to Hemswell. The Washington was pressurized, comfortable for its crews, carried a much larger bombload further, and was better defended (by ten .5 machine guns), and 3 Group lorded it over 1 Group and its Lincolns for a time. This lead was not to last, however, as in May 1951 101 Sqn at Binbrook received the RAF's first jet bomber, the Canberra, the very first being delivered by English Electric's Chief Test Pilot, Roly Beamont. Mr R A Lord of Nottingham remembers that:

'...he scared the daylight out of us as he screamed round the airfield without any warning; the noise was so ear-shattering to us... Secondly the Canberra was so new to us, the crew and the groundcrew were scared stiff of the things; and the rumours! – Don't stand too close to the air intakes, someone was sucked in once etc, etc... Whether the crews were not used to the new jet power, or the aircraft could be manhandled more than the ageing Canberras we now see, but many is the time I've seen the rubber bumper under the tailplane smoking on take-off'. (Letter to the author)

A few teething troubles resulted in some early crashes, not unexpected with such a technical advance, but the Canberra soon proved to be a winner, even being ordered by the USAF! The Canberra was thus a welcome boost to Bomber Command and by

The first English Electric Canberra B2, and the first jet bomber for the RAF, was delivered to 101 Squadron at Binbrook in 1951, piloted by EEC's Chief Test Pilot, Roly Beamont; here he taxies the aircraft in past the control tower. P H T Green

1952 all four Binbrook squadrons were flying the Canberra and were joined, in August, by 50 Sqn. Alf Tyson, of Chippenham, joined 101 Sqn as a navigator in 1953:

'We used to fly over the tower at Grimsby docks, then along Freeman Street. This would bring us nicely in line with runway 22 at Binbrook. Incidentally, there was a nudist camp on this approach, and whenever we passed, we used to look out to see what the inmates were up to. Of course, the best known Lincolnshire landmark is Lincoln Cathedral itself. I can remember flying back after a night flight. Dawn broke and we saw Lincolnshire was covered with fog as far as the eye could see. Standing up out of the fog, in the early morning light, was the Cathedral – it looked like a fairy castle built on top of the clouds. It was a sight I'll never forget!' (Letter to the author)

Scampton, which since the war had housed 230 OCU, training Lincoln crews for Bomber Command, and the Command's Instrument Rating & Examining Flight, replaced these with four Canberra squadrons during 1953, Nos 10, 18, 21 and 27; Coningsby's Washingtons (intended as a stopgap until the Canberra arrived) were replaced in the same year and it was only at Hemswell that the Lincoln soldiered on, with 83 and 97 Sqns. Hemswell's role, in the early 1950s, was an important one in Bomber Command as the Lincolns and two

Mosquito squadrons, 109 and 139, provided the Pathfinder Force while 199 Sqn, with its Lincolns, joined them in April 1952 to carry out electronic countermeasures, as 101 Sqn at Ludford had done during the war. Canberras re-equipped 109, 139 and 199 Squadrons in 1953/54. By 1955, 1 Group had nine Canberra units, one squadron with Canberras and Lincolns, and two Lincoln squadrons, Coningsby having lost its units during 1954.

A pathfinder force was no longer required, so 83 and 97 Sqns disbanded in January 1956; however they were perpetuated in two new Lincoln units, Antler and Arrow Sqns (symbols taken from the 83 and 97 Sqn crests), which were formed to train navigators. 199 Sqn's Lincolns transferred to them when it received Canberras and they became 1321 Lincoln Conversion Flight (as 230 OCU was now training Vulcan crews), moving to Lindholme in April 1958. As the Canberra squadrons had already left, Hemswell was now free to become the base for the Nuclear Weapons Task Force, which was to be used to monitor the Christmas Island H-Bomb tests. This Force had two Canberra units, 76 and 542 Sqns, for taking high-altitude air samples, and 1439 Flight with Varsities and Whirlwind helicopters for communications support, all moving to the Pacific in August 1957 for the trials; they

returned to Hemswell when these finished, 1439 Flt disbanding in November 1957 and the Canberras leaving in July of the following year. This marked the end of Hemswell as an operational airfield.

The life of a bomber crew in the period from the war up to 1955 consisted mainly of training for a 'hot' war with the USSR, of course, but with overseas flights to the many parts of the world still under British sovereignty where, quite often, operations were undertaken - against the Mau-Mau in Kenya, dissident tribesmen in the Aden Protectorate and, chiefly, against the communist terrorists in Malaya. Each squadron was detached in turn to meet these needs, thus spreading operational experience. With the arrival of the Canberra, training intensified, a feature of this being the 'Lone Ranger' flights offered to crews who had gained a laid-down proficiency level in bombing, navigation and general experience. These flights operated singly to such places as El Adem, Libya; Nicosia, Cyprus; Rhodesia; Germany;

Luqa, Malta; Gibraltar; Eastleigh, Kenya; the Canal Zone, Egypt; Habbaniyah, Iraq; and Khormaksar, Aden (where the author remembers a Canberra of the Binbrook Wing delivering a sack of brussels sprouts – very welcome!). 'Showing the Flag' flights were also made, 12 Sqn touring South America and the West Indies in 1952. The strength of each squadron was made up to ten aircraft, thus increasing 1 Group's strength impressively. 1956 saw the RAF's post-war strength reach its peak the first of the new jet heavy bombers, (the V-Bombers as they were called), having entered service in 1955; this was the Vickers Valiant, issued to 3 Group on its East Anglian bases. The Valiant was actually a 'standby' type, and the first of the really advanced pair of V-Bombers, the Avro Vulcan, was destined for 1 Group. Scampton and Waddington had both been reconstructed during 1954-56, with stronger dispersals and taxiways, specialist buildings and, most notably, a long single runway to replace the wartime triangular pattern, entailing closing or altering several roads including the A15 north of Lincoln. The Vulcan initially carried the 'Blue Danube' A-bomb and special shelters were needed to house these dangerous and secret weapons, both at the airfields and at a central storage site constructed on part of Faldingworth airfield; 92 MU moved into this, from Wickenby, in 1956-57, and the site

resembled an American State Penitentiary, surrounded by walls, barbed wire, watch towers plus, later, closed circuit TV. Sixty small brick sheds, rather resembling outside toilets, could each house a detonator, and had combination locked doors, the combination being changed frequently. Components of the nuclear bombs were taken to the airfields for final assembly. Although Maintenance Command looked after the conventional bombs on the site, the nuclear weapons were seemingly the responsibility of a Bomber Command detachment from Scampton.

The first Vulcans were delivered to the crew training unit, 230 Operational Conversion Unit (OCU) at Waddington, which was reformed in August 1956, displacing two Canberra squadrons, 21 and 27. The OCU's first Vulcan was XA897 which, proudly displaying Lincoln city's coat of arms on its fin, flew to Australia in 23 hours, 9 minutes, in September. XA897 flew non-stop from Boscombe Down to Aden in seven hours, presumably the first UK-Aden non-stop flight, but this achievement was marred when the aircraft crashed at London Airport on its return to the UK in October, killing four of the six crew. An unfortunate aspect of the accident was that many people thought that the flight should have been diverted from the bad weather at Heathrow to Waddington, where the conditions were much better.

A lively Lincoln! SX958, a B2 of 9 Squadron, gets airborne from Binbrook in June 1950, displaying a transparent radome for its H2S radar and, interestingly, still carrying World War Two style roundels and fin flash. The Lincoln was the mainstay of the county bomber units into the 1950s. P H T Green

Each of theses innocuous-looking brick huts at Faldingworth's 92 MU housed the detonator for the nuclear bombs stored there for use, if required, by the Vulcan squadrons; each hut had its own combination lock and the MU was heavily guarded. This photo was taken in the winter of 2000. Author

Although obviously not Lincolnshire (even Mablethorpe!) this shot is of the county's first Vulcan; XA897 of 230 OCU taxies in at RAF Khormaksar, Aden, on 9th September 1956 on its way to Singapore. Sadly, on its return to the UK on 1st October the aircraft crashed at London Airport, killing four of the six crew. Author

Almost certainly the largest aircraft type to land in Lincolnshire up to that date was this USAF Douglas C-133 Cargomaster delivering a Thor ICBM to Hemswell in 1958.

October 1956 saw the outbreak of the Suez war and the Lincolnshire Canberras were heavily involved in the bombing of Egyptian airfields. 9, 12, 101 and 109 Sqns from Binbrook were based in Malta, while 27 Sqn from Waddington was at Nicosia, Cyprus. The debacle of Suez, diplomatic rather than military, saw a drastic rethink in defence policy and the infamous Sandys White Paper of 1957 which forecast that future air wars would be fought by missiles – thus the number of aircraft could be drastically reduced, so that the 187 squadrons which existed in 1955 were down to 135 by 1960, to 100 by 1965 and to 84 by 1970. However, in 1957 the emphasis was still on the nuclear deterrent and by the end of the year Waddington had its first Vulcan Squadron, 83, while Scampton reopened in 1958 to receive 617 Sqn in May. Coningsby still flew Canberras, forming 45 Sqn for Far East service and 249 for the Near East Bomber Wing in Cyprus. Binbrook housed 9, 12 and 139 Sqns but the Canberra force generally was being run down.

The 1957 White Paper's emphasis on missiles saw the delivery to the RAF, during 1958, of the Thor Intercontinental Ballistic Missile (ICBM), with nuclear warheads; these were to be housed in four complexes in the eastern counties of England, each complex having four dispersed sites in addition to an HQ. The HQs were situated at permanent stations whilst the dispersed sites were on disused airfields. Lincolnshire was selected to house one of the HQs and Hemswell, whose Canberras had departed in 1956, was selected, the Thors and their associated equipment being flown in by USAF Globemaster and Cargomaster transports, probably the largest aircraft seen in the county up to that time; by May 1959 178 such flights had been made into Hemswell.

Squadrons, each with three missiles, were placed on the five sites, Hemswell (97 Sqn), Bardney (106 Sqn), Caistor (269 Sqn), Coleby Grange (142 Sqn) and Ludford (104 Sqn), whilst the Thor site at Folkingham (223 Sqn) came under the control of North Luffenham HQ, Rutland.

Each site had three launch pads, the Thors being stored horizontally under large sheds, which slid back to allow the missile to be raised to the vertical for launching. This was frequently practised by the 39 personnel on each dispersed site which included an RAF Launch Control Officer, who held one set of the launch keys, and a USAF officer who held the second set; theoretically the Thors could not be launched without both sets being used, as the USAF still controlled the warheads, but there were unofficial plans to get round this in the event of the Americans not wishing to retaliate against a strike on the UK only. There were, of course, more personnel at the Hemswell Missile Control Centre, including a USAF Lt Colonel and Major.

According to a BBC TV documentary broadcast in 1999, there was a serious accident at Ludford site on 7th December 1960, when a Thor was being fuelled; liquid oxygen overflowed and covered the immediate area, with a grave risk of explosion which, had it happened, would not have exploded the warhead but would have spread radioactive material over the surrounding area. Fortunately the RAF and local fire brigades managed to avoid such an explosion. All sites were operational by 1960 and during the Cuba crisis of 1962 were at a high state of readiness with the Thors vertical and armed, an alarming sight for the locals. The Lincolnshire Vulcan force was also at a high state of readiness at the time, and by now comprised 83 and 617 Sqns at Scampton and 44 Sqn at Waddington, backed up by Coningsby's Canberras of 9 and 12 Sqns.

1960 saw the end of National Service and, thus, the disappearance of the National Service airman, who had formed a large part of Lincolnshire personnel since 1946. The complexity of the new aircraft coming into service required a professional RAF, and this was particularly so with the V-Force, which continued to expand during the early 1960s. The Vulcan B2 entered service with 83 Sqn at Waddington in 1960, and was a great improvement on the B1, carrying the Yellow Sun hydrogen bomb while Scampton Wing

had the Blue Steel stand-off missile, 617 Sqn being its first carrier from February 1963. (Victors also carried Blue Steel). This weapon was powered by a rocket motor, allowing the Vulcan to launch it many miles from the target and then turn for safety; its size meant that the Vulcan's bomb-bay doors were cut away, the Blue Steel's bottom half being exposed, and the fuel was very volatile (as was the Thor's), necessitating careful handling by, and protective clothing for, the ground crew. Each dispersal was provided with a small water tank in which contaminated airmen could immerse themselves in the event of an accident, and it was the job of the patrolling RAF Police to break the ice on these in winter! By 1963 the vulnerability of the Thors to counter-attack was obvious and the force disbanded, the USAF transports returning them to the States where many were later used in the space programme; the personnel who manned the Thor sites must surely have had one of the most boring jobs in the RAF but they made a valuable contribution to the 'Deterrent' and their work was enlivened by frequent checks on their security, often taking the form of 'raids' by personnel from other sites; for example a team of three airmen from Hemswell penetrated vital areas of 269 Sqn's site at Caistor in December 1960, but Hemswell hardly had time to gloat before

This poor but rare photo, although taken just over the border at the Melton Mowbray Thor site in Leicestershire, does show an upright missile, illustrating the sight that would have met many Lincolnshire residents during the Cuba crisis in 1962. Author

two officers from Bardney site hid themselves in a missile checkout trailer and entered Hemswell. The anti-contamination measures were more sophisticated than those of the V-Force, each missile launch-pad having a galvanised iron shower which was operated by opening its gate. The disused airfields returned to their former state, whilst Hemswell ceased to perform an operational role.

1965 saw Waddington's Vulcan Wing comprising 44, 50 and 101 Sqns whilst at Scampton there were 27, 83 and 617 Sqns with their Blue Steels, and a third Wing at Coningsby consisting of 9, 12 and 35 Sqns. At each of the two stations not equipped with Blue Steel were stored 24 free-fall nuclear bombs but Coningsby Wing was quite short-lived, operating only from 1962 until November 1964, when the squadrons moved to Cottesmore in Rutland. During the 1960s the V-Bombers were a highly professional force, with training at a very high pitch and a

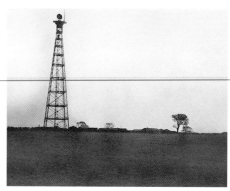

Skendleby's 250ft high mast carrying the 'P' radar head, c1956.
Dennis Caton

Skendleby Rotor Station as it was in 1955, with eight radar scanners.
Information from Dennis Caton, map by Tony Hancock

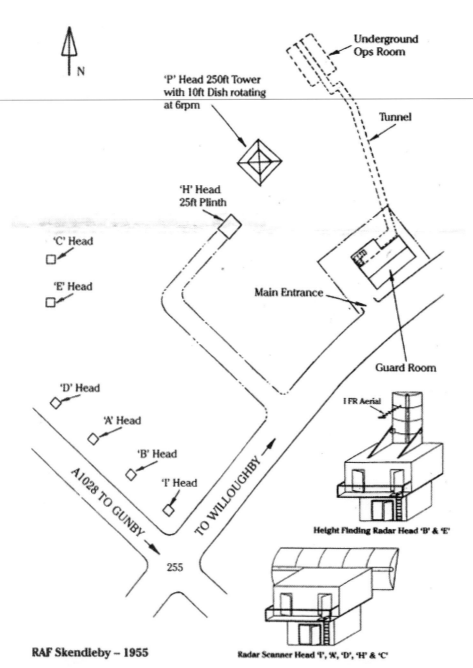

N

Underground Ops Room

'P' Head 250ft Tower with 10ft Dish rotating at 6rpm

Tunnel

'H' Head 25ft Plinth

'C' Head

'E' Head

Main Entrance

Guard Room

'D' Head

'A' Head

A1028 TO GUNBY

'B' Head

'I' Head

TO WILLOUGHBY

255

I FR Aerial

Height Finding Radar Head 'B' & 'E'

Radar Scanner Head 'I', 'A', 'D', 'H' & 'C'

RAF Skendleby – 1955

Royal Observer Corps personnel in Lincolnshire were rarely short of aircraft to plot, as this crew from 15 Group, Charlie One post, at Sturton-by-Stow illustrate. Although this photo was taken in the 1950s, not long before the Corps went underground and stopped aircraft reporting, everything (with the possible exception of the uniforms) would have been familiar to wartime Observers.
Jack Shanks via Charles Parker

destructive power far outweighing that of the World War Two Bomber Command. 27 Sqn had reformed at Scampton on 1st April 1964, and all three Wings, as in the Canberra days, placed great emphasis on global mobility with 'Lone Ranger' flights to many parts of the world, now including Strategic Air Command bases in the USA; the Vulcans took part in the annual SAC bombing competition, usually obtaining good results. These visits became such a regular feature that Goose Bay RCAF base, in Labrador, became a sub-station of Waddington, remaining as such until the end of the V-Force. Visits to Australia were also fairly common and air displays all over the world asked for Vulcan participation because it was a very spectacular display aircraft. 1963 saw the end of Squadron groundcrew, as 'centralized servicing' was deemed to be more economic and efficient; all aircraft

were allocated to a station and only the aircrew belonged to a squadron, a fact much regretted by all concerned as squadron 'esprit de corps' had played a very large part in RAF tradition. Happily, the Air Staff realised its error and the old system returned in the early 1970s; by this time the squadrons came under No1 (Bomber) Group of the new Strike Command, which had taken over Bomber Command on 1st April 1968. 1 Group's HQ was just over the border at Bawtry Hall.

Because the V-Force was so professional its personnel were pushed very hard and when the Vulcans were forced, because of the efficiency of Soviet surface-to-air missiles (as proved by the shooting down of Gary Powers' U-2), to operate at low-level, they realised that their mission would be a one-way trip, with not enough fuel to return to the UK after delivering their weapon.

However, the writing was on the wall for the RAF's nuclear deterrent and from 1969 the nuclear role was handed over to the Royal Navy's Polaris submarines. Several factors caused this. The Harold Wilson government, when it came to power in 1965, cancelled the aircraft intended to replace the Vulcan, the TSR2, which bore all the signs of being a worthy successor to the 'Tin Triangle'. (Coningsby was in the process of being reconstructed to be the first station to operate it.) The American F-111 was ordered to replace the TSR2 but this order too was cancelled, as was the Anglo-French variable-geometry aircraft intended to replace the F-111, leaving the Vulcan's replacement, now to be the Tornado, some twelve years in the future. This fiasco meant that the Vulcan had to soldier on.

The Americans also contributed to the demise of the RAF's deterrent when its Government cancelled development of the Skybolt missile, which was to have replaced the Blue Steel with the Vulcan force. Blue Steel, now obsolete, was withdrawn in 1969 and the Vulcans became conventional bombers. The morale of the V-Force crews understandably plummeted and, just before the deterrent role was transferred to the RN, matters came to a head at an official dinner for the crews, held at Waddington Officers' Mess. Already feeling aggrieved by the events listed above, the crews were kept waiting by the official guests, the C-in-C and the then Defence Secretary, Denis Healey, and were in no mood to listen to the standard speeches; jeering started, and bread rolls and 'thunderflashes' thrown, whereupon the crews were ordered back to their stations.

Returning to 1945 and the ensuing cutback, the RAF had a great many surplus bombs and much ammunition, not to mention all the other equipment now no longer needed. Particular care had to be taken with the explosives and the three MUs at Norton Disney, Market Stainton and South Witham were fully engaged in their disposal, with German prisoners-of-war drafted in to help. 233 MU at Market Stainton took over Caistor, Goxhill and Wickenby for bomb storage but moved to Wickenby, after clearing its own site, in November 1948, disbanding a month later to become part of 93 MU. At Norton Disney the incendiaries were sent by rail to ICI at Cairnryan and Kilmarnock while the 4,000 gas bombs stored but, thankfully, never used, were burnt on site until their storage area on Spalford Road could be closed, in June 1947. (As late as 1997 the RAF were

called in to check possible contamination in the area). During that month 1,400 250/500lb bombs were sent to Pembrey in Wales whilst the tail units and fins were sent for scrap metal. 93 MU moved its HQ to Wickenby in January 1949 and was joined there by the personnel of 233 and 100 MUs (Market Stainton and South Witham), controlling Maintenance Sub-Units at Caistor, Goxhill, South Witham, North Witham, North Killingholme, Elsham Wolds, East Kirkby, Ludford Magna, Norton Disney, Metheringham, Skellingthorpe, Fulbeck, Fiskerton and Faldingworth, as well as some other sites outside Lincolnshire. 900 personnel were engaged in the work of the MU, with roadside clearance the top priority, and the work progressed sufficiently well for 93 MU to move to Newton, Notts, in January 1951, leaving a sub-unit at Wickenby until that became 92 MU in 1952, serving the remaining bomber stations in the county.

Mr R N Kenroy arrived at Wickenby as a National Serviceman in June 1950 and recalls that by this time all the explosives had been moved to the MSUs where they were being inspected and classified ready for disposal. The bombs were stored along

the runways and included Grand Slams and Tallboys, with large numbers being transported to Snelland Station and thence to West Freugh in Scotland, where they were loaded on to ships and dumped in the Irish Sea.

Surplus equipment, being rather more stealable than bombs, was kept in the hangars until sold or otherwise disposed of, the parent units being equipment MUs situated some distance away, notably 16 MU at Stafford and 61 MU at Handforth, Cheshire. Locals remember that at Fiskerton one of the hangars was full of bicycles.

Air Defence
Digby's last fighter unit, 441 (RCAF) Sqn, left in July 1945 and proved to be the last Lincolnshire fighter unit for almost two decades; the station's sector operations room was reactivated for a time, because most of Blankney Hall was destroyed by fire in the summer of 1945, but returned to its wartime home in an undamaged wing of the Hall, becoming Lincolnshire Sector HQ in September, with its GCI at Langtoft. In March 1946, Lincolnshire Fighter Sector merged with Yorkshire Fighter Sector at

Church Fenton, leading to the closure of Blankney Hall in April. Blankney had still taken part in exercises, as on October 2nd 1945 when

'...a small force of Lancasters operated as hostiles, escorted by Mustangs. 19 and 124 Sqns (Mustangs and Meteors) flew defensive sorties under Langtoft. Both units made quite a satisfactory interception'.

Langtoft became 966 Signals Unit and Stenigot 178 SU, continuing its role as a CH and a GEE slave station, with Humberston and Skendleby also still operational, but the threat of nuclear attack and the advent of much improved equipment brought new plans for Britain's air defence radar. This was the Rotor Plan under which, between 1950-55, the radar chain went underground into concrete bunkers 40 to 50 feet below the surface; the new radars had greater range so some stations were closed, including Humberston, but Skendleby and Langtoft went underground, Langtoft to a site some two miles east; Stenigot remained on the surface. SAC Dennis Caton was stationed at Skendleby from 1955 to June 1957 by which time, he remembers, the 'Marconi' station, opened in 1955 '...was already obsolete'. The airmen manning Skendleby lived at Strubby and entered the underground

bunker via the innocuous 'bungalow' still to be seen, which in fact was the guardroom; after walking through an underground tunnel, blast-proof steel doors led into the operations room. Above ground one 250ft-high tower mounted a revolving 10ft dish, which had a range sufficient to cover as far as northern France, whilst five shorter range scanners were mounted around the site; two others were height finders, and all of these were mounted on 25ft plinths.

As Dennis Caton intimates, radar development proceeded apace and another large increase in range soon rendered the Rotor Plan obsolete; the CH stations all closed immediately, including Stenigot. Langtoft and Skendleby were not amongst the few former GCI stations to receive the new radar, all the Lincolnshire radar stations having closed by 1960.

Although the Royal Observer Corps had been stood down on 12th May 1945, it had not been disbanded and when the RAF realised that the USSR had bombers which could reach the UK from eastern Europe, it pressed for the ROC to be reactivated, this happening in January 1947. Lincoln Centre moved into buildings at RAF Waddington in March and the Corps operated much as it had in 1945, supplementing the radar by visual and aural means. A reorganization in

Although Binbrook's fighter period will always be associated with the Lightning, these were predated by the Gloster Javelin FAW9 delta-wing all-weather fighters of 64 Squadron, seen here from the control tower during the mid-1960s. Binbrook's BK code can be seen on the grass. Tony Foster

1953 saw the Centre move to Derby, with Waddington a 'secondary training base' from which the Lincoln Centre observers went to Derby for exercises, sometimes involving hundreds of aircraft. However, the writing was on the wall for the ROC as the new jets came into service, flying high and fast, and in 1955 the Government announced a change of role, with the ROC becoming responsible for the detection of nuclear attacks and the subsequent reporting of the arrival and spread of radioactive fallout. This meant that the corps followed the radar stations underground and the Lincoln Group operations room returned from Derby to one of the first ROC underground bunkers, built on the old Fiskerton airfield in 1960, the posts also going subterranean over the next few years. The last aircraft reporting exercise took place in July 1963. Plans were also made for the government of the country after a nuclear attack, with Regional Seats of Government being established in underground bunkers, that for the East Midlands taking over the Rotor station at Skendleby, something that was top secret for many years.

It was the establishment of the nuclear deterrent that led to air defence units returning to the county, as the Vulcan bases and Thor sites demanded protection; in line with the Sandys view, this was to be provided by surface-to-air guided missiles, in the form of the Bloodhound Mk1. Like the Thors, most of the Bloodhound squadrons were sited on part of disused airfields, in Lincolnshire's case 222 Sqn at Woodhall Spa and 141 Sqn at Dunholme Lodge. The missile had been pioneered into service at North Coates, where 264 Sqn formed in April 1958, followed by 148 (Air Defence Missile) Wing in May 1960, this controlling the three sites. Wing Commander Bill Newton of Boston was the engineering officer of 222 Sqn and remembers that it had some 120 personnel (who were billeted at Coningsby) to service and control the two Flights of 12 Bloodhounds, each flight having its own radar and control room, and a Servicing Flight. The Bloodhound was a passive system, in which the radar illuminated the target and the missile homed on to the returns from it and when 222 Sqn was operational it maintained 24 hour surveillance on a three-watch system, with advance radar warning coming mainly from Patrington Master Radar near Hull. The Squadron's own radar could pick up a target at about 200 miles and, if it had been identified as hostile, a Bloodhound would have been launched as soon as the hostile came within the missile's range of about 100 miles, 20 seconds being the timespan from the order to the launch itself. Because the Bloodhounds 'at rest' pointed to the east the public thought they were aimed at the USSR – the true reason was more mundane, says Bill – if one was launched accidentally its track would take it out to sea between Boston and Skegness! Bloodhounds did not carry nuclear warheads. They were of a high-explosive fragmentation type, designed to throw out pieces of whirling metal which it was hoped would cut the wings off the incoming bomber. Bill remembers that the Russians, as one would suppose, were very interested in the Bloodhound, particularly in the radar frequency on which it operated, and the Russian air attaché was a not infrequent visitor to the perimeter fence; fortunately our intelligence could normally warn the site of his arrival and all radar and radio would be switched off until he departed back to London. The Squadron was nominally allowed one live-firing once a year at Aberporth in South Wales but cost-cutting meant that this was rarely achieved. An unexpected problem was that the many electrical cables on the site were buried in ducts, which became quite warm and attracted the local rodents,

which then took a liking to the cable sheathing and occasionally gnawed through it!

The Bloodhound Mk1 sites closed following the demise of the Thor, except at North Coates; 264 Sqn disbanded in November 1962 and 148 Wing in 1963 but the Bloodhound Mk2, a much improved version, had been ordered for the RAF and 17 Joint Services Trials Unit formed to introduce this to Fighter Command. The Mk2 had a guidance system much harder to jam and was intended to be mobile, as fixed sites were vulnerable to attack; however, North Coates became operational again when 25 Sqn formed on the new missile in October 1963. From structures which can now be examined at North Coates, it is obvious that 'hardened' launchers were considered at some stage, but these were never used operationally and the Bloodhounds stood out in the open, close to the large scanners of their associated radars. Woodhall Spa presented a similar picture when 112 Sqn and its Mk2s moved in in 1964, but the site was abandoned when 112 moved out to Cyprus in October 1967.

Fighter Command took over Binbrook, then on Care and Maintenance, in April 1960 but it was not until June 1962 that the C&M came to an end and the airfield once more resounded to the noise of jet engines, these being the Armstrong-Siddeley Sapphires of 64 Sqn's Gloster Javelins. These large delta-wing all-weather fighters joined the Bloodhounds in defending the Vulcan bases and were themselves joined, in October, by the Central Fighter Establishment. The purpose of the CFE was to evolve new fighter tactics and weapons to tie in with any new types or versions of existing types about to enter service, and it was equipped with Hunters, Javelins and Lightnings, the latter to be forever associated with Binbrook. In the following May 85 Sqn arrived with its Canberras and Meteors, its task being to tow targets for air-to-air firing by the Binbrook fighters and to provide high-speed targets against which the aircraft and their radar stations could practice interceptions. The three units operated together until 64 Sqn was posted to Singapore in April 1965; its replacement unit, 5 Sqn, arrived in October, equipped with the much more potent Lightning F6. The Lightning was the RAF's first supersonic fighter and 5 Sqn was one of its oldest squadrons, having served most of its time in India, until independence in 1947. It re-formed in Germany in 1952, from whence it came to Binbrook.

The CFE disbanded on 1st February 1966, but one of its component parts, the Air Fighting Development Squadron, was renamed the Fighter Command Trials Unit and continued to serve at Binbrook, with the Lightning, until it too disbanded in June 1967. In the following year Fighter Command itself was consigned to history when it became 11 (Fighter) Group of the new Strike Command, formed on 1st April; 11 Group con-

trolled just three stations, Binbrook, Leuchars, Scotland, and Wattisham, Suffolk, all Lightning equipped, and reflecting the low priority now given to air defence against nuclear attack.

To help fill the gap left by the cancellation of the TSR2 and its intended replacements, the Government ordered the American Phantom fighter-bomber and Coningsby, left in something of a vacuum following the various cancellations, was selected as the first Phantom station. The British Phantom was redesigned to take Rolls-Royce Spey engines and other British equipment and 5 School of Technical Training formed at Coningsby in March 1967 to train the groundcrew for the new aircraft, followed by 228 OCU, in February 1968, to train the pilots and navigators. The station came under the newly formed Air Support Command, as the Phantom's initial role was ground attack and reconnaissance. It was a complex aircraft and serviceability in the early days was very poor, so it was with some difficulty that 228 OCU turned out enough crews to form the first Squadron, No 6, in May 1969, followed by 54 Sqn in September, the three units making Coningsby a very busy station. In its first year, 6 Sqn undertook weapons training, simulated attack profiles, reconnaissance, low-level flying and flight-refuelling, pioneering these for the Phantom; in addition, because the RAF wished to show off its new aircraft, the Squadron took part in the flypast over Caernarvon for the investiture of the Prince of Wales, and was detached to Germany, Cyprus and Norway. It is apparent that the air and groundcrews had a steep learning curve!

Flying Training
19 Flying Training School formed at Cranwell in May 1945, replacing 17 SFTS which had just moved across to Grantham; 19 FTS had 86 Harvards and 43 Tiger Moths on strength, necessitating the use of Wellingore and Coleby Grange as Relief Landing Grounds; Digby came into use for the Tiger Moths after two Harvards collided in Cranwell's circuit, with fatal results, on 18th January 1946. However, it was to be expected that the RAF would once more want its own College and on 16th October 1946, the RAF College re-formed and absorbed 19 FTS the following April. As in its pre-war days, the RAFC trained career aircrew officers, using Harvards and Tiger Moths, replaced by Prentices, Chipmunks, Provosts and Balliols in the 1940s and early 1950s they, in turn, being replaced by the jet Meteor T7s and Vampire T11s in the late 1950s. Navigators were finally recognized as 'officers and gentlemen' in 1955 and started to train at the College, flying in Ansons, followed by Valettas and Varsities. The later aircraft needed hard runways so the relief landing grounds became Barkston Heath, Folkingham and Fulbeck (where many historic aircraft, both British and captured German, were stored

and, unbelievably, often destroyed during the 1950s), with Grantham in use 1951-61 for the lighter aircraft. No1 Radio School used Ansons until it lost its flying task and moved to Locking in October 1950, its apprentices remaining at Cranwell to form 6 Radio School, but this was shortlived and disbanded in 1952, leaving Cranwell entirely to the College. Much building took place and the last World War One wooden hut finally disappeared in 1960. The large Trenchard Hall was built to house the student engineers from the RAF Technical College, Henlow, which merged with the RAFC on 1st January 1966.

Grantham, having had 17 SFTS transferred from Cranwell as the war in Europe ended, flew Oxfords, Harvards, a few Spitfires, Beauforts and Ansons, using Harlaxton as its RLG, its numbers gradually reducing until it was retitled No1 FTS in June 1947, now with Harvards and Tiger Moths. 1 FTS trained a large Dutch contingent (following the example of its predecessor, 17 SFTS, which trained some Turkish pilots) before disbanding in February 1948. Grantham also operated as a radio beam station and was much used at this time as a navigational aid. However, being a grass airfield, Grantham's days as a flying station were numbered, although it was used as an RLG by Cranwell until 1961, and it was home to a succession of ground units from 1948 onwards – the Officer Cadet Training Unit (for non-career officers) 1948-54, RAF Mess Staff School, 1949-57, HQ 24 Group, Technical Training Command, 1954-58, RAF School of Education 1954-58, RAF Central Library 1955-58, Secretarial Officers' School 1959, and HQ 3 RAF Police District (renamed HQ Provost and Security Services) 1959-60. In 1960 a degree of stability returned as the Women's Royal Air Force Depot formed, responsible for recruit training, this remaining for the next 14 years.

Manby continued its work as the Empire Air Armament School after the war, using Strubby as an RLG, but in July 1949, its name now considered inappropriate, it became the RAF Flying College which also absorbed the Empire Flying School from Hullavington. The RAFFC performed many tasks, including armament, navigation and refresher flying training. Lincolns were flown too and

used for several long-distance navigation trips, such as that by an aircraft named *Aries III* which flew a 29,000 mile world trip. The Lincolns and Valettas formed 1 Sqn at Manby while the Meteors, Vampires and Athenas (of which the RAFFC had the only examples) were with 2 Sqn at Strubby. Later, Hastings, Varsities and Hunter fighters arrived, whilst Manby Canberras broke several records – *Aries IV* the London-Capetown in December 1953, with *Aries V* setting a transatlantic record plus one for Tokyo-London. Research and development was also undertaken here, including the preparation of the pilot's notes for new types entering service with the British forces, thus ensuring a myriad of different types at the two airfields. However, in 1954 this task was passed to Boscombe Down and in July 1962 the RAFFC became the RAF College of Air Warfare; using Meteors and Canberras it taught new techniques and tactics, as well as giving refresher flying training to pilots returning from ground appointments, the latter having become the responsibility of 4 Sqn in 1958, using Provosts.

The 1960s saw different types arrive, the Hunters and Lincolns having gone by 1961 and Jet Provosts replacing the Provosts and Varsities with the School of Refresher Flying, which had become a separate unit after the CAW formed. 1965 saw the last Meteor depart, with the Canberras leaving the next year, being replaced by the first of the RAF's new Dominie T1 navigation trainers. Manby was now becoming increasingly 'civilianized' with Airwork Ltd taking over many of the airmen's tasks, and the last WRAF left the station in 1965.

Although Cranwell's aircraft used the airfield at Digby, no flying units were actually based there immediately after the war, the station becoming No1 Officer's Advanced Training School, which trained senior officers for command and staff duties, and junior officers for Flight Commander posts. As at Grantham, these ground units tended to move around quite quickly and 1 OATS was replaced by the Secretarial Branch Training School and Equipment Officers' School during 1947, in turn being replaced, the following year, by the Aircrew Educational Unit and Aircrew Transit Unit. Then came No1 Initial Training School (for officers), which moved to the Isle of Man in 1950 and was replaced by 2 ITS. In 1951 flying returned with the Tiger Moths of No2 Grading School, which assessed would-be pilots for aptitude before passing them on for flying training and was staffed by civilian instructors employed by Airwork Ltd, although the Tigers belonged to the RAF. 2 ITS and 2 GS lasted rather longer at Digby before they too moved out, in 1953, the station entering a period of Care & Maintenance. A complete change of role came in January 1955 when Digby became a communications base, aerial masts springing up all over the old airfield; 399 Signals Unit took

up residence, followed by 591 SU in July, the work of both of these units being top secret. They were joined in September 1959 by the Wireless Operators' School and the Aerial Erectors' School, the former moving to North Luffenham in 1964; a third SU, 54 from the Far East, arrived in February 1969.

1660 HCU at Swinderby continued to train Lancaster crews after the war, though the Base system disbanded in October 1945. Personnel were trained for their return to civilian life – for example three WAAFs at a time occupied, for one week, a cottage on the WAAF site where they had to budget, shop and cook for themselves; there was no feminist movement then! By November 1946, 1660 HCU had moved to Lindholme, Yorks, and its place was taken by 17 OTU from Silverstone, Northants (soon to become the famous racing car circuit). 17 OTU was equipped with Wellingtons and it operated as the wartime OTUs had done, introducing new crews to large, operational aircraft and operational techniques. An RAF restructuring transferred this role to Flying Training Command in May 1947 and the OTU was retitled 201 Advanced Flying School (AFS), training pilots, navigators and air signallers. 202 AFS arrived to amalgamate with 201 and in 1950 204 AFS, with Mosquitos, flew in, the subsequent overcrowding necessitating the reopening of Wigsley as an RLG. One of 204 AFS's students was Ted Hooton, who arrived there:

'...in October 1950 as a newly "winged" and sprog Pilot Officer navigator. I was posted to 204 AFS for my initial training on Mosquitos – very nice. We shared the airfield with the larger Wellington AFS, they had Wellington T10 aircraft. There was a dreadful crash while I was there, two Wimpies collided while coming in to land, and finished up as an inferno of flames on the main runway, alongside the Fosse Way. It was during an air defence exercise, and they had taken realism too far by banning all radio calls, so neither aircraft knew the other was there. There was one survivor, and I saw the whole thing – it has never really gone out of my mind. I loved Mossies. We flew T3 and FB6 types. Pilot familiarisation, circuits and bumps (mostly at that ghastly place Wigsley), and nav exercises cross-country – mostly about 3-hr trips.

'I went on to further training in Yorkshire in January 1951, and wound up on 23 Sqn in Norfolk – night fighters. My pilot and I would often sneak a Mossie off, to fly over Lincoln, where my pilot had a girl-friend who was a nurse. The hospital must have been close to the Cathedral, because I have vivid memories of the latter when we used to "buzz" the city – quite low, but not illegally so!' (Letter to the author)

The next month saw the award of the George Medal to Flying Officer Harvey who assisted other members of his crew from a crashed Wellington despite his broken back. The Wellingtons were replaced, in 1951, by the new Vickers Varsity crew trainer, 22 being on strength by March 1952. February saw 204 AFS depart for Bassingbourn, leaving the Varsities in sole occupa-

tion, and as these were a new type Swinderby hosted the aviation press, also flying its aircraft around 18 Battle of Britain displays in September. Like many other new aircraft, the Varsity had problems and was grounded, because of a fault in the tailplane, during the winter; in fact, after several crashes the Varsity had a jinx reputation in the RAF but, by 1954, the problems had been overcome and it gave excellent service for another 22 years. 201 AFS became 11 FTS in June 1954 and in November of that year the air signaller part of its curriculum transferred to Thorney Island, followed by the rest of the School in June the following year.

The sound of jet engines replaced that of the heavy pistons when 8 FTS moved in during August, equipped with single and two-seat Vampires, its task to train fighter pilots. New buildings sprang up, including a modern control tower, and trees at the end of the runway were felled to give a clear approach. The station now came under 25 Group, rather than 21 Group as it had in the Varsity days; 21 Gp's HQ had been at Morton Hall and this now closed. 8 FTS had a student population of 120, courses starting at nine-week intervals; the students had already completed training on the Provost and some, recalling the (P) AFUs of World War Two, were acclimatized to British methods after training in Canada. FAA and foreign pilots were included and the airfield became very busy, flying 4,000 hours a month at its peak. An experimental change in methods came when eight Provosts

arrived and all-through training on the same unit was initiated, with students moving up to the Vampire for jet training. The all-through experiment concluded, apparently a failure, and the Provosts left Swinderby. Two Vampire aerobatic teams were formed and did tours of the Battle of Britain displays. With the reduction in size of the RAF the numbers of students dropped and Wigsley, the RLG, closed in 1958, with Winthorpe, the satellite, closing the next year. After a threat of closure, the delayed introduction into service of the Gnat, which was to replace the Vampire, gave 8 FTS a reprieve and it became busy again, but this was only temporary and in March 1964 8 FTS disbanded. Eric Sower was stationed at Swinderby in 1954/55 and remembers that there was a demonstration at the airfield of a quick pressure-refuelling turnround, a new procedure at that time:

'The VIPs arrived, mainly foreign air force officers, and lined up on the control tower balcony (the old tower) to witness the demonstration. The aircraft, a Hunter, I do not know where from, duly arrived and did a fast run past the tower, did a circuit, and then flew past the tower, and VIPs, at low speed with undercarriage down. The aircraft was then seen to start losing height and vanished doing a left turn, behind some trees about half a mile across the other side of the Fosse Way. A minute or so passed, no Hunter, and then various red-faced RAF officers started dashing in and out of the tower and the crash wagons departed out of the gate. The visiting VIPs were then ushered away, no doubt to the Officer's Mess, and the blood-wagon dashed off

One of several accidents which happened to Swinderby's Wellington T10s, as evidenced by the slogan 'Accident prevention concerns you' which is painted above and below the serial number of this example; NB131 of 201 AFS, had its undercarriage collapse on landing, on 20th December 1948, damaging its flaps so severely that it was written off.
R A Palmer via P H T Green

When the Vickers Varsity T1 replaced the Wellingtons with 201 AFS it too had some accidents, but survived to become a well used and liked type for many years, training crews for multi-engined aircraft. Eric Sower

WA271 was one of 8 FTSs Vampire FB (T) 5s, seen here in a Swinderby hangar (note the curved roof), 1959. The FB (T) 5 was a trainer version of the fighter-bomber, having the four cannon removed. P H T Green

down the road. The Hunter was lying in a muddy field, up to its intakes, the pilot unhurt, having suffered a flame-out of the engine!'
(Letter to the author)

Owing to the proximity of Waddington and Cranwell circuits no more flying at Swinderby was envisaged and it was transferred to Technical Training Command.

The new Command sent in No7 School of Recruit Training, its first intake arriving in June, with further intakes every eight weeks as the previous one 'passed out'. A shortage

De Havilland Tiger Moth T2s of No1 Initial Training School at Kirton-in-Lindsey, 1954.
John Walls

of accommodation meant that No2 Wing went to Hemswell during the winter, remaining there until May 1967. July 1970 saw the number 7 disappear from the school's title as it became the only School of Recruit Training in the diminishing RAF, and all adult airmen now entered the Service through Swinderby.

Kirton-in-Lindsey received 7 SFTS from Peterborough in April 1946, this absorbing 5 (P) AFU which had just arrived at Hibaldstow, its Spitfires and Harvards, still flying from Hibaldstow, being added to the Oxfords and Harvards of 7 SFTS. The School left in August 1948 and, because of Kirton's grass surface, was replaced by the Central Synthetic Training Establishment and the Aircrew Transit Unit until 1949. More ground units succeeded each other, the Aircrew Educational School (1949-50) and Link Trainer School (1950-52), before flying returned in the shape of the Tiger Moth, which positively needed grass runways. The Tigers belonged to 2 Initial Training School, training would-be aircrew officers in the basics of RAF life before passing them on for flying training, their aptitude being tested in the Tigers. It became No1 ITS in 1954 and remained until 1957, when Kirton went on to the familiar Care & Maintenance. In August 1959 No7 School of Technical Training formed to train airmen in the Supply trade, and the Air Movement's School was in residence from January to December 1963. The airfield itself was used from 1960 by No2

Gliding Centre, operating a variety of gliders for Air Training Corps use and, when this left for Grantham in 1965, 7 School of Technical Training became Kirton's last RAF unit, leaving in 1965, after which the Royal Artillery moved in.

At Sutton Bridge 7 SFTS and its Oxfords trained pilots (many of them French), until the School moved from Peterborough to Kirton in April 1946 and flying ceased. The station went onto 'Care & Maintenance' until 58 Maintenance Unit arrived in July 1954 to salvage crashed aircraft in the region but its stay was brief and it disbanded in November 1957, bringing RAF Sutton Bridge's long history to a close.

The Korean war saw a rapid expansion of Flying Training Command and part of this was the establishment of Advanced Flying Schools to train jet fighter pilots; 215 AFS was at Finningley and Blyton was selected as its RLG, operating from February 1952 to January 1954.

In an earlier part of this book I recorded the 'write-offs' in Lincolnshire which occurred in 1939, the last year of peace. It seems appropriate now to record the 'write-offs' of the first full year of peace, which

were fairly disastrous, 950 aircraft being written off in accidents and some 750 airmen killed worldwide. Those crashes which happened in Lincolnshire are listed below:

8th Jan Lancaster, 300 Sqn, Faldingworth, hit tree at Normanby, 4 killed.
18th Jan Two 19 FTS Harvards collided in circuit, Cranwell, 2 killed.
23rd Jan Two Martinets of 2 APS collided in Spilsby circuit, 2 killed.
24th Jan Spitfire V of 17 SFTS, Grantham, force-landed near Manby.
28th Jan Mosquito B16 of 109 Sqn, Hemswell, lost so crew bailed out, 1 killed.
30th Jan Harvard of 7 SFTS, Peterborough, flew into ground during snowstorm near Harlaxton, 1 killed.
7th Feb Tiger Moth of 19 FTS, Cranwell, blown over while taxying at Digby.
14th Mar Lancaster of 300 Sqn, Faldingworth, force-landed near base.
15th Mar Mosquito B16 of 139 Sqn, Hemswell, engine cut on approach and crashlanded.
21st Mar Harvard of 17 SFTS, Grantham, engine cut on approach and crashlanded.
27th Mar Hurricane II of 1687 BDTF, Hemswell, crashed near Bassingham.
28th Mar Spitfire F16 of 17 SFTS, Grantham, belly landed Harlaxton after engine cut.
4th Apr Harvard of 19 SFTS, Cranwell, into sea off Theddlethorpe, 1 killed.

6th Apr Spitfire V of 1687 BDTF, Hemswell, hit vehicle while taxying at Binbrook.

10th Apr Oxford of 17 SFTS, Grantham, crashed on overshoot at base.

16th Apr Anson of 19 SFTS, Cranwell, crashed on take-off at base.

30th Apr Spitfire of 17 SFTS, Grantham, collided near Digby.

7th May Lancaster of 300 Sqn, Faldingworth, crashed on take-off from base.

14th May Master II of EAAS, Manby, undershot landing at base.

22nd May Spitfire, 7 SFTS, Kirton-in-Lindsey, crashed on take-off, Hibaldstow.

5th Jun Spitfire F16 of 17 SFTS, Grantham, engine cut on approach to Barkston Heath.

14th Jun Spitfire F16, 17 SFTS, Grantham, engine cut on approach to Harlaxton.

20th Jun Mosquito FB6 of 13 OTU, Middleton St George, hit HT cables at Holbeach Drove, 2 killed.

1st Jul Spitfire V of 1687 BDTF, Hemswell, crashed landing at Binbrook.

16th Aug Harvard of 7 SFTS, Kirton, hit ground near Hibaldstow during a low-level roll, 2 killed.

19th Aug Oxford of 19 FTS, Cranwell, burnt out after engine fire, base.

27th Aug Wellington XIII of EAAS, Manby, crash-landed at base.

28th Aug Lincoln B2 of 61 Sqn, Waddington, undercarriage collapsed.

29th Aug Lincoln B2 of 97 Sqn, Coningsby, caught fire in hangar at base.

2nd Sep Lancaster of 1660 HCU, Swinderby, crashed on take-off from base, 1 killed.

17th Sep Harvard of 7 SFTS, Kirton, hit control van on take-off at base.

19th Sep Mosquito PR34 of 8 OTU, Mount Farm, lost control in cloud, crashed at Pilsgate, 2 killed.

2nd Oct Harvard of 17 SFTS, Grantham, crashed landing at base.

19th Oct Proctor of 23 Group Comms Flt, Halton, ran out of fuel and crew baled out, Surfleet.

31st Oct Oxford of 7 SFTS, Kirton, force-landed near Barton.

3rd Dec Mosquito B16 of 139 Sqn, Hemswell, bird strike on take-off

Most of these crashes, as can be seen, occurred in training units and involved a variety of aircraft types. Such a crash rate would not be tolerated today but it must be remembered that the RAF had many more aircraft, and flew many more hours than it does today.

Miscellanea

The bombing ranges at Theddlethorpe, Wainfleet and Holbeach continued to operate for the post-war RAF (although Donna Nook closed) and there were sometimes rather inaccurately placed practice bombs, to the consternation of local residents; on one such occasion a Lincoln bomb-aimer dropped a practice bomb on the circle of lights he thought to be at Wainfleet range but was actually at a traffic island just inland, demolishing the outside toilet of a garage. Ted Hooton was training as a navigator at No1 Air Navigation School, Hullavington, and remembers that:

'...we used to fly up to the bombing ranges between Donna Nook and Mablethorpe. This was in 1950 when we were using the Wellington T10. There were (if I remember correctly) 3 triangular targets mounted on stilts on the long beach up there. There were sighting stations mounted on the dunes which would take bearings on the bombs we dropped from the Wimpies. They were 25lb practice bombs, smoke by day, flash for night work. We carried 24 of them on a normal sortie, and with two trainee navs we got to drop 12 each. On the first sorties we would drop them singly...once we got the hang of that, then we went on to practising dropping "sticks"... I often used to think as we droned over the

Moored near HMS Apollo, *a fast minelayer of the Royal Navy in Immingham Dock, are HSLs 2740 and 2743 of 110 Marine Craft Unit, c1953. Much smaller is the range safety pinnace 1510.*
C Hutt via Graham Chaters

top of Mablethorpe with our bomb doors open [we did our "run-up" always from the south, parallel with the coast], 'I wouldn't like to live down there'. You can imagine that I was highly amused when, on leave in Croydon, I saw a poster in our local railway station: "Come to Sunny Mablethorpe for your holidays!"

'There was one memorable bombing trip up there. We had a very good sergeant staff pilot on the Wimpies. He was Scottish, and he hated dummy runs. A dummy run was where you spent all the time running up to the target ["Left, left, steady... steady, right"... etc], then got it wrong at the last moment, and had to announce "dummy run, bomb doors closed" [ie, no bombs left the aircraft]. If you did this to that particular pilot, he had a long broomstick handle, and he would deal you a hefty clout on the rear end – he could reach you from his seat... He was a smashing pilot, and I loved flying with him. He would do anything to help us young lads get good assessments on our nav trips, whereas a few of the staff pilots were really mean'. (Letter to the author)

The amount of flying engendered by the ranges required air-sea-rescue cover, range safety, and target repair launches; as 22 MCU at Grimsby had disbanded in December 1945, two new Marine Craft Units were formed during 1948/49. 1109 MCU was responsible for the Wash ranges and its launches operated from the Haven at Boston Docks, their crews being housed in huts on South End Park in the town. The MCU was parented by Coningsby and its task was largely routine but, in May 1950, a launch was out looking for a West Raynham Meteor which had crashed in the Wash. The wreckage was located and buoyed, and the pilot's body was found on 13th June.

1110 MCU was based on Immingham Docks and was responsible for Theddle-thorpe Range, having a large launch for long-range work. Its 42 airmen were par-ented by Manby but lived in a camp in the town; again its work was routine for the most part but it too had an emergency when a Vampire crashed one mile off Mable-thorpe in March 1950. A launch sailed at 15.20, arriving in the area at 16.48, but a communications failure both with HQ 18 Group and the search aircraft hampered the search and nothing was found. The two MCUs operated until helicopters made them redundant, 1110 disbanding in February 1958 whilst 1109 carried on until July, though both units had had airborne assistance from 275 Sqn's detachment of Sycamore heli-copters at North Coates from 1954 to 1957. These were the only aircraft based at North Coates after VE Day and the station became a storage sub-site until No1 Initial Training School formed in May 1946, training cadet officers until it moved to Bridgnorth in December, returning in January for a longer spell before disbanding in October 1947. After a period of Care & Maintenance, North Coates became the home of the School of Explosive Inspection in May 1948, training armourers in Aeronautical Inspection Ser-vices (Explosives), officers of the Equipment

Branch in 'explosives and fuels', and War-rant Officers and airmen in 'explosives han-dling'. In August the Bomb Disposal School arrived and the various schools amalga-mated in October under the title of 15 School of Technical Training; in 1950 the Junior Armament (Foreign) Officers Spe-cialization Course was added, all no doubt using the old bombing range on the sands at Donna Nook. Training was interrupted by the East Coast floods of 1953, the station being under three feet of water and the units being transferred out, but they returned after a month. 15 SoTT disbanded in August and was replaced by 54 Maintenance Unit, which salvaged wrecked aircraft until it moved to Hucknall, Notts, in July 1956, when the station again went onto Care & Maintenance. The buildings at Donna Nook had housed the Master Provisions Office just after the war but this soon closed and the site became a prisoner of war camp, some prisoners being Polish personnel con-scripted by the Germans.

Although aircraft from the Polish squad-rons took part in the Victory flypast over Lon-don in 1945, no Polish soldiers were allowed in the parade beneath, because Poland was now a Soviet satellite and the British gov-ernment did not wish to upset the USSR! Many of the Poles serving with the Allied forces did not wish to return to a Poland thus controlled and the RAF's Polish squadrons carried on for some time after the war ended, new personnel being trained by the Polish School of Technical Training at Cam-meringham (Ingham), which opened in June 1945 and became 16 SoTT (Polish) in July. 107 staff trained 293 Polish airmen to become wireless-operators, air gunners, armourers, flight mechanics, wireless and radar mechanics, electricians and cooks, and 47 WAAFs to become electricians or cooks. November 1945 saw No4 Personnel Holding Unit (Polish) established to look after the increasing number of Poles await-ing demob and as the airfield itself was no longer required it was released for cultiva-tion in February 1946.

Civilian training courses started in July, on building, dressmaking, carpentry etc, and by October the military training ceased and 16 SoTT disbanded in December to be retitled No1 Polish Resettlement Unit. 1 Polish RU and its Lincolnshire sister unit, 3 Polish RU at Dunholme Lodge, arranged repatriation to Poland or other countries, gave English classes and the other courses as already mentioned; as the Poles were demobbed they were absorbed into what was known as the Polish Resettlement Corps until they were settled into civilian life in the UK. No1 Polish RU disbanded in February 1948 when the Polish Record Office moved to Dun-holme to join 3 Polish RU, Ingham then clos-ing, but 3 PRU continued its important work until it too closed in 1949, some 3,300 Poles being 'on strength' during August 1949.

In 1947 Rauceby Hospital was returned to

its original role of psychiatric hospital for south Lincolnshire, but the large number of RAF stations in the county meant that an alternative had to be found locally; this need was satisfied by Nocton Hall which had been converted to a hospital during World War Two by the US Army, casualties from Europe having been flown into Methering-ham. Nocton Hall was taken over by the RAF in 1947 and provided medical services for the East Midlands stations, the wards being wooden huts in the grounds and the per-sonnel accommodated in the Hall itself.

Although the Americans moved out of their Lincolnshire bases soon after the war, the Cold War saw their return, in limited numbers, during the 1950s, when several war built airfields were taken over by the USAF as 'reserve' bases. Blyton, East Kirkby, Sandtoft, Spilsby, and Sturgate were used for this purpose but only one or two saw active use, as at Sturgate when the 508th Strategic Fighter Wing flew in its F84F Thun-derstreaks after a non-stop transatlantic flight in 1954. The wing stayed only for a short time, having demonstrated that quick reinforcement worked. At East Kirkby were based a succession of C47 Dakota squad-rons for communications and air-sea res-cue, both airfields having their runways strengthened and extended before the USAF closed all its 'reserve' bases in 1958. Sturgate did remain as a USAF supply depot until 1964.

The two and a half decades following World War Two had seen great changes in the RAF in our county but as it entered the 1970s the service, even when deprived of its nuclear deterrent role, still had many chal-lenges to face.

The Republic F-84F Thunderstreaks of the 508th Strategic Fighter Wing, during their visit to Sturgate, 1954. Steve Payne

Huts like these could be seen at all the Lincolnshire stations but these at Normanby-by-Spital transmitter station were rather special because from here would have been sent the signal for Armageddon. Twelve airmen manned the site in the 1950s and 60s, making sure the 10 short-wave transmitters were all working satisfactorily to send out coded messages every 30 minutes from Bomber Command to its airborne V-bombers, which the aircraft's AEOs had to log. Should the USSR have attacked, the message for nuclear retaliation would have been transmitted. This photo was taken c1989 with the site still in use for unknown purposes. There would have been eight more aerials in its heyday. Information Tony Cunnane, photo Charles Parker.

Chapter Six

Turbulent Times
1971-2004

The Bombers

By 1970 the Vulcan was the only heavy bomber on the RAF's strength, the Victors having been converted to tankers following the withdrawal from service of the Valiant in 1965 due to metal fatigue. Two Vulcan squadrons were at Akrotiri in Cyprus but the rest were all Lincolnshire-based, 44, 50 and 101 at Waddington and 27 and 617, plus 230 OCU, at Scampton. The OCU also flew the RAF's last four Hastings, affectionately known as '1066 Sqn', which were used as radar trainers for the Vulcan navigators. As the Vulcans no longer had a strategic nuclear role, this having been taken over by the Royal Navy's Polaris submarines, the Yellow Sun Mk2 hydrogen bombs which they had carried were withdrawn, enabling 92 MU at Faldingworth to close down in November 1972. (The site has since been used for explosives manufacturing, testing and storage by BMARC of Grantham, then by BMARC's successor, Astra, and finally by BAe Royal Ordnance, who closed it, apart from the range facility, in March 2000). In March 1972 27 Sqn disbanded but was reformed at Scampton in November of the following year with a special version of the Vulcan, the B2 (MRR), which was used for maritime radar reconnaissance; 27's aircraft sometimes carried pods under their wings, with which they obtained air samples at high altitude.

Although the RAF had lost the nuclear deterrent there was still considered to be a need for an air-delivered tactical nuclear weapon, and so the WE177B bomb was developed, entering service with the Waddington Wing during 1967/8 and the Scampton Wing during 1970/1; this was a comparatively small bomb, weighing 950lb and with a length of 11ft 1in. When the Turks invaded Cyprus in 1974, 9 and 35 Sqns were ordered back to the UK and took up residence at Scampton (35) and Waddington (9). These were also able to carry the WE177B. All of No1 Group's Vulcans, now Lincolnshire-based and numbering seven squadrons, were under the command of the Supreme Allied Commander Europe (SACEUR) and were a formidable force.

The crews were, of course, kept on their toes by constant training which, Rod Wetton remembers:

'Could be an air display at an international air show, or a basic training requirement (BTR) sortie to practise high/low level navigation, bombing with 28lb practice bombs or real 1,000-pounders. It could be a 'Ranger' to Cyprus or Goose Bay, Labrador, or a radar reconnaissance sortie in co-operation with the Royal Navy. It might even be an around the world trip, stopping off at Cyprus, Bahrain, Gan, Singapore, Darwin, Guam, Wake, Honolulu, California, Nebraska, Goose Bay and taking several weeks.

'And then there were the Strike Command or SACEUR generated exercises, with exotic names like "Mickey Finn", "Spring Train" and so on'

Rod was an Air Electronics Officer and flew on Vulcans from 1970 to 1982 with various squadrons and the OCU. I am grateful to him for the following recollections about the Vulcan force.

'A Vulcan crew consisted of five men – a pilot (who was almost invariably the Captain and under whose name the crew was identified (eg the Smith crew), a Co-pilot, a Navigator Plotter (responsible for navigation), a Navigator Radar (responsible for dropping the bomb) and an AEO (responsible for communications, electrical systems and electronic and other counter measures). Ages ranged from 20 to 55, in a few cases even older. These five men came together on an almost casual basis, initially at the OCU stage, and usually stayed together unless there was serious disharmony. It was accepted that a co-pilot or an AEO could substitute with another crew when necessary but captains and navs were rarely substituted...

'Let me tell you of one sortie by one crew – mine. They were: Captain-Steve, Co-Pilot-Bill, Nav Plot-Alf, Nav-Rad-Spike, AEO-me. We were Crew 5 on 617 Sqn and were detailed to fly Exercise Capricorn on 7th June 1972. Our aircraft was Vulcan B2 XL426...

'Exercise Capricorn was a SACEUR exercise, designed to test the UK's air defences, with the Vulcan fleet acting as aggressors. The plan was for 48 Vulcan B2s to fly from their UK bases to designated rendezvous points (RV) over Denmark and Holland. From the RV they would fly, with strict timing, to a descent point (DP) and then they would descend to low-level to carry out a broad front low-level attack on designated targets in the UK. Accurate route-flying and time-keeping are obviously essential in such exercises, otherwise disaster is very near. Simulated bomb runs were to be scored by Radar Bomb Score Units (RBSUs). Crew Five, however, were given a different task. We were to fly with the bomber stream to the DP but we would then climb to high level around 45,000ft and accelerate to M.9 and maintain this height and speed to carry out a simulated bomb release on a specific target...

'Specialist briefings are given... The meteorological forecaster had his say... crews would have a short "crew brief"... and when all were happy it's off to the aircrew feeder for a preflight meal. Pilot and Co-Pilot were supposed to have different meals in case of food poisoning... I had steak, egg and chips, Spike a full fry... Alf ate curry and rice.

'The meal over we board the crew bus to ferry us to XL426... All aboard, aeroplane wound up, everything appears to work so away we go. Airborne, gear up, spot on time. Routine passage to the RV, on time. DP on time, commence climb and accelerate. So far, so good. A few minutes later we are at our designated height and speed when Alf announces that he has to go to the toilet... This is a problem. Apart from a so-called P-tube at each crew station there were no toilet facilities in a Vulcan – and Alf is obviously in some discomfort. What shall we do? Abort the sortie – pointless. Divert somewhere – equally pointless. Alf needs a quick solution. The answer lies in the in-flight ration boxes... Alf removes the contents of two boxes, reinforces one with the other and-hey presto, a suitable container. Having removed his parachute, taken off his immersion suit and his air-ventilated suit Alf, clutching his emergency toilet, crawled up the bomb-aimer's tunnel, which runs forward under the pilots ejection seats... Meanwhile the rest of the crew have put on their oxygen masts and selected 100% pure oxygen!

'Spike and I kept an eye on the navigation and timing until a mightily relieved Alf was able to re-don his kit and resume his duties. The box was carefully stored on the floor near to the crew exit door.

'It was at this moment when the fickle finger of fate pointed directly at XL426 and Crew 5. I received a coded/authenticated message from the Bomber Controller at 1 Group HQ. This told us to complete our mission and then divert to Kinloss where we should complete a quick turn-around ready for re-tasking...

'We completed our bomb-run, and incidentally the RBSU scored it a direct hit (DH), and turned for Kinloss. As soon as we contacted Kinloss Approach control a message from Wing Commander Operations at Kinloss was relayed to us. He was obviously concerned that we might be carrying live bombs or even a live nuclear weapon. The question asked was "Do you have a hazardous cargo on board?" The immediate reply – and I will not reveal who transmitted it – was "Affirmative". Much ribald comment and hilarity amongst the crew ensued and no-one thought to put the matter right. We landed at Kinloss three hours and forty minutes after take-off from Scampton and followed the "Follow me" vehicle to a remote dispersal, accompanied by fire engines and RAF Police Landrovers. We shut XL426 down, opened the crew door and lowered the ladder. First out, clutching his box, was Alf. He was met by WingCo Ops and his specialist weapons officers, police with guard dogs and fire crews. In retrospect we should have expected the reaction of the Kinloss authorities – a total sense of humour failure! ...Suffice it to say we returned to Scampton under a bit of a cloud, and the

punishment of a couple of extra Station Duty Officers was probably worth it...

'Looking back on this story now I think it demonstrates three things. Firstly the sort of task that Vulcan crews were given, with unexpected changes thrown in. Secondly the resourcefulness shown by an ordinary Vulcan crew when faced with an awful dilemma but still completing the task. And finally that bizarre, perhaps even macabre, sense of humour that seems to be shared by all aircrew of all nations of all eras'. (Rod Wetton, letter to the author)

During 1977 the Hastings of '1066' Sqn were retired, having flown several patrols over the North Atlantic during the so-called 'Cod War' with Iceland, leaving the Vulcan as the sole aircraft type at Scampton and Waddington. By the late 1970s the Vulcan had been in service for some 20 years; designed as a high altitude nuclear bomber, the soundness of its design, its strength and the skill of its crews had allowed it to be used in the low-level role for 15 of those years. However, its design dated from the 1940s and although, where possible, its avionics and weapon systems had been updated, it was now due for replacement. The Lancaster, in comparison, had served as a bomber for a mere six years, the Lincoln for eleven, and the Canberra for 21. Operational and financial considerations meant that there was no longer a place for the long-range strategic bomber in the RAF so there was no direct replacement for the Vulcan; instead the RAF's offensive capability was to be undertaken by the Tornado GR1 low-level strike aircraft against tactical targets,

and it entered service with the Tri-Service Tornado Training Establishment, at Cottesmore, Leics, in 1981. Therefore, in that year the rundown of the Vulcan force commenced, with 230 OCU being, logically, the first unit to disband, in August, and then Scampton's squadrons; 617, the Dambusters, in January 1982, 35 Sqn in February and, finally, 27 in March. Passers-by could see the melancholy sight of Vulcans being broken up for scrap.

It was now the turn of Waddington's units but on 1st April 1982, Argentinean forces invaded the Falkland Islands; at Waddington most personnel thought that there was no role for the Vulcan but, just before Easter leave, rumours were heard (and treated with disbelief), of Vulcans undertaking air-to-air refuelling, and some crews were placed on stand-by. When the bulk of Waddington's personnel returned from leave the rumours became reality and the aircrews were told that any action in the Falklands would involve dropping 1,000lb bombs, as used in World War Two. As Vulcans had practised with the WE177 since the mid-70s and had not trained in AAR during the same period, there were few personnel left in the force with relevant experience. Luckily, Squadron Leader Williams had had the most experience with conventional bombs and was still at Waddington, albeit in a ground appointment, so was immediately tasked with training the selected crews, which came from 44, 50 and 101 Sqns, 9 Sqn being already in the process of disbandment. The three

Hastings T5 TG517 of '1066' Squadron, 230 Operational Training Unit, Scampton, airborne on a radar training flight c1975. Its use in a more active role, that of fishery patrols during the 'Cod War' with Iceland, is signified by four 'fish' symbols on the nose. These were the last Hastings in RAF service.
Middleton, Lincoln

finally chosen were captained by Squadron Leader Montgomery, Squadron Leader Reeve and Flight Lieutenant Withers, with Squadron Leader McDougall as reserve.

AAR training started on 14th April by day and night, and after five trips they were judged to be qualified; bombing training then began by dropping 28lb practice bombs on splash targets in the Wash and near the Isle of Man to calibrate the radar bombing equipment, after which the primary crews bombed with 21 1,000-pounders, the reserve being allowed only five! On 18th April the crews were told that their target would be Port Stanley airfield, and after further training at high and low altitudes, and the addition of Victor pilots to each crew for their tanking expertise, the Vulcans flew to Ascension Island on 28th and 29th April.

On 30th April the first operation took place, Squadron Leader Reeve's crew being given the task but, after five minutes, his aircraft suffered a pressurization fault and had to turn back, so Flight Lieutenant Withers and his crew, the reserve, became respon-

The Falklands bomber. XM607, the Vulcan which bombed and hit Port Stanley airfield on 30th April 1982, the longest bombing raid in RAF history. She is now preserved at RAF Waddington on a site which, sadly, cannot be seen by the public. Mike Ingham

sible for 'Black Buck 1'. Nine Victor tankers accompanied the sole Vulcan as it flew down the South Atlantic, the tanking being a complex operation which, not unexpectedly, hit some snags, leaving the Vulcan 8000lb short of the fuel it needed and placing at risk the last Victor, which gave the bomber more fuel than it was safe to do, relying on meeting another Victor from Ascension before it itself ran out of fuel. Flight Lieutenant Withers dropped to 250ft as he neared the Falklands until, 40 miles from the target, he pulled up to 10,000ft and started to release the 21 bombs two miles from Port Stanley airfield, on a heading of 30 degrees to the runway, this having been calculated to give the best chance of hitting it with at least one bomb. The tired crew turned back to Ascension and, refuelling without undue problems, landed back to learn that one bomb had indeed hit the runway. A second attack, by Squadron Leader Reeves two days later, narrowly missed it. On 30th May Squadron Leader McDougall carried out a radar suppression raid with Shrike anti-radar missiles, which the Vulcan had been hastily modified to carry, and one further such sortie was carried out, during

which the Vulcan's refuelling probe snapped whilst refuelling from a Victor, meaning that Squadron Leader McDougall, in order to save his aircraft and crew, had to divert to Rio de Janeiro in Brazil. The Brazilians initially impounded the aircraft but after a week of diplomacy, it was allowed to fly back to Ascension. Flight Lieutenant Withers, after a spell back at Waddington to train up other crews, carried out the last 'Black Buck' bombing raid on 12th June, against Port Stanley airfield once more, and the Argentineans surrendered two days later as the Army and Marines closed in. Ironically, the Vulcan had, on the very eve of its retirement, dropped bombs in anger for the first time in its career. The raids were probably the longest ever carried out, certainly by the RAF, involving some 16-17 hours over 7,200 miles of very inhospitable ocean.

Back at Waddington things got back to normal, and the disbandments carried on – 9 Sqn in May, 101 in August, and 44, the last strategic bomber squadron in the RAF, in December 1982. However, 50 Sqn received a stay of execution because the Falklands war had placed great demands on the Victor tankers which, even after the surrender,

were still heavily involved in refuelling Hercules, VC10s and other types flying from Ascension to Port Stanley. This left the UK's air-defence fighters very short of tankers and several VC10s which had been stored at Abingdon for a number of years began a hasty tanker conversion programme as did some ex-airliner TriStars. In the meantime it proved reasonably simple to convert six Vulcans into tankers which could support the fighters; the conversion involved the removal of the ECM equipment in the tailcone, which was replaced by a Hose Drum Unit (HDU) with, underneath, a box of ungainly appearance housing the signal lights and drogue. The bomb-bay was filled with three standard Vulcan long-range tanks, spotlights were fitted under the wings, and a periscope and tanker paint-job

The business end of a Vulcan B2 (K) tanker conversion, seen on XH561 of 50 Squadron, 1983. The hose-drum unit is housed in the white box beneath the tail cone, with the refuelling drogue on the end of the hose, left. Note Lincoln City's coat of arms on the fin, above the 50 Squadron symbol.
Charles Parker

on the undersurface completed the conversion. Retitled the Vulcan B2K (or sometimes K2) these conversions served with 50 Sqn, along with four standard aircraft for training, from June 1982, patrolling out over the North Sea to refuel Lightnings and Phantoms in the UK Air Defence Region.

The first VC10s entered service in May 1984 but by then 50 Sqn's usefulness was deemed over and the Squadron disbanded on 31st March. Several Vulcans were presented to air museums throughout the country and at Waddington XM607, Flight Lieutenant Withers' crew's aircraft, is preserved as gate guardian. In a rare moment of sentimentality the Ministry of Defence even allowed one Vulcan to keep flying, forming the Vulcan Display Flight which, from April 1984 to its disbandment in September 1994, thrilled crowds at air displays all over the UK and Europe. Eventually the accountants won and after overflying several old Vulcan

bases and the city of Lincoln, the very last flying Vulcan, carrying a poignant 'Farewell' painted on its bomb doors, flew to Bruntingthorpe in Leicestershire, where it can still be seen to taxi under its own 'steam' (and, at the time of writing, might even fly again!). So ended the era of the strategic bomber, both in the RAF and in Lincolnshire, where such bombers had been based since 1926. Even the Tornado was not scheduled to come to the county and so 1984 saw the end of Bomber County, as the remaining Lincolnshire bases became involved in air defence or training, much as they had been during World War One.

Air Defence
Binbrook entered the Seventies with the Lightnings of 5 Sqn and the Canberra target aircraft of 85 Sqn, but in January 1972 85 Sqn left for Norfolk and the airfield became an all-Lightning base, with the arrival of 11 Sqn in March; like 5 Sqn, 11 had spent much of its existence overseas, in the Far East, Middle East and, latterly, Germany. Both Squadrons were part of the UK Air Defence Force, tasked with the interception of unidentified aircraft picked up by UK radar. In Binbrook's case this was the Master Radar at Patrington, near Hull, all the Lincolnshire radars having now closed. Two aircraft were kept on 24 hour Quick Reaction Alert, ready to scram-

ble when required. Trips were sometimes made to Malta for armament training, the last of these being in 1978, after which Cyprus was used. Rare detachments were also made to Valley in Anglesey, where pilots could fire a Red Top AAM 'for real'. The Lightning F1s used by the Binbrook Target Facilities Flight were parked out on the airfield after the flight disbanded in December 1973, as 'decoy' targets for any attacking Soviet aircraft and such attacks were often simulated in exercises, whereupon the Lightning F3 and F6s would demonstrate their amazing take-offs, much to the delight of watching enthusiasts.

As the Lightning began to be superseded by the Phantom the Lightning OCU, 229, disbanded at Coltishall in September 1974, and was replaced by the Lightning Training Flight, which formed at Binbrook the following month to train pilots for the two front-line Squadrons. In 1979 the new Conservative Government professed to be concerned about the depleted state of the UK air defences and decided to form a third Lightning squadron at the base, rumoured to be 45 Sqn; in the event, as so often happens with politicians, there was no third squadron but in June the Instant Readiness Reserve Unit formed, changing its title in 1981 to the Lightning Augmentation Unit which disbanded the following year. Thus

the UK air defences remained the same and 5, 11 and the LTF operated the Lightning, the other three fighter stations now having the Phantom. The Lightning was a superlative fighter but had the disadvantage of having a very short endurance, often meaning that a tanker had to be scrambled at the same time; it was also prone to fires, and several Binbrook aircraft were lost in this way. With the advent of the new Tornado fighters, the Lightning's days were numbered and in April 1987, with no further requirement for new pilots, the LTF was disbanded, followed by 5 Sqn in December and 11 Sqn in April 1988, 11 having the honour to operate the last RAF all-British fighter.

Binbrook's days as an RAF station were also over, as Leeming in Yorkshire had been rebuilt as an air defence station and now took over; the reason behind this was possibly that Binbrook had always been more than usually subject to bad weather and, in addition, Leeming was geographically more to the north from where the Russian threat was likely to come; Binbrook's Lightnings had occasionally intercepted their Tupolev Bear reconnaissance aircraft out over the North Sea. For a time the airfield was used as a relief landing ground for CFS at Scampton and in 1991 643 Volunteer Gliding School arrived to train the county's Air Cadets, but this left again in October 1992 and Binbrook's use by the RAF ceased. Civil regis-

tered Jet Provosts were based there for a time and enthusiasts from all over the country assembled at the airfield in 1989 when it was used as a location for the film The Memphis Belle, with some half-dozen B-17 Fortresses filling the skies around. The camp itself was sold for housing and took on the identity of the 'new' village of Brookenby.

At Coningsby in 1970 228 OCU was turning out crews for the ground-attack Phantoms, with 6 and 54 Sqns also flying from the base, joined by 41 Sqn (with a reconnaissance role), which reformed in April 1972. However, the ground-attack role was only intended to be a temporary one for the Phantom and as the dedicated ground-attack Jaguar began to enter service, from 1973 on, the Phantom shifted to air-defence, 228 OCU changing its training to this new role in 1974, after which most of the RAF's fighter squadrons rotated through Coningsby to convert to the Phantom. The first resident Phantom fighter unit was 29 Sqn, which arrived in December 1974 and was one of the RAF's oldest fighter squadrons; it replaced 6 and 54 which had both disbanded to reform on the Jaguar, with 41 following suit in 1977, leaving 29 and 228 OCU as the sole occupants. In the early 1980s hardened aircraft shelters were built on the east side of the airfield to house 29 Sqn's 15 aircraft.

A 5 Squadron Lightning F6 taxies for take-off at Binbrook, 1986, wearing the type's last camouflage scheme of two-tone grey. Author

Not a World War Two shot but one of the B-17 Fortresses starring in the film 'The Memphis Belle', many of the flying sequences being shot at Binbrook in the summer of 1989. Author

Long resident at Coningsby was 29 Squadron and its Phantom FGR2s, one of which, XV487, is seen here in pristine condition at Coningsby's Photo Day in June 1987. Author

The Phantom, whilst not so manoeuvrable as the Lightning, had a two-man crew, reducing the workload, and a much increased armament, namely four Skyflash AAMs carried beneath the fuselage and four Sidewinders under the wings, with the option of a 20mm Vulcan multi-barrel cannon pod; the Lightning had two 30mm cannon and just two Red Top AAMs. With three long-range tanks under wings and fuselage, the Phantom could carry 10 tons of fuel, thus eliminating the shortage experienced by the Lightning pilots. 29 Sqn shared the Southern QRA with Binbrook and another Phantom station at Wattisham and when it was Coningsby's turn two Phantoms were fully armed, with the crew kitted up in immersion gear and flying suits; other tasks

included the defence of naval units in the eastern Atlantic, shared with another Phantom unit. Once a year 29 Sqn visited Deccimomanu, the NATO air combat range off Sardinia, where they practised with other NATO air forces and aircraft and, like the Lightnings, they went to Akrotiri in Cyprus for gunnery training, and Valley for AAM firing. Crews served for around five years with the Squadron and, during that time, spent four months with 23 Sqn in the Falklands where, for a change, they could gaze at the South Atlantic rather than the North Sea whilst they patrolled!

228 OCU trained all pilots and navigators for the Phantom squadrons, and at Coningsby they crewed up and spent 60 hours converting to the aircraft and learning the basics of the air-defence 'trade'; after some six months the crew joined an operational squadron. The OCU also retrained crews already experienced on the Phantom but who had been in a ground job; their course lasted only three months. In the event of a 'national emergency' the OCU aircraft and instructors would have become 64 Sqn, and the aircraft carried this unit's markings.

Somewhat older aircraft arrived at Coningsby in March 1976 when, after much lobbying by Lincolnshire enthusiasts, the Battle of Britain Memorial Flight took up residence in one of the hangars; the Flight's Lancaster, Hurricanes and Spitfires soon became familiar and welcome sights in the sur-

rounding skies and have remained ever since, with the addition of a Dakota and two Chipmunks in recent years. In 1986 a joint initiative with Lincolnshire County Council resulted in a Visitors' Centre which was established adjacent to the Flight's hangar, and parties are now shown around the hangar by experienced guides each weekday.

The Phantom had entered service with the USN in the late 1950s and was thus not a new aircraft and in November 1984 its intended successor, the Tornado F2, entered service at Coningsby with a second OCU, No 229. A variant of the strike Tornado, the fighter version was designed to operate out over the North Sea for long periods and to destroy incoming Russian bombers before they could launch their stand-off missiles against UK targets. The F2 only equipped the OCU and it was quickly replaced by a developed version the F3. After early problems with its Foxhunter radar, the Tornado proved very capable in this role, with a weapons fit of four Skyflash and four Sidewinder, plus a 27mm cannon; the missiles are being replaced by ASRAAM (Advance Short range) and AMRAAM (Advanced Medium range) missiles, plus a JTIDS data link and laser Inertial Navigation System (INS) to take the aircraft into the 21st century as a still very potent interceptor. Unfortunately its original role disappeared with the end of the Cold War and the aircraft

5 Squadron was the last operational Tornado F3 squadron at Coningsby. ZE760 was with the Squadron during the late 1980s and is seen here at Waddington's Photomeet in May 1988. Sadly, the colourful squadron markings have been toned down over recent years. Author

has received misguided criticism concerning its ability as a dogfighter, for which task it was not designed. The Tornado F3 Operational Evaluation Unit formed at Coningsby in April 1987 and, under the auspices of the Air Warfare Centre at Waddington, continues to work out the roles and tactics for the F3 squadrons, while the F3 replaced the F2 in the OCU by 1988.

As the number of Tornados at the airfield increased it was time for the Phantoms to leave and 228 OCU departed for Leuchars in April 1987, just after 29 Sqn disbanded; a good Squadron cannot be kept down, though, and 29 reformed almost immediately as a Tornado F3 unit, reoccupying its HASs. However, its seniority was soon challenged when 5 Sqn arrived, fresh from Binbrook and Lightnings, to take up residence as Coningsby's second operational Tornado squadron. These two units were in Cyprus for armament training in August 1990 and twelve Tornados were sent 'to hold the line' in the Gulf after the Iraqi invasion of Kuwait. The aircraft were not really combat ready,

being without chaff or flares for defence against AAMs, or the latest versions of their own missiles or radar and their crews were not optimistic if it came to fighting the Iraqi's Russian-built fighters. The groundcrew arrived in Dhahran on 11th August and the first Combat Air Patrols (CAP) were flown on the 12th.

Fortunately, the Iraqis did not attack Saudi-Arabia and by late August the most up-to-date F3s arrived from Leeming, their crews being a mixture of 5, 11, 25, and 29 Squadrons who took the name of 'The Desert Eagles'. When the War started the F3s flew 4½ air-defence sorties, the crews flying 60 hours a month, but because the Iraqi Air Force made little attempt to attack Allied aircraft their skills were not put to the test and their efforts little publicized. Coningsby also supplied three F3s for 1435 Flt in the Falklands and when the aircraft were exchanged for major servicing, their crews faced a long and uncomfortable flight over the South Atlantic; however, in January 2000 two F3s were loaded into the capacious hold of a Russian Antonov 124 transport, on hire to a British company, and when the RAF received its large Boeing Globemaster transports, these took over the task, their first use in this role being in 2001.

A third squadron was nominally added to Coningsby's strength in 1992 because, as the end of the Cold War brought a rapid rundown in the number of RAF squadrons, it

was decided to perpetuate some of the famous units by giving their numbers to OCUs, with the title Reserve Sqn. Thus 229 OCU became, in July 1992, 56 (Reserve) Sqn and carried the Phoenix badge on its Tornados. 56 (R) Sqn's main task was the Long Course, which converted newly winged pilots fresh from Hawks at 4 FTS as well as pilots experienced on other aircraft types plus, of course, their navigators, who were also a mixture of novice and experienced personnel. 56 is the largest fast-jet unit in the RAF and its 20 or so aircraft and 44 instructors take the student crews through 46 sorties for pilots and 44 for navigators, starting with 11 covering general handling, after which the pilots and navigators teamed up for the next six sorties teaching basic interception, each of the student crew flying with an instructor in separate aircraft. The crew then flew together for five sorties covering basic fighter manoeuvres, splitting up again for six flights using more advanced interception techniques; further phases of the training followed, taking the crews (still flying separately) through to one-to-two interceptions and, eventually, two versus two.

About 12%, on average, failed but the rest were then posted to one of the five F3 Squadrons where their skills were further refined. There is also a shorter course for F3 crews returning to the aircraft after a break, and 56 also trained the Qualified Weapons Instructors for the F3 units, these being

Built at many operational airfields in the UK during the 1980s, these hardened aircraft shelters (HAS) were designed to withstand very near misses from air attack; only Coningsby, of the Lincolnshire stations, has them, and this one was sheltering a 29 Squadron Phantom in 1985. Curiously, in 2001, three open sided/ ended shelters were erected on Coningsby's flight line, resembling the sun shades found on airfields in warmer climes, but were removed again in 2003! Author

experienced crews who undertook an 18 week course covering advanced tactics, air-to-air and air-to-ground gunnery, and missile camp at Valley. As part of the Labour government's Strategic Defence Review 29 Sqn was disbanded in October 1998, leaving 5 and 56 (Reserve) as Coningsby's air-defence units. The Italian Air Force also sent crews to 56 Sqn, as it has some former RAF Tornado F3s on lease until it receives the Eurofighter in the first decade of the new century. IAF aircraft were thus regular visitors to Coningsby.

5 Sqn, like the other air defence units, had a busy schedule; during September/October 2000, it was in Saudi-Arabia on Operation Bolton, and on its return prepared for its Evaluation in December, followed by a visit from French Mirage F1s for low-level training. January 2001 saw four crews taking part in the multi-national leadership programme

in Belgium, while the remainder of the Squadron had ACMI training with FAA Sea Harriers, and practice missile-firing at RAF Valley on Anglesey, shooting-down a Jindivik target-drone. Training during February and March involved FAA helicopters, RAF low-level strike aircraft, USAF F15 Eagles and Dutch F16s, honing the Sqn's skills in preparation for a 'Red Flag' exercise in the USA; this two-week day and night flying exercise in Nevada was reached via the Azores, Halifax in Canada, and Albuquerque. On its return to Coningsby 5 Sqn had gunnery training and a visit to Iceland during April, undertook its stint of Quick Reaction Alert, and started to train for its next detachment to Saudi-Arabia, whilst during the summer of 2001 it was in Oman for a major exercise, Safe Sareera. With Coningsby due to close for runway resurfacing in March 2003, and thereafter operating the Typhoon, 5 Squadron disbanded in September 2002, but will reform at Waddington during 2005. The BBMF moved to Barkston Heath during the resurfacing and the F3 OEU to Waddington.

When Wattisham transferred to the Army Air Corps in 1992 Coningsby became the most southerly air defence airfield, the other two being Leeming and Leuchars, and big changes are afoot for the station in the new century as, just as it pioneered the Phantom and Tornado fighter into RAF service, so it will the Eurofighter Typhoon. This aircraft will replace most of the RAF's Tornado fighters and the Jaguars and will be one of the world's most advanced fighter ground attack aircraft; from 2004/2005 it will equip an Operational Evaluation Unit, numbered 17 Sqn, at Coningsby, and a new OCU/Reserve Sqn, (welcome back to 29 Sqn) followed by the operational units, two of these being scheduled for Coningsby. 56 (R) Sqn, having been displaced by these units, moved to Leuchars in March 2003 to continued its Tornado training.

Serving alongside the Typhoon units will be the Fast Jet Operational Evaluation Unit, formed from the resident F3 OEU and the Strike Attack OEU (from Boscombe Down) in the spring of 2004, and flying Tornado F3 and GR4, Harrier GR7 and Jaguar GR3 to evolve new tactics and test new weapons.

Arriving at Coningsby in 1984-85 was a Territorial Army unit, 219 Field Squadron (ADR) of the Royal Engineers, which became responsible for repairing Coningsby's runways in the event of an attack and was equipped with various civil-engineering plant and vehicles for this purpose; with the cut-back in the TA in the late 1990s the Sqn was disbanded in June 1999.

It practised its work at the outstation of Coningsby on the old Woodhall Spa airfield where, as the Phantom entered service, an engine test and engineering facility had been built on the former Bloodhound SAM site (and 627 Sqn dispersal!); it continued this role for the Tornado but, as the last Tornados left in 2003, the site closed. Closer to Coningsby, on Kirkby Lane, are the RAF Police Dog kennels, once a Radar Bomb Score Unit.

Fighter aircraft are only able to provide the nation with its air defence if they can find the attackers and, with today's high perfor-

Rarely photographed are the three BAe Nimrod R1s of 51 Squadron, whose role is highly classified and which can be distinguished from the maritime patrol Nimrods by the many aerials on the fuselage, and the lack of the MAD tailcone. This example, carrying the Squadron's 'red goose' symbol on its fin, departed Waddington during the 1998 air display. Author

A Boeing Sentry AEW1, to give it its correct RAF designation rather than the American E-3D, is seen on approach to Waddington in 1992 with 'everything down', and displaying 8 Squadron's fighter-style blue, yellow and red squadron marking, once carried by Venoms and Hunters in Aden. The Sentries are always busy and have seen active service over Bosnia, Kosovo, Afghanistan and Iraq. Author

mance aircraft, this is only possible if they are under radar control – at least until their own radar is within range. As already stated it was Patrington in East Yorkshire which guided the Lincolnshire squadrons in the 1970s but this too closed in the early 1980s, and Neatishead, Norfolk, together with Boulmer, Northumberland, took over the task. In January 1972 the RAF had formed its first airborne radar station, equipped with converted Shackleton anti-submarine aircraft. Both aircraft and radar were already elderly but, nevertheless, made an important contribution to our defences, flying from Lossiemouth in Scotland. During the 1980s the whole UK air defence radar system was scheduled to be re-equipped and upgraded, including the airborne factor.

Waddington, empty since 50 Sqn had disbanded, (although it was far from disused as it was still an active airfield – in 1986 the NATO Tactical Fighter Meet took place there), became the home of the Nimrod Airborne Early Warning Joint Trials Unit, tasked with introducing into service the new version of the Nimrod maritime reconnaissance aircraft which was to replace the venerable Shackleton. The Nimrod itself was a very successful aircraft, based on the famous Comet airliner, and 11 conversions were to be made using a brand new Marconi radar which would be able to direct the Tornados on to targets over a very wide area of the North Sea; in addition it could plot

enemy shipping and direct Tornados or Buccaneers on to these targets. Unhappily, despite much work and tribulation by the JTU, an effective marriage could not be made between radar and aircraft, nor could the radar be made to work to specification and so, after three years, it was decided to abandon the project and those Nimrods already converted were flown away to various other airfields, never to fly again. The cost was enormous but the RAF was still without a replacement for the Shacks and so it was decided to order the aircraft which had been turned down by the MoD in 1977, because of disagreements within NATO – the Boeing E3 Sentry. At least the delay meant that the seven Sentries ordered for the RAF could incorporate all the upgrades then available, including advanced fanjet engines which much reduced the decibel level compared to the Vulcan. Waddington was selected as the base for the Sentry and much work was carried out, adding to the cost; a very large new hangar at the north end, capable of housing three Sentries, new buildings for training and last but not least, wider taxiways to allow for the outboard underwing engine pods of the new aircraft. As the Sentry was already in service with NATO and the USAF the type, with its mushroom radar, was quite often seen at the base before the RAF received its first Sentry in the summer of 1991, the groundwork having been already carried out by the Sentry Train-

ing Squadron, formed in June of the previous year. 8 Sqn's remaining Shackletons flew down to Waddington and a few days later, in July 1991, left for disposal, and the Squadron reformed on its new state-of-the-art aircraft.

With just seven aircraft, and also providing the aircraft for the STS, the Squadron was soon in action over Bosnia, flying from a forward base in Italy which became a permanent detachment during the 1990s; this resulted in severe overstretch for 8 Sqn and, although there were no extra aircraft, 23 Sqn formed at Waddington in April 1996. 23 took over the training role and provided extra personnel for operations, the Sentries thus carrying 8 Sqn's Arabian dagger on one side of the fin and 23's Eagles on the other.

A typical mission for a Sentry crew starts the previous day, with a three-hour briefing; these are large crews, with the captain, co-pilot, flight engineer and navigator forming the flight crew; two weapons controllers, a fighter allocator, surveillance controller, ESM operator, data-link manager, two surveillance operators and tactical director forming the mission crew; and three air technicians and a communications operator, a total of 17 altogether recently increased to 18. The mission normally lasts about eight hours, comprising an hour to establish the equipment, six hours on operations, and an hour to close everything down; however, if required, this could be

extended to 72 hours with the aid of in-flight refuelling and a double crew, a crew joke being that the limiting factor is then the toilet capacity! When crews (which now contain female members) come to train on the Sentry all are already qualified in their respective branches except those in the two new aircrew categories established for the aircraft, air technician and airborne controller, who receive their brevets at the end of the six month OCU course with 23 Sqn. To assist the OCU training and continuity train-

2503 (County of Lincoln) Squadron, RAuxAF Regiment, formed at Scampton in 1979 with the task of defending Waddington from ground attack, a role it still performs in 2004; these airmen take up position in front of a Scampton Vulcan, c1980. 2503 Squadron

Pictured at Waddington in 1985, these 30mm anti-aircraft guns were captured from the Argentineans during the Falklands war, and later pressed into service with 2729 (City of Lincoln) Squadron, RAuxAF Regiment to give close-range AA defence for the station; similarly equipped was 2890 Squadron at Coningsby, but both units were disbanded in 1994. Author

The Bloodhound SAM2s of 85 Squadron's B Flight at North Coates; although an elderly system by the time this photo was taken in 1987, the Bloodhound was still a quite potent weapon for medium-range air defence.
Charles Parker

ing, there is a flight simulator and a mission simulator, the former also used by crews from the French Air Force, which also has Sentries. The detachment in Italy came under intense pressure in 1999 when the Kosovo air operations required RAF, USAF and NATO Sentries to operate over the Adriatic constantly and since then the Sentries have been very active over Afganistan and Iraq. The two units are probably the busiest in 3 Group and the Sentry will be in service until 2020/25, with upgrades to its sophisticated equipment.

Another flying unit arrived at Waddington in April 1995, with the role of 'eavesdropping' by electronic means wherever required by the Government; 51 Squadron flies the Nimrod R1, of which it has three examples, and these aircraft are equipped with highly secret electronics, evidenced by the number of aerials they carry and the size of their crews (24). 51 Sqn has been engaged on such duties since 1958 and nothing more can be said about its role except that a Squadron Nimrod carried out 27 consecutive sorties during the 2003 Iraq war.

In 2005, according to current plans, 8, 23 and 51 will be joined by a reformed 5 Squadron flying much modified, Canadian Global Express executive jets, named the Sentinel R1 by the RAF; these will carry a new Advanced Stand-off Radar (ASTOR) which will enable the aircraft to plot ground traffic in the same way as the Sentry plots that in

the air, enabling generals to know what is happening on and behind their battlefronts. The new squadron will have five of these highly sophisticated aircraft.

Waddington is thus one of the RAF's most important bases and its future seems assured well into the 21st Century. Its aircraft are essential but few in number and their protection on the ground at the base, in times of tension or war, is paramount; responsible for this protection is 2503 (County of Lincoln) Sqn, Royal Auxiliary Air Force Regiment. The RAuxAF Regiment was reformed in 1979 comprised of three Squadrons, one of which was 2503, tasked to protect Waddington from attack by saboteurs and Russian paratroops; the number 2503 perpetuated the Auxiliary flying squadron (503) based at Waddington pre-war. Men and women were recruited from the local area to serve as spare-time members and are trained, by Regular and Auxiliary instructors, to handle all the normal infantry weapons up to the 66mm anti-tank rocket launcher and the mortar. Initially the Squadron was based at Scampton because of shortage of accommodation at Waddington, but in February 1985 it moved to Waddo, where its personnel attend weekly training meetings; weekend camps are a monthly occurrence, and they are expected to take part in the annual 15-day summer camp in this country or abroad.

In April 1985 2503 was joined at Waddington by 2729 (City of Lincoln) Sqn, RAuxAF

Regiment, this unit having an anti-aircraft role; its equipment comprised twelve A-A field guns, each mounting twin 35mm Oerlikon cannons, controlled by their associated Skyguard radar, all having been captured from the Argentinean army in the Falklands (and, ironically, made by BMARC at Grantham!) They were very effective systems, the guns firing 3,300 rounds per minute, and would have given a warm reception to any low-level attacking aircraft; 14 regulars and 96 auxiliaries provided the personnel but, once more, the end of the Cold War meant that the Squadron's raison d'être had disappeared and 2729 was disbanded on 1st April 1994, as was 2890 Sqn, its sister unit formed in 1989, together with their controlling Wing 1339.

More sophisticated and longer-range anti-aircraft defence was to be found at North Coates where the Bloodhound 2 surface-to-air missiles of 25 Sqn's detachment pointed out over the North Sea; however, in December 1970 25 Sqn moved its SAMs to Germany to cover the RAF's 'clutch' airfields and North Coates began to run down, as had happened so often in its history. A reversal took place as the RAF withdrew from Singapore and reduced its presence in Cyprus, resulting in the return to the UK of Bloodhounds used at these bases. 85 Sqn took these over and reformed at West Raynham, Norfolk, with two dispersed Flights, B Flt at North Coates and C at Bawdsey, Suffolk. B Flt had 24 missiles, split into three sections,

each with its own radar-tracking set and Launch Control Post (LCP), and targets were assigned by the engagement controller. Once launched the Bloodhound's own guidance locked on to the reflected radar energy from the target; it was an potent system and when 25 Sqn was withdrawn from RAF Germany in 1983 it became the second UK unit, arriving at Wyton in March of that year and forming its A Flight on a new site on the north side of Barkston Heath airfield, still being used as an RLG by Cranwell. The LCPs here were old armoured personnel carriers, buried in earth mounds, and there were two of these to control the two sections of A Flt. The two Lincolnshire sites continued to protect the county's airfields until 1989 when 25 Sqn became a Tornado F3 unit, and 85 Sqn took over all the Bloodhound flights, Barkston Heath becoming its G Flt.

During the 1980s the Bloodhounds and their radars had been upgraded but, nevertheless, were one of the first casualties of the end of the Cold War, both sites being vacated in 1990, after which North Coates quickly closed; this time the closure was final and after use as a light aircraft airfield during the 1990s it is scheduled to be returned to agriculture early in the new century, although a light aircraft strip will remain. The RAF retains the site at Barkston Heath, which is used for training Cranwell's student officers.

The RAux AF anti-aircraft squadrons at

Waddington were replaced by 27 Sqn RAF Regiment, equipped with the short-range Rapier surface-to-air missiles and manned by auxiliaries plus a few regulars, which arrived from Scampton when that station closed, with 48 Sqn, similarly manned, joining it from Lossiemouth in July 1996. These were comparatively short-lived, both disbanding in September 1998, to be replaced by a Regular RAF Regiment Sqn, 26, which brought its Rapier SAMs to Waddington from Laarbruch, Germany, in December of that year. These Rapiers are of the latest Field Standard C, capable of all-weather operation and able to engage two targets simultaneously at low and medium levels. Although based at Waddington the Squadron is part of the Joint Rapid Deployment Force and so can be called away to anywhere in the world at short notice; it also carries out four-month detachments to the Falklands every 16 months and served in Iraq. A further RAuxAF unit on the station was 7644 (Media) Sqn but this left in 2000 and was replaced by 7006 (VR) Intelligence Sqn and 7010 (VR) Photo-Intelligence Sqn which provides photo-intelligence to JARIC and 13 and 14 Sqns.

The idea of the RAuxAF was originally based, by Trenchard, on the Territorial Army, and the TA came to Waddington in April 1987 in the shape of 267 Field Sqn, Royal Engineers (Volunteers), with the responsibility of repairing the airfield runways and taxiways after any air attack – their

heavy equipment and rolls of runway matting being clearly visible from the A15. This role assumed less importance with the end of the Cold War and the Squadron became an air support sqn with a more flexible role but this did not save it from disbandment at the end of 1999 as part of the general cuts in the TA.

Many new buildings have sprung up at Waddington over the past decade, including a new control tower (is the station unique in having examples of three towers?), NCOs' mess, offices etc but, apart from the Sentry hangar, the most impressive is the Thomson Building, erected to house the Air Warfare Centre HQ, which arrived in September 1995. The AWC had been formed in October 1993 as a result of experience gained in the Gulf War and has three main functions:

a) The development of doctrine and provision of practical and theoretical air warfare training for all personnel who might be involved in operations, from crews to commanders.
b) The provision of electronic warfare operational support to all three Services.
c) The execution of trials and operational evaluations of new and in-service equipment.

Commanded by an Air Commodore, the AWC carries out this work from 11 different locations but the main two are at Waddington and Cranwell; at Waddington the personnel concentrate on operational doctrine, tactics and electronic warfare, and operational analysis.

Electronic warfare is also the responsibility of the Electronic Warfare and Avionics Detachment (EWAD), which occupies one of the hangars and moved from Wyton in 1995; it is a detachment of the RAF Signals Engineering Establishment, based at Henlow, Beds, and enables the RAF to design, develop and install avionic equipment to match operational priorities and time scales in all RAF, FAA and AAC aircraft. About 230 personnel, two thirds of them civilians, serve with the unit, its primary task being the support of 51 Sqn but encompassing the above. Like most present-day RAF stations Waddington has grown and become home to more diverse units then hitherto – its per-

sonnel number around 2,800, 220 of which are civilians.

Waddington could now reasonably be described as the 'Eyes and ears of the RAF', electronically, but in World War Two and up to the 1950s this was the recruiting slogan of the Royal Observer Corps which, in the 1970s, continued in its warning and monitoring role; it was now controlled by the Home Office, and its links with the RAF gradually diminished, although ROC Cells were active in all of the Service HQs. At Fiskerton and in the monitoring posts dotted, at 10-15 miles, around Lincolnshire, the observers practised their nuclear defence role and during the early 1980s more sophisticated equipment, particularly computerised com-

munications, made the corps more efficient. Apart from the HQ of 15 (Lincoln) Group the underground bunker at Fiskerton housed HQ Midland Sector of the UK Warning and Monitoring Organization. The Government deemed that there was no use for the ROC with the end of the Cold War and it was stood down in September 1991, in a rather shoddy way which upset many of its volunteer observers and which meant redundancy for its few full-time officers and staff. So passed into history a unique organisation. The Sub-Regional HQ in the old radar station at Skendleby (thankfully never used) was also redundant.

Although not an RAF organization mention must be made of the BA Systems Air

Representative of the foreign air forces which regularly visit Waddington to use the ACMI facilities is this Mirage 2000 of the French Air Force's famous 'Cigogne' (Stork) Escadrille, taxying for take-off in the spring of 1994. The missile-like object under the wing is the acquisition pod, necessary to use the range's facilities. Author

During the 1970 and 80s Cranwell had its own aerobatic team, 'The Poachers', and its Jet Provost T5a s are here flying over the main College building, c1980. RAF Cranwell

The Scottish Aviation Jetstream T1 is responsible for training the RAF pilots destined to fly multi-engined aircraft, and they are operated by 45 (Reserve) Squadron, part of Cranwell's 3 FTS; XX493 carries the Squadron's marking on the top of its fin, 2000. RAF Cranwell

Combat and Manoeuvring Range (ACMI), the Waddington base of which was established in the south-east corner of the airfield in 1990. BAe erected four radar towers in the North Sea off the Lincolnshire coast and these transmit back to Waddington, Coningsby, Lakenheath, Suffolk and Holland, radar pictures of the air combats which take place above them; pilots are thus able to relive their dogfights and see where and if they made mistakes by watching video playbacks on the radar screens at the four bases. This invaluable training is 'rented out' to the RAF, FAA and any other air forces which are willing to pay, resulting in visits each year from, in particular, FAA Sea Harriers, French Mirages, and Belgian F16s, whilst other air forces have included the Swiss and Austrians. These visits put considerable pressure on the Waddington Aircraft Viewing Enclosure, built as a joint venture by local councils, businesses and the RAF on the east side of the A15 at the airfield. This admirable facility enables enthusiasts and less committed but interested spectators to see Waddington's based aircraft and visitors from the safety of a proper carpark, with toilets and a small cafe and shop. A chance to see a more formal air display has been provided each year since 1996 when Waddington took over, from the closed Finningley, as the venue for the RAF's main annual air display, the sole English successor to the much lamented Battle of Britain displays held at so many airfields in the 1950s and 60s. Easily seen from the Viewing Enclosure was the MBB 105 helicopter of the Lincolnshire and Nottinghamshire Air Ambulance, now replaced by a Boeing Explorer, which is based on the old 9 Sqn dispersal by the A15 and performs a valuable service to the county. Visitors there on 2nd March 2000 would have seen the rare sight of a Chilean Air Force Boeing 707, which called to take the dictator General Pinochet back to Chile.

Training

By 1971 the RAF College at Cranwell no longer acted as the RAF's own university; prospective officers now attended the university of their choice, perhaps serving with

Also part of 3 FTS is 55 (Reserve) Squadron, whose Dominie T1s (which first entered service at Manby in 1966 but which have been updated) are used to train all non-pilot aircrew; XS712 sports the smart new gloss-black and white finish currently deemed to be the most visible scheme for trainers, 2000. RAF Cranwell

the Air Squadron, before coming to Cranwell to train as RAF officers of any branch; they were joined there by trainees from many overseas air forces. All of these were given the rank of acting pilot officer, the term 'cadet' having disappeared in September 1970. December 1973 saw the College of Air Warfare at Manby moved to Cranwell to become the College's Department of Air Warfare, still flying the CAW's Dominies and, as a result of more defence cuts, the HQ of the Central Flying School arrived from Little Rissington in April 1976, along with its Jet Provost Squadron, which trained the instructors destined for the JP. The other parts of the CFS were scattered about the country and this proved unsatisfactory, resulting in the CFS and its Jet Provosts leaving for Leeming in November 1977 whilst the Dominies were transferred to 6 FTS, leaving only Cranwell's own JPs flying from the airfield. A major change came about in August 1979 when the RAF College ceased to be a flying training establishment, concentrating on its officer training role which, from April 1980, now included the non-graduate students formerly trained by the Officer Cadet Training Unit at Henlow, Beds. This meant that all officers, whether career or short-service, men or women, now did their training at the College.

The airfield itself became the home of the Basic Flying Training School, which took over the JPs operated by the College; it was not numbered, rumour had it, because No1 FTS already existed and an FTS at Cranwell was not prepared to accept a lesser number! It operated in the same way as the RAF's other two basic flying training units, at Linton-on-Ouse and Church Fenton, and comprised four squadrons, one of which undertook instructor standardization, whilst the other three were responsible for basic flying training; students came from the FSS at Swinderby or from a University Air Squadron, and their courses lasted 33 to 36 weeks, flying the Jet Provost T5a. The successful students, depending on aptitude and the needs of the Service, moved on to fast-jet training (90%) on Hawks at Valley, multi-engine training on Jetstreams at Finningley, or rotary-wing training on Gazelles at Shawbury. The airfield was very busy, with 35 based JPs, so Barkston Heath continued as a satellite airfield. The courses contained RN, Commonwealth and foreign students as required, and provided flying experience for the student engineer officers.

The BFTS was finally allocated a number in February 1989, when it became 3 FTS, a unit well-known to Lincolnshire from its years at Grantham between the wars, and during 1991 the venerable Jet Provosts were replaced by the RAF's new basic trainer, the Shorts Tucano T1. The Tucano was originally a Brazilian design, but had been extensively modified to suit it to the RAF (despite the politician's claim of 'an off-the-shelf purchase'!). To the outsider it might have

seemed a retrograde step because it was, and is, a propeller-driven aircraft – however, the propeller is powered by a turbo-prop engine which gives a performance very similar to that of the Jet Provost, but with a greatly increased endurance, and at a greatly reduced cost.

The end of the Cold War saw a rapid rundown of the RAF and the Government's priority was 'Front-line First', meaning that flying training suffered a great upheaval, with much of it being privatized. The much reduced need for pilots meant that only one basic flying school was required, this being 1 FTS at Linton-on-Ouse, and Cranwell's last Tucano course finished in March 1996, the aircraft then being transferred to 1 FTS. However, this did not mean the end of 3 FTS – during 1995 it had already taken on the Central Flying School's Bulldog Squadron (now replaced by Grob Tutors), when it moved from Scampton and in the same year, with the closure of 6 FTS at Finningley, took over its role. This is split between two Reserve Squadrons, 45 and 55; the Jetstream T1s of 45 Reserve Sqn are used to train those pilots destined for the RAF's Hercules, Nimrods, VC10s, Sentries and TriStars, whilst the recently upgraded Dominie T1s of 55 Reserve Sqn give flying training to all RAF non-pilot aircrew – navigators, air electronic operators, air loadmasters, air engineers and air signallers. The Flying Wing is completed by a Tutor unit, the RAF College Air Squadron, which gives flying instructor and basic navigation training, and the Wing also provides general service training for the FTS's student officers, some 200 of whom pass through each year. A Ground School gives academic training for all student pilots, whether RAF, Fleet Air Arm or Army Air Corps, numbering 550 a year, and is also responsible for the Navigator and Airmen Aircrew School, which provides ground training for the categories mentioned above; apart from the navigators, most students will be NCOs. From May 2003 all non-pilot aircrew are known as Weapons System Operators, an Americanism which does give a more accurate description of their work; thus the terms Navigator, Air Electronics Operator, etc will pass into RAF history once the present holders of such brevets retire.

3 FTS is, however, a 'lodger' unit at Cranwell and the station's traditional role is as the RAF College which was, until recently, divided into three Directorates, namely Recruiting and Selection (DRS), Specialist Ground Training (DGST) and Initial Officer Training (DIOT), which trained all those destined to be commissioned into the RAF (and some foreign air forces). During 2003, however, a reorganisation saw a major break with RAF tradition as the DIOT was renamed the Officer and Aircrew Cadet Training Unit; O&ACTU still runs the 24-week course for prospective officers and an eight-week course for those officers entering branches

The Grob Tutor now equips all the University Air Squadrons and Air Experience Flights; they are civilian operated, by V-T Aerospace, and are civilian-registered though wearing RAF roundels. This example belongs to the Central Flying School Tutor Squadron, which trains instructors for the UAS/AEFs, and is seen at Cranwell in 2000. RAF Cranwell

A busy scene on Swinderby's flight line, as two Elementary Flying Training School Chipmunk T10s are topped up ready for their next students, 1985. Author

A Raytheon Super Kingair B200 nears Cranwell on its delivery flight to 45 (Reserve) Sqn, December 2003, bearing the unit's red and blue diamond marking across its fin. The Kingairs, civilian-registered and operated by Serco Ltd, but with RAF instructors, will replace 45's 30-year-old Jetstreams by March, 2004.

The Joint Elementary Flying Training School, with HQ at Barkston Heath, provided basic flying training for all RAF, FAA and AAC pilots, from several sites and the instructors are a mixture of Service and civilian. The aircraft used is the Slingsby Firefly, as seen here, a very good type for the purpose but, like the Tutors, civilian registered. The winged hunting horn on the fin was the symbol of the Hunting Company which ran the School. In 2003 the RAF withdrew and it became the Defence EFTS run by Babcock. RAF Cranwell

for which they have already had specialist training, such as lawyers, doctors and chaplains. The break with tradition comes because O&ACTU also runs a 12-week initial training course for those entering the RAF as NCO (ie sergeant) non-pilot aircrew, hitherto performed by 3 FTS, to which they move for flying training after the College.

DOIT was briefly known as the Dept. of Recruitment, Selection and Initial Officer Training when, in 1997, it took over the duties of the Dept. of Recruiting and Aircrew Selection, which had arrived on the station in September 1992; however, reflecting the rapid changes of the 1990s, the DRSIOT became two separate entities again in 1999. DRS is thus once more responsible for the Officer and Aircrew Selection Centre (OASC) which had been at Cranwell since 1992 and to which all aspiring aircrew, for whichever Service, come for the aptitude tests which will determine whether their hopes will be realised; OASC also selects or rejects those wishing to become officers in the RAF. After O&ACTU those newly commissioned officers who wish to become engineers or supply officers move onto the DGST which, apart from this initial training, also runs more advanced courses for RAF officers already serving in these branches and from the other Services and the Civil Service.

Cranwell also houses various other units; HQ University Air Squadrons, which had been at Cranwell since 1971, combined with HQ Air Cadets when it moved from Newton, Notts in July 1995, to become the HQ University and Air Cadets. However, this HQ was also short lived and in 1998 split again to become HQ Air Cadets and the HQ Elementary Flying Training. HQ Air Cadets controls the activities of the Air Training Corps squadrons around the country, whilst HQ EFT is responsible for the 15 University Air Squadrons and the Joint Elementary Flying Training School at Barkston Heath. During 1999 the UAS/AEFs began to receive the new German-built Grob Tutor trainers, which were initially operated by the Bombardier company, the contract being taken over later by VT Aerospace, and which are civilian-registered, unlike the Bulldogs which they had replaced by 2001.

In July 2003 the RAF withdrew from JEFTS and now trains all its undergraduate pilots at the UASs prior to coming for officer training at the College, direct non-University pilots going on to a UAS for training after their initial training at the College. As a result, HQ EFT changed its name to No1 Elementary Flying Training School, also setting the syllabus for the FAA and AAC students at Barkston Heath. One such UAS is the East Midlands UAS/7 Air Experience Flight equipped, as are all the UASs, with the Tutor, which moved to Cranwell when its previous home, RAF Newton, closed in 2000. It has its administrative and ground training school at Nottingham but does flying training from Cranwell; its 80-odd students, who have

expressed an interest in the RAF as a career and joined the RAFVR, are drawn mainly from Leicester, Lincoln and Nottingham Universities. They are given a 60-hour flying course, spread over two years, and when they graduate they will, if selected, go on to the College for officer training; coming into the UAS in the opposite direction may be non-graduate or direct entrant recently commissioned officers from Cranwell to do the same 60-hour course. 7 AEF, using the UAS's Tutors, gives flying experience to the RAF's other prospective recruits, Air Cadets from around the East Midlands.

As various other stations closed during the 1990s, Cranwell became home to more and more 'lodger' units; despite an earlier, seemingly unsuccessful stay, the HQ, Central Flying School arrived from Scampton in June 1995, having been preceded by the CFS Bulldog Squadron from the same base, in March. They were followed by the most famous component of the CFS, the RAF Aerobatic Team (the Red Arrows), in February of the following year, although the 'Arrows', because of limited airspace at Cranwell, still did their training flights largely over Scampton, before moving back there permanently in January 2001.

After its arrival at its new home CFS quickly became responsible for training and/or checking all RAF flying instructors (rather than just the pilots) so it now covers Pilot Navigation Instructor (QPNI), Navigator Instructor (QNI), Helicopter Navigator Instructor (QHNI), Helicopter Crewman

Instructor (QHCI), Tactics Instructor (QTI) and Weapons Instructor (QWI). Most of this work is carried out at other airfields around the country and the only flying unit of the CFS at Cranwell was the Bulldog Sqn which trained Bulldog instructors – but as the Bulldog was replaced by the Grob Tutor the unit was retitled the CFS Tutor Sqn in December 2000.

The Air Warfare Centre, Cranwell, which arrived in the mid-90s, is parented by the Air Warfare Centre at Waddington, and provides training in air power, warfare, and advanced avionics, replacing the College's Dept. of Air Warfare.

The Band of the RAF College was formed in April 1920 and has been at the forefront of RAF music ever since; in 1973 the control of the band transferred to the MoD, and as only five RAF bands then remained it has become much travelled, although still based at Cranwell. When RAF Germany disbanded, the musicians from its band joined Cranwell, and there are now some 40 personnel; lest it be thought that these are solely musicians, the bandsmen and women performed their wartime task as medical assistants and stretcher bearers during the recent wars. Recently, the RAF College Band has been joined at Cranwell by the RAF Regiment Band. Finally, HQ Provost and Security Service (Central Region) provides such services as counter intelligence, special investigation, drug investigation and many others, for RAF stations in East Anglia and the Midlands.

An unusual view, from Scampton's control tower, of the Red Arrows Hawks formating on the ground as they taxi out for a flypast over a Swinderby passing-out parade in early 1984. Author

Thus, Cranwell is a very large station, its personnel numbering, in 1999, 1160 RAF, 440 civil servants and 700 civilian contractors, who provide catering and motor transport; those under training add 790 to the total and to house all of these a large building programme was undertaken in the 1990s. Mention must be made of the College Library which, as well as housing the college's own records and those of the RAF in general, has also to provide learning materials (increasingly IT based) for the College itself and all of the other units now at Cranwell.

Lincolnshire's second RAF college, the College of Air Warfare at Manby, with a satellite at Strubby, continued to run its specialist courses but the writing was on the wall and Strubby closed in September 1972, owing to the poor state of its runways. The College's Jet Provosts and Dominies then operated entirely from Manby but in December 1973 the CAW, victim of more defence cuts, moved to Cranwell to become the RAF College's Dept of Air Warfare, whilst the School of Refresher Flying went to Leeming. Manby closed in March 1974, many of its buildings being used by East Lindsey DC, whilst Strubby housed a heliport to operate the North Sea rig supply helicopters of Bond Helicopters, this moving to Humberside Airport in the mid 1990s.

At Swinderby the RAF School of Recruit Training was the only such School in the RAF and all adult airmen recruits started their service in Lincolnshire. Training covered drill, lectures on service knowledge, security and general defence training (some of which was undertaken in Sherwood Forest), and PT, each course lasting for six weeks. October 1982 saw the School take on the training of women recruits, no doubt to the delight of the males; it was transferred from RAF Hereford but, before that had been undertaken at Grantham so the wheel had turned full circle. Swinderby now took all the RAF's adult non-officer recruits and as Cranwell, by this time, took all officer recruits, few could enter the RAF without serving in Lincolnshire. The WRAFs' training was identical to the men's apart from rifle-drill. In the 1970s it was common to see the recruits, in uniform, in the streets of Lincoln, distinguishable by their pale-blue capbands, but the activities of the IRA meant that all Service personnel were banned from wearing uniform outside their stations, a ban which was only lifted in 1999. The 1990s' rundown of the Services saw a reorganization of the RAF's ground training and No1 School of Technical Training at Halton (the successor to the famous Trenchard Brats), moved, leaving that camp empty and the MoD decided to move to it the School of Recruit Training, the last recruits leaving Swinderby in July 1993.

Although the airfield at Swinderby had been used occasionally by visiting communications aircraft, and by the East Midlands UAS and 7 Air Experience Flight during 1977 because of the bad surface at Newton, the re-appearance of a based flying unit in July 1979 came as something of a surprise. It happened because the RAF was concerned about the wastage rate during basic flying training on the Jet Provost, which was proving expensive; hitherto potential pilots were tested for aptitude at the Selection Centre at Biggin Hill, and after completing officer training, went straight on to the JP at the Flying Training Schools, but in 1974 trials were undertaken whereby aptitude was also tested in the air using Chipmunk aircraft, which were readily available. The 'Chippie' was also cheap to operate and, like all good trainers, difficult to fly well, especially during take-off and landing, when its tailwheel undercarriage made it prone to swing. The 1974 trial, carefully monitored, proved a success and it was decided that, in future, all airmen selected for pilot training but with no previous flying experience would fly 14 hours on Chipmunks at the Flying Selection Squadron.

As all officers now did their initial training at Cranwell it was logical that the FSS should be based in the vicinity, but not so close as

to interfere with Cranwell's own Jet Provosts. Swinderby, still very much an RAF station but with its runways virtually unused, was the obvious choice and the Flying Selection Squadron formed there in July 1979, administratively under Swinderby but tasked by the FTS at Cranwell. As the Chipmunk was no longer in service, except at the Air Experience Flights (where it was flown by RAFVR officers), there were few instructors still qualified to fly it and the pilots posted to the FSS tended to be very experienced and towards the end of their flying careers – thus the Squadron was unkindly referred to as the 'Geriatric Squadron'! The students arrived from Cranwell for a six-week course and received limited instruction, exactly the same for each student, in the basics of flying. On average, 25% failed and were offered careers as navigators or in other branches; had they gone straight to the JP much time and money would have been wasted.

In 1985 the FSS began to operate, as an experiment, as an Elementary Flying Training School, the students now undertaking a 16-week course which included 65 flying hours on the Chipmunk; this had the effect of reducing the flying time needed on the Jet Provost at the FTSs, giving considerably reduced fuel costs, and in fact cutting the JP stage out altogether for prospective helicopter pilots. With the experiment considered a success, the FSS became the Elementary Flying Training Squadron in June 1987 and its Chipmunks were a familiar sight until April 1993 when the EFTS disbanded. Swinderby RAF station closed in July 1993 and was quickly sold; the domestic site was demolished in early 1999 and the married quarters became, as at Binbrook, a 'new' village, in this case called Witham St Hugh's.

The EFTS was not disbanded because its role had disappeared or because its base was also to disappear; it was disbanded because, in the wake of the Cold War, the Conservative government decided to save on the defence budget by privatizing many of the RAF's second line units. The Hunting company was the successful bidder to run the RAF's elementary flying training and the Joint Elementary Flying Training School was formed by them at Topcliffe, Yorks, on 1st April 1993, taking over immediately from the EFTS. The 'Joint' part of its title signified that it also trained Fleet Air Arm pilots. Just as the mixed Service and civilian instructors, and civilian ground staff, were settling in at Topcliffe the RAF moved the School to Barkston Heath, in April 1995. JEFTS was equipped with 17 civilian-registered Slingsby Fireflies, an aircraft highly thought of by the instructors and, as well as RAF and FAA pilots, the School also trains Commonwealth and foreign air force pilots on a commercial basis. Extra Fireflies were purchased in 1996/97 to cope with increased demand and from April 1997 JEFTS became responsible for training

Army Air Corps pilots too, operating 25 aircraft in total. Hunting's original five year contract was renewed for another five years in 1998 so that the company has now built permanent accommodation at Barkston to replace the Portakabins used hitherto.

So busy had Barkston become that the RAF contingent moved to Church Fenton in January 1999, with AAC grading being carried out at Newton, then Middle Wallop, and the RAF's multi-engine lead-in course taking place at Cranwell, the Fireflies used by the latter having full airways avionics. FAA pilots arrive at JEFTS having carried out grading flights in the RN College's Grob Herons (basically the same as the UAS Tutors), and joined the RAF students, who had no previous flying experience; both had six weeks of ground school at Cranwell, the FAA students then moving to Barkston and the RAF to Church Fenton, where they did the same 62 hour flying course consisting of general handling, navigation, formation flying and instrument flying. AAC students come to Barkston from their 13-hour grading flying, on Fireflies, at Middle Wallop, which includes the first twelve sorties of the basic syllabus. The Army then decides if they have the aptitude to go on to further training and, if so, they come to Barkston for a 40-hour course which, because the vast majority will fly helicopters operationally, contains no formation flying or solo aerobatics.

However, big changes came about in July 2003 when the RAF transferred its elementary flying training to the UASs as previously described. JEFTS then changed its name to the Defence EFTS, continuing to train FAA pilots, now as 703 Naval Air Squadron, and those from the Army, now known as 674 Sqn, Army Air Corps; the courses remained the same as described.

After DEFTS the newly qualified pilots go on to further training with their own Service but the experience of working with each other is a valuable by-product of the School. The DEFTS does still have some input into RAF pilot training as to it come those newly-qualified pilots destined to fly multi-engined aircraft; in airways-equipped Fireflies at Cranwell the Multi-Engine Lead-In Course consists of 30 hours of multi-crew operation, with the emphasis on formation, navigation and night-flying. DEFTS has a mixture of FAA, AAC and civilian instructors, the latter trained in-house, all other personnel being civilians employed by the Babcock Group, who took Hunting over in 2001.

Scampton's future was uncertain following the demise of the Vulcan squadrons and at one time it was under consideration as a USAF tanker base but, in the event, it transferred to Support Command. The first unit to arrive was the RAF Aerobatic Team, the famous 'Red Arrows', which flew in to the base in March 1983 from their previous station at Kemble in Gloucestershire, scheduled to close after yet more defence cuts. People in the neighbourhood soon got used

to seeing the Arrows practising their routines over Scampton, particularly during the winter months when each year's intake of three new team members are trained. The new boys start practising on the Hawks during October while the rest of the team are enjoying a well-deserved rest after their hectic display season and it is November when the six experienced pilots return and training starts in earnest; even then some of the Hawks are undergoing maintenance at any one time so only four aircraft are in use initially, with a formation which could look like this.

```
        1
         2
          4
           8
```

instead of the full

The largest formation to be seen over Lincoln for many years was the arrival of the Central Flying School at Scampton on 19th September 1984. A Vampire T11 and two Meteor T7s of the 'Vintage Pair', sadly lost in fatal accidents later, lead, followed by Jet Provost T3As (with tip tanks), and T5As. A photographer's Hawk turns overhead.
(Ken James via Lincolnshire Echo).

```
        1
      3   2
    5   6   4
      9   8
        7
```

This gives rise to some strange formations as the pilots still fly in the positions they will assume throughout the year. As the aircraft return from servicing the number builds up to six and these will include the two 'singletons' who perform separately from the main Team for part of each display; the formation may then look like this.

```
        1
         2
      6     4
          8
          7
```

and it is 6 and 7 who are the 'singletons'. The pilot flying number 6 is normally in his third and final year with the Team, while number 7 is a second-year pilot who will move up to number 6 in his final year, thus ensuring continuity. It will be noted that whatever positions are flown there will always be a 'number one' who is, of course, the team leader and it is on his aircraft that all the other eight formate – thus explaining why practices can be flown without all nine aircraft.

A Central Flying School Bulldog T1 from Scampton poses in the line-up at the Waddington Photomeet in 1988. The Bulldog finally left RAF service during 2001. Author

Given the weather the Arrows do two practices per day, which are videoed from the ground and the tape played back at the debrief. The practise flights consist of an half-hour briefing, 15-minute flight preparation, half-hour flight, 15 minutes back to the crewroom and a half-hour debrief, making a two-hour session in total. The team practises three routines, the full display up to 4,500 feet, the rolling display up to 2,500 feet, and the flat display which needs 1,000 feet, and it is the cloud at each display which decides which of the three is to be used; sometimes the leader must juggle elements of all! By early spring the team is almost ready for the new season and goes to Cyprus for the final 'polish up', the better weather allowing three flights a day, after which, with final approval of the display from the AOC, the Red Arrows start their display season. Apart from the pilots there are a team manager, PRO, adjutant and admin. team, plus some 80 ground crew, 27 of whom travel with the Team to displays, the rest doing major maintenance as required – there is only one spare Hawk! In 1989 several Euro-

pean military aerobatic teams visited Scampton to help the Arrows celebrate their Silver Jubilee, an event open to an appreciative public.

As previously told, the 'Arrows' had to move from Scampton when the airfield closed and were based at Cranwell; that this was not entirely satisfactory is evidenced by the fact that the team still performed most of its practices over Scampton because of the crowded airspace around Cranwell, so the airfield at Scampton was still active. When the team moved to Cranwell the MoD stated that it was a temporary measure and that their permanent home would be at the Norfolk Tornado base at Marham. Most enthusiasts said at that time that this would not work and have been proved right because, in January 2001 the 'Arrows' returned to Scampton!

The Red Arrows are a part of the Central Flying School, the oldest military flying training establishment in the world, having been formed at Upavon, Wilts, in 1912. At that time it was responsible for the advanced training of pilots who, in those early days of aviation, had already obtained a Royal Aero Club Certificate at their own expense; this was refunded in part if they successfully completed their Royal Flying Corps training at CFS. Its role was greatly expanded by the

needs of World War One, pilots now arriving from 'ab initio' training at the Reserve Squadrons, such as those based at Scampton, Waddington and South Carlton. The methods of instruction introduced by Major Smith-Barry in 1917, which standardized and immensely improved pilot training, led to the CFS becoming responsible, in April 1918, for the training of flying instructors for the newly-formed RAF and it has continued this role ever since. However, it was not based in Lincolnshire until 1976 though it was, for several years between the wars, based at Wittering just south of Stamford and its aircraft were thus a familiar sight over the south of the county; particularly eye-catching were the colourful Avro Tutors of the CFS Aerobatic Team, which established the tradition currently undertaken by the 'Red Arrows'.

The CFS's stay in Lincolnshire during the 1970s was brief, as it moved to Leeming in 1977 but it was decided that Leeming was to be developed as an air defence station to replace Binbrook so the CFS was again looking for a new home and Scampton was selected; on 19th September 1984 the biggest flypast over Lincoln for many years took place as the CFS arrived, comprising nine Bulldogs, 16 Jet Provosts, two Meteor T7s and a Vampire T11. (The Meteors and

A smart new Shorts Tucano T1 of the CFS, just coming into service as the Jet Provost 's replacement, basks in the sun at the Red Arrow's 21st Anniversary party in 1989. Tucanos still visit Scampton, for their major overhauls by V-T Aerospace, but are now in the black and white colour scheme.Author

Who'd have thought it? A Sukhoi Su27 (Flanker in NATO parlance) of the 'Russian Knights' aerobatic team, on approach to Scampton to visit the Red Arrows, 1991. Such a sight would have been unthinkable even five years earlier. Author

Vampire were the RAF's first jet trainers and formed the Vintage Pair, Support Command's Historic Flight, performing a delightful routine at airshows around the country until all were destroyed in fatal accidents during the 1980s). With the arrival of CFS Scampton regained some of its previous activity, the CFS's elements comprising the Bulldog Squadron, responsible for training Bulldog instructors, and Nos 1 and 2 Jet Provost Squadrons flying the JP T3a and T5a, which trained instructors for Nos 1 and 7 FTSs and the BFTS at Cranwell. Other CFS squadrons were based at Valley with Hawks

and at Shawbury, Salop, where helicopter instructors are trained.

Five courses a year operated at the CFS, each lasting for 25 weeks, of which five were spent in ground school and the rest flying, and there were approximately 25 students on each course of whom two were likely to be from a foreign air force. Eighteen one-hour trips in the Jet Provost T3a to convert fully to it were followed by a flight with the Staff QFI to check on the student's handling skills. This was followed by the 12 basic pre-solo exercises as given to a student pilot by an instructor, in this case the QFI; the trainee instructor then practised the exercises on another trainee after which he/she returned the exercise to the QFI who flew as a student might, wandering off track or descending slightly. A successful trainee then passed on to the Jet Provost T5a for more advanced training, with aerobatic exercises and, after some 90 hours flying, a final handling test – if completed they then became a QFI Grade B2 and were posted to their FTS. The procedure for Bulldog instructors was broadly the same. All instructors returned to CFS to be upgraded to QFI B1, A2 and the coveted A1 categories, the latter two being tested by staff of the Examining Wing, whose role may be described as 'Maintaining the highest standard of flying instruction within Royal

Air Force Support Command and of pure flying throughout the Royal Air Force' and it carried this out in several ways, of which one has already been mentioned, the upgrading of QFIs to A categories; secondly, the Wing's staff visited all Support Command flying bases annually to check on their standards, with each QFI being checked at least once every two years to maintain his/her category. Whilst at Scampton the Wing was also responsible for developing a training programme for the RAF's new basic trainer, the Shorts Tucano T1, which entered RAF service at Scampton in 1988, soon replacing the Jet Provosts. The training of instructors on the Tucano was similar to that on the JP and carried on until the CFS Tucano Squadron moved north to Linton-on-Ouse and the HQ and Bulldog Squadron moved to Cranwell, in the spring of 1995.

A memorable and historic event occurred at Scampton in September 1991, one which would have been unthinkable even five years earlier; hundreds of enthusiasts lined the station to see the arrival of the Russian Air Force's 'Blue Knights' aerobatic team, preceded by their Ilyushin 76 transport, and escorted by Coningsby Tornados. The team flew Russia's latest fighter, the Sukhoi Su27 Flanker, and their visit was a celebration of 'Perestroika'. Other Russian transports vis-

ited Scampton subsequently, notably Antonov 72s, because a lodger unit at the base, from July 1990 to May 1996, was the Joint Arms Control Implementation Group (JACIG), whose job it was to make sure that the Warsaw Pact countries were implementing the various disarmament treaties. The Russian visitors were making sure that the British were doing the same! In fact JACIG was the last unit to leave Scampton but, because of the Red Arrows practice flights, as described earlier, the airfield remained open and the camp unoccupied, though some of the married quarters began to be sold in the late nineties. The uncertainty surrounding Scampton's future was a cause for concern to the Local Authorities who, through local MPs, pressed the Government for a decision so that they could plan for future uses of the site; Save Our Scampton became the rallying call of the Lincolnshire Echo. In November 1999 the MoD announced that the airfield would reopen as a relief airfield for 3 FTS at Cranwell, to alleviate the evident overcrowding in the airspace surrounding Cranwell and Barkston Heath, this being followed by the return of the Red Arrows, announced in 2000. The selling of married quarters has been suspended because of the perceived need for housing for Waddington when the

Astor squadron arrives. Also using Scampton's facilities are Hawker Hunter Aviation Ltd, which uses one of the hangars for storage, and V-T Aerospace which overhauls the RAF's Tucano fleet in another hangar.

Non-Flying Units

The RAF Hospital at Nocton Hall continued to provide medical services to the RAF in Lincolnshire and the North throughout the 1970s and any spare capacity was used by the NHS; thus many people had reason to be grateful to the Hospital and its staff. When it was announced that the RAF intended to close Nocton and centralize medical services at RAF Hospital, Ely, local people organized a petition to keep it open but this, of course, had little effect and Nocton closed as a hospital in March 1983. (Ely also closed in the 1990s and there are now no RAF Hospitals). A small out-patients' department remained and the USAF took over the building as a wartime emergency hospital, recalling its use in World War Two by the US Army. With the coming of Perestroika its use in this role looked unlikely but then Saddam Hussein invaded Kuwait and Nocton was quickly activated, with equipment being flown into Waddington in USAF C141 Starlifters. Happily, the expected number of casualties did not materialize and Nocton was little used, which probably hastened its end as the USAF closed it down in 1995; the site is now being used for housing.

The 1970s saw Digby continuing to form an important part of the RAF's communications system although one of its resident units, 54 SU, left in 1974; its work is highly classified, apart from that of one of its units, the Aerial Erectors' School. The RAF's airfields, radio and radar stations rely on aerials of various types and heights for their

communications and when these need to be erected, repaired or dismantled it is the responsibility of the RAF's small band of aerial erectors.

Apart from their technical expertise these airmen/women must have a good head for heights and the aspiring aerial erector is one of the few recruits to be tested for aptitude before actually enlisting, the test being a remarkably basic one – climbing the one remaining 360ft-high ex-radar mast at Stenigot! While simply doing this would daunt most people even more exacting tests have to be performed at the platforms on the mast, at 50ft, 90ft and 200ft; at 90ft, for example, recruits must walk out from the platform with each foot on beams about two feet apart, then bend forward so that that their hands are also on the beams and they are staring straight down at the ground beneath; from this position they get astride a single 6in-wide metal beam and hotch along this until they reach one of the four massive legs.

The next step is to work their way around the leg to its outside and then shin down it, monkey fashion, to the 50ft platform below. Whilst all this is happening the recruit is being watched by the instructors and is attached to the structure by a safety harness and rope but, even so, such tests deter those with vertigo! The 200ft platform is the limit for these aptitude tests but if the recruit passes, they return to Digby after basic training and undertake trade training which includes an ascent to the very small (and swaying) platform 360ft above the ground. The eight-week course also includes technical training and further climbing, stressing the safety aspect, after which the newly fledged erector joins his/her unit ready for work on any RAF station requiring their services.

As the number of RAF erectors requiring training shrinks, in line with the rest of the Service, the school now takes Royal Signals personnel, other RAF people who may be required to work at heights, and civilians from such organisations as British Gas, Civil Aviation Authority etc. When an RAF erector has been working for 4-5 years he/she comes back to Digby for a further 15½ week training course on which will depend promotion to Corporal and above, and this covers actually carrying out the job, working out the equipment needed and so on. Thus Stenigot mast, now a very rare relic of World War Two, remains because it still performs a useful service for today's RAF. The large 'elephant ear' dish aerials on the same site were part of a NATO communications system remotely operated by Royal Signals personnel and were not part of the RAF presence at Stenigot. No longer needed after the end of the Cold War, they were demolished around 1997.

The School, as a lodger unit, came under the newly formed Personnel and Training Command in the mid 1990s, with the rest of the station being in the also newly-formed Logistics Command. The end of the Cold War also brought change to Digby as, with the closure of Berlin signals centre in Germany, Royal Signals soldiers came to join 399 Signals Unit in 1994, plus some from Cyprus, numbering about 200 in total. Following from this, as part of the MoD's policy of centralizing similar functions at one station and joining personnel from all three Services doing similar work together under one roof, Digby has become the major RAF communications unit; reflecting this, 399 SU was recently retitled the Joint Service Signal Unit, and is manned by RAF, Army and Royal Navy specialists, together with some 50 Americans from all three of their Services and some British and US civilian technicians. The Royal Navy detachment is known as the Maritime Cryptological Integration Centre. The JSSU is responsible for research and development in the communications field for all three Services. The other unit at Digby is 591 Signals Unit which executes defensive information operations in support of air operations and is responsible to the Air Warfare Centre at Waddington. In December 2001 Digby became the first Lincolnshire RAF station to have a female Commanding Officer. .

Owing to the enthusiasm of a small group of Digby's personnel the World War Two Operations Room, which had been emptied in 1940 when it was transferred to Blankney Hall, was restored to its original condition after its more recent role as the station's nuclear, biological and chemical warfare centre came to an end in the early 1990s. The operations room, as it was in 1939, is now open to the public at agreed times, a marvellous relic of Digby's historic past.

It might have been expected that one or more of the RAF's three Lincolnshire air weapons ranges would have been surplus to requirements, as the end of the Cold War caused a big run-down in the number of RAF aircraft and, more particularly, the number of USAF aircraft, using them; A-10 Thunderbolts and F-111s were regular and impressive visitors. However, this has not been the case and it is ranges in other parts of the country which have closed, including Cowden on the East Yorkshire coast; out of the seven remaining, three are in Lincolnshire, perhaps reflecting Lincolnshire folk's traditional tolerance of the RAF and its attendant noise – it is hard to imagine those in Kent, for example, putting up with it! The RAF did make an effort to reduce the noise over Mablethorpe when it closed Theddlethorpe Range in December 1973, transferring it further up the coast to the less-inhabited sands of Donna Nook, last used in World War Two. Since then Donna, Wainfleet and Holbeach have continued to provide bombing and gunnery targets, the major change being when, as in so many other parts of the RAF, they were civilianized during the 1990s, so that the RAF camps at the sites were closed; the COs are retired RAF officers. The gunnery targets are canvas screens erected on the beaches or mudflats, whilst for bombing Holbeach has old ships; other targets are developed as required and Wainfleet is the only one of the three which is designated as a night range and which can also be used for TIALD (Thermal Imaging and Laser Desig-

nator) bombing. It must be emphasised that live ammunition is not used on any of the Lincolnshire AWRs, the bombs being of the smoke variety, giving a puff of smoke on impact which is plotted from three quadrant towers to give the position in relation to the target; this is then faxed to the pilot's squadron for his debrief. In 1997 Holbeach was the busiest range in the UK, with 19,500 movements, whilst Donna had 13,000 and Wainfleet 7,800. The ranges are essential to the RAF and, whilst noisy, do keep the coastline in its original state – at Donna Nook every November hundreds of seals gather to pup and then to mate, completely unconcerned as Harriers, Tornados and Jaguars roar overhead!

The Future

In 2014 there will have been 100 years of military flying in Lincolnshire and who, in 1914, could have seen that 86 years later the fabric and wire aeroplanes would have been replaced by aircraft which could fly faster than sound and deliver their weapons with uncanny accuracy? It would therefore be unwise of me to try to look far into the future – it does seem that Western Europe, at least, has finally learnt to live in peace and the RAF has been deprived of its raison d'être of 40 years, the threat from the USSR. The Conservative Government of the first half of the 1990s, keen for a 'peace dividend', imposed cuts which, together with much 'civilianization', has drastically altered the face of the RAF, making the 1990s one of its most turbulent decades; one has only to look at the rapid changes of HQs, etc, at Cranwell to realize that not all the decisions taken were wise ones, the closure of Scampton being another example. In November 1999, Logistics Command, only in existence for five years, was disbanded.

Unfortunately for the politicians, the RAF has seen more action since the end of the Cold War than it did during it – the Gulf, Bosnia, Kosovo, Afghanistan and Iraq all making great demands on its much reduced human and technical resources. The new Labour Government of 1996 seemed to have recognised this and with its Strategic Defence Review has attempted to match resources to commitments. Thus it seems unlikely that any of the bases current in 2004 will close in the foreseeable future, with Waddington assuming even greater importance than now, Coningsby receiving the Eurofighter Typhoon, Digby being at the centre of the RAF's communications, Barkston Heath continuing to train pilots, Scampton housing 'The Red Arrows', and Cranwell being the major training base.

However, as this book closed for press in 2004 the Government had announced another Defence Review, the details of which were not given, but it seems likely that the number of Typhoons on order will be reduced, perhaps meaning one less

squadron at Coningsby. On the credit side, there were also proposals to move several ground units, from other areas, into Scampton and/or Coningsby.

And so this story of the RAF in Lincolnshire during the 20th Century closes – who knows what challenges the Service will face in the 21st? What is certain is that as long as there are RAF stations in the county, the close links with the people of Lincolnshire, forged over 90 years, will continue.

The Eurofighter Typhoon F2 will play a large part in the RAF's future, both nationally and in Lincolnshire. It will replace the Tornado F3 and the Jaguar now in service and represents a quantum leap over these types; the first is scheduled to come into service at Coningsby during 2005. BAE Systems

Map of Airfields in Lincolshire

New Holland
Goxhill
Alkborough
Killingholme
Winterton
North Killingholme
Harbrough
Immingham Docks
Elsham Wolds
Greenland Top
Elsham
Grimsby
Broughton
Kirmington
Grimsby/Waltham
Humberston
Sandtoft
North Coates
Manton Common
Hibaldstow
Caistor
Kirton
Holton-le-Moor
Donna Nook Range
Kirton-in-Lindsey
Cuxwold
Donna Nook
Ludborough
Roman Hill
Skidbrooke
Blyton
Blyboro Elg
Bainbrook
Theddlethorpe
Kelstern
Hemswell
Hamilton Hill
Harpswell
Ludford Magna
Gainsborough
Louth
Manby
Lea Marsh
Sturgate
Cockthorne
Ingham
Strubby
Faldingworth
Wickenby
Sienigot
Scampton
Anderby Creek
Dunholme Lodge
Market Stainton
Fenton
South Carlton
Lingoln Stores
Bardney
West Common
Skendleby
Fiskerton
Ingoldmells
Skellingthorpe
Bucknall
Orby
Bracebridge Heath
Spilsby
Skegness
Mere
Waddington
Nocton Hall Hospital
Moorby
Morton Hall
Metheringham
Swinderby
East Kirby
Norton Disney
Coleby Grange
Woodhall Spa
Gibraltar Point
Bassingham Fen
Digby (Scopwick)
Wellingore
Coningsby
Wainfleet
Leadenham
Anwick
Fulbeck
Cranwell
Leverton
Rauceby
Willoughby Hills
Barkston Heath
Boston Docks
Belton Park
Freiston
Braceby
St Vincents
Grantham
Harlaxton
Holbeach
Spitalgate
Folkingham
Gosberton
Swayfield
Swinstead
Sutton Bridge
North Witham
Grimsthorpe
Tydd St Mary
Buckminster
South Witham
Langtoft
Market Deeping

The Stations

ALKBOROUGH
OS sheet 112. 883231. 1m W of the village on River Trent.
WW2 Bombing Range for 1 Group.

ALMA PARK
See Belton Park.

ANDERBY CREEK
OS sheet 122. 554760. N of village, on coast.
WW2 RAF Regiment Gunnery Range.
5 Group Anti-Aircraft School
Oct 1944 to 1945.

ANWICK
OS sheet 121. 110515. 0.75m NE of village on minor road.
WW1 Emergency Landing Ground
for 38 and 90 Squadrons.

BARDNEY
OS sheet 121. 132706. 1m NE of village on minor road.
Opened Apr 1943.
9 Squadron
Lancaster, Apr 1943 to Jul 1945.
53 Base Sub-station
Nov 1943, disbanded Nov 1945.
227 Squadron
Lancaster, formed Oct to Oct 1944.

189 Squadron
Lancaster, formed Oct to Nov 1944, returned Apr to Oct 1945.
Bomber Command Film Flight Unit
Lancaster and Mosquito 20 & 25, formed Mar to Apr 1945.
106 Squadron
Thor ICBM, formed Jul 1959, disbanded May 1963.
Closed 1963.

American 82nd Airborne Division glider pilots in front of a suitably inscribed GC-4a Hadrian glider at Barkston Heath, 1944. Herman Brooks

BARKSTON HEATH
OS sheet 130. 960410. 1m SSW of village, W
   of B6403.
Opened 1937.
Relief Landing Ground for RAF College
   Cranwell to Apr 1943.
Runways constructed Apr 1943 to Jan 1944.
No5 Group Commando School
   May to Dec 1943 (trained aircrews in
   escape and evasion).
61st Troop Carrier Group USAAF
C-47 Dakota and GC4a Hadrian, Feb 1944 to
   Mar 1945.
349th Troop Carrier Group USAAF
   C-46 Commando, Mar to Apr 1945.
RAF Regiment Sub-depot
   May 1945 to 1946.
No7 Equipment Disposal Depot
   Formed Jun 45, became **256 MU**, dis-
   banded Dec 1948.
Relief Landing Ground for Cranwell, Feb
   1949 to Apr 1995.
25 Squadron
   A Flt, Bloodhound SAM2, formed May
   1983, became **85 Sqn G Flt in 1989**, dis-
   banded 1990.
Joint Elementary Flying Training School
   Firefly, Apr 1995 to July 2003.
   became **Defence EFTS** to present, 2004.
703 Sqn, FAA, formed July 2003 to present.

*A USAAF dance band, the 'Skymasters',
perform on the main steps of Belton House,
near Grantham (now a National Trust
property). The House was used for recreational
purposes by the locally-based Americans.*
Herman Brooks

674 Sqn AAC, formed July 2003 to present.
BBMF, Mar to Oct, 2003.

BASSINGHAM
OS sheet 121. 943612.
WW2 Night Decoy for Swinderby.

BASSINGHAM FEN
OS sheet 121. 927587. 1m S of village.
WW2 Bombing Range for 5 Group.
In use by Cranwell, 1950s.

BECKINGHAM
OS sheet 121. 870545. N of village.
Range and Exercise Area for Army and
   RAF. In use by Cranwell, 1950s.

BELTON
OS sheet 112. 759100.
WW2 Night Decoy for Finningley.

BELTON PARK/ALMA PARK
OS sheet 130. 930380. S of village, E of A607.
Opened Dec 1941.
RAF Regiment Depot
Dec 1941 to Aug 1946.
2730 Squadron RAF Regiment, May to Jun
   1944.
2841 Squadron RAF Regiment, Jan, disbanded Feb 1945.
2849 Squadron RAF Regiment, May to Jun
   1944.
2957 Squadron RAF Regiment, May to Jun
   1944.
Closed 1946.

BINBROOK
OS sheet 113. 186956. 1m NNW of village,
   N of minor road to Rothwell.
Opened June 1940.
12 Squadron
Battle, Jul to Sep 1940, Wellington II, III (42),
   Sep 1940 to Sep 1942.
142 Squadron
Battle, Jul to Aug 1940, Wellington II, Sep
   1940 to Nov 1941.
No1 Group Target Towing Flight
Lysander, Nov 1941, became **1481 TTF**,
   formed Nov 1941, added Whitley, to Nov
   1942.

The control balconies of Digby Sector operations room, Blankney Hall; this view does show some of the Hall's wooden ceiling supports, at top. RAF Digby via David Curry

Air Bomber Training Flight
Formed Jun to Sep 1942.
Runways built Sep 1942 to May 1943.
2842 Squadron RAF Regiment, 1943.
12 Base
Formed May 1943, disbanded Apr 1945.
460 (Australian) Squadron
Lancaster, formed May 1943 to Jul 1945.
1481 Target Towing Flight
Wellington and Martinet, May 1943 to Mar 1944.
12 Squadron
Lancaster, Lincoln (46), Sep 1945 to Jul 1946
101 Squadron
Lancaster, Lincoln (46), Canberra B2 (51), B6 (54), Oct 1945, disbanded Feb 1957.
12 Squadron
Lincoln, Sep 1946 to Jan 1948.
9 Squadron
Lancaster, Lincoln (46), Canberra B2 (51), B6 (55), Apr 1946, disbanded Jun 1959.
617 Squadron
Lancaster, Lincoln (46), Canberra B2 (52), B6 (55), May 1946, disbanded Dec 1955.
50 Squadron
Lincoln, Aug to Dec 1947.

12 Squadron
Lincoln, Canberra B2 (52), B6 (56), B2 (57), Mar 1948 to Jul 1959.
Bomber Command Jet Conversion Flight
Meteor F4, T7; Formed Dec 1950 to Jul 1952.
Bomber Command Aircraft Modification Unit
Formed Jul 1952 to Nov 1953.
50 Squadron
Canberra B2; Aug 1952 to Jan 1956.
139 Squadron
Canberra B6; Jan 1956 to Dec 1959.
109 Squadron
Canberra B6; Jan 1956, disbanded Feb 1957.
Bomber Command Supply Unit
Formed Oct to Nov 1955.
Care & Maintenance 1959 to 1962.
Re-opened 1962.
64 Squadron
Javelin FAW9; Aug 1962 to Apr 1965.
Central Fighter Establishment
Oct 1962, disbanded Feb 1966.
Day Fighter Conversion Squadron
Hunter T7; Nov 1962, disbanded Nov 1965.

85 Squadron
Canberra T11, T19, TT18, Meteor F8; Apr 1963 to Jan 1972.
5 Squadron
Lightning F3, F6; formed Oct 1965, disbanded Dec 1987.

Air Fighting Development Squadron
Lightning; formed Feb 1966, became **Fighter Command Trials Unit** 1967, disbanded Jun 1967.
Target Facilities Flight
Lightning F1a; formed Feb 1966, disbanded Dec 1973.
11 Squadron
Lightning F3, F6; Mar 1972, disbanded Apr 1988.
Lightning Training Flight
Lightning F3, F6, T5; formed Oct 1975, disbanded Apr 1987.

Instant Readiness Reserve Unit
Lightning F3; formed Jun 1979, became **Lightning Augmentation Unit** 1981, disbanded 1982.
Closed 1988 but runways used as **RLG** for Scampton 1988 to 1992.
643 Volunteer Gliding School
Viking T1; Jun 1991 to Oct 1992.

BLANKNEY HALL
OS sheet 121.068600. S of village, E of B1188.
Opened 1940.
Digby Sector Operations Room
1940 to Jul 1945, became **Lincolnshire Sector HQ** Aug 1945 to Mar 1946.
Closed Apr 1946.

BLYBOROUGH
OS sheet 112. 945945. E of B1398, 0.25m N of village turn.
WW1 Emergency Landing Ground
1916-19, for 33 Squadron.

BLYTON
OS sheet 112. 863955. NE of village, E of A159.
Opened Nov 1942.
199 Squadron
Wellington III; formed Nov 1942 to Feb 1943.
Air Bomber Training Flight (1 Group)
Sep to Nov 1942.
1662 Heavy Conversion Unit
Lancaster & Halifax I, II, V; formed Jan 1943, disbanded Apr 1945.
No1 Lancaster Finishing School B Flight
Formed Nov 1943 to Feb 1944.

11 Base Sub-station
Sep 1943, became **71 Base Sub-station** Nov 1944, disbanded Oct 1945.
No7 Aircrew Holding Unit
1945, disbanded Jan 1946.
61 MU Sub-site
Mar 1946 to 1951.
Relief Landing Ground for 101 Refresher Flying School, Finningley. Wellington T10, Spitfire 16, Meteor F4, T7; Oct 1951 to Feb 1952.
Relief Landing Ground for 215 Advanced Flying School, Finningley. Meteor F4, T7; Feb 1952 to Jan 1954.
USAF Reserve Airfield
May 1953 to Nov 1956.
Closed 1956.

BOOTHBY PAGNELL
OS sheet 130. 965315.
WW2 Night Decoy for Grantham.

BOSTON DOCKS
OS sheet 131. 330430.
Opened late 1940s.
1109 Marine Craft Unit
Formed 1948?, disbanded Jul 1958.
Closed 1958.

BRACEBRIDGE HEATH
OS sheet 121. 986673. E of village, E of A15.
Robey's Test Aerodrome
Opened as RAF 1918.
120 Squadron
Aug to Nov 1918.

No4 Aircraft Acceptance Park
1919, disbanded 1919.
Closed 1920.

BRACEBY
OS sheet 130. 015355. Between village and A52.
WW1 Emergency Landing Ground
1916-19, for 38 & 90 Squadrons.

BRANSTON FEN
OS sheet 121. 078693.
WW2 Night Decoy for Waddington.
077689. **WW2 Night Decoy** for Lincoln City

BRANT BROUGHTON
OS Sheet 121. 905552.
WW2 Night Decoy for Swinderby.

BRATTLEBY See Scampton.

BROUGHTON/BRIGG
OS sheet 112. 955105. 0.25m N of village, E of B1207.
Opened Apr 1943.
209 Maintenance Unit
Formed Apr 1943, disbanded Feb 1946.
Closed 1946.

BRUMBY
OS sheet 112. 849096.
WW2 Night Decoy for Scunthorpe.

These mighty blast walls at Caistor once surrounded a Thor ICBM of 269 Squadron, and are still in existence in 2004. Author

BUCKMINSTER
OS sheet 130. 893235. 1m ENE of village on minor road to A1.
Opened 1916.
38 Squadron B Flight
FE2b; Oct 1916 to May 1918.
90 Squadron
Avro 504 NF; Aug 1918, disbanded Jun 1919.
Closed 1919.

BUCKNALL
OS sheet 121. 170700. 1m N of village, W of minor road.
WW1 Emergency Landing Ground
1916-19 for 33 Squadron.

BURNHAM
OS sheet 112. 044177.
WW2 Night Decoy for Goxhill.

CADNEY
OS sheet 112. 015050.
WW2 Night Decoy for Kirton-in-Lindsey.

CAENBY
OS sheet 121. map ref not known.
WW2 Night Decoy for Hemswell.

CAISTOR
OS sheet 112. 081017. 2m W of town, N of minor road to North Kelsey.
Opened 1941.

Relief Landing Ground for Kirton-in-Lindsey to May 1942.
Relief Landing Ground for 15 (P) AFU, Leconfield, Oxford; May to Nov 1942.
Relief Landing Ground for Manby Dec 1942 to Jun 1943.
Relief Landing Ground for Cranwell Jun 1943 to Feb 1945.
US Army
Nov 1943 to Feb 1944.
5354 Airfield Construction Wing 1945.
233 Maintenance Unit Sub-site
Feb 1945 to Sep 1948.
93 Maintenance Unit Sub-site
Dec 1948 to Dec 1950.
269 Squadron
Thor ICBM; formed Jul 1959, disbanded May 1963. (Hemswell Complex).
Closed 1963.

CAMMERINGHAM See Ingham.

CANWICK
OS sheet 121. 011694.
WW2 Night Decoy for Lincoln.

COCKTHORNE
OS sheet 121. 075875. 1m N of Faldingworth, W of A46.
WW1 Emergency Landing Ground
1916-19 for 33 Squadron.

COLEBY GRANGE
OS sheet 121. 000600. W of A15, N of B1202.
Opened 1940.
Relief Landing Ground for Cranwell, Kirton-in-Lindsey and Waddington, 1940 to 1941.
409 (Canadian) Squadron
Defiant I, Beaufighter IIf, VIf (42); Jul 1941 to Feb 1943.
410 (Canadian) Squadron
Mosquito II; Feb to Oct 1943.
264 Squadron
Mosquito II; Nov to Dec 1943.
288 Squadron
Spitfire V & 9, Martinet; Nov to Nov 1943.
409 (Canadian) Squadron
Beaufighter VIf; Dec 1943 to Feb 1944.
68 Squadron
Beaufighter VIf; Feb to Mar 1944.
307 (Polish) Squadron
Mosquito XII; Mar to May 1944.
Relief Landing Ground for Cranwell, Oct 1944 to May 45.
1515 Beam Approach Training Flight
Oxford; Feb 45, disbanded Jun 1945.
Relief Landing Ground for Grantham, May 1945 to Nov 1946.
107 Gliding School
Cadet; Jun 1945 to Jun 1946.

142 Squadron
Thor ICBM; formed Jul 1959, disbanded May 1963 (Hemswell Complex).
Closed 1963.

CONINGSBY
OS sheet 122. 216562. S of village, W of minor road to Dogdyke.
Opened Nov 1940.
106 Squadron
Hampden, Manchester (42), Lancaster (42); Feb 1941 to Sep 1942.
97 Squadron
Hampden, Manchester (42), Lancaster (42); Mar 1941 to Mar 1942.
No5 Group Training Flight
Various types; Mar to Aug 1941, Oct, disbanded Oct 1941.

Coleby Grange has the best preserved World War Two control tower of any of the disused Lincolnshire airfields and there have been several schemes mooted to restore it, all of which have come to nought. It stands alongside the A15 as a reminder of this busy night-fighter station. Author

The Spitfire LFIXe, a Hurricane II painted as a MkI, and the mighty Lancaster sit outside the Battle of Britain Memorial Flight hangar at Coningsby ready for engine runs, summer 2000. Inside the hangar will be the other Hurricane, a IIc, the Spitfire II, Vb and two PR19s, two Chipmunks, and the Dakota, which together constitute the Flight. Author

No5 Group Target Towing Flight
Various types; Apr 1941 became **1485 TTF**, Lysander, Whitley and Wellington; formed Oct 1941 to Aug 1942.
14 Beam Approach Training Flight
Oxford; formed Sep 1941 became **1514 BATF**, formed Oct 1941 to Mar 1943.
No5 Group GEE Equipment School
1942 to 1943.
Bomber Command Field Cookery School
1942 to 1943.
Runways built 1942 to 1943.
617 Squadron
Lancaster; Aug 1943 to Jan 1944.
1514 Beam Approach Training Flight
Oxford; Aug 1943 to Jan 1944.
2756 Squadron RAF Regiment, 1944.
619 Squadron
Lancaster; Jan to Apr 1944.
61 Squadron
Lancaster; Jan to Apr 1944.
54 Base
Formed Jan 1944, disbanded Nov 1945.
83 Squadron
Lancaster, Lincoln (46); Apr 1944 to Oct 1946.
97 Squadron
Lancaster, Lincoln (46); Apr 1944 to Nov 1946.
Highball Training Flight
Mosquito IV, FB6, Sea Mosquito TR33; Jun 1946 to Nov 1947.
109 Squadron
Mosquito B16, B35 (48); Nov 1946 to Mar 1950.
139 Squadron
Mosquito B16, B35 (48); Nov 1946 to Apr 1950.

231 Operational Conversion Unit
Mosquito T3, B16; formed Aug 1947 to Dec 1949.
149 Squadron
Washington B1, Canberra B2 (53); Oct 1950 to May 1954.
15 Squadron
Washington B1, Canberra B2 (53); Feb 1951 to May 1954.
44 Squadron
Washington B1, Canberra B2 (53); Apr 1951 to May 1954.
57 Squadron
Washington B1, Canberra B2 (53); Apr 1952 to May 1954.
Bomber Command Jet Conversion Unit
Meteor F4, T7; Apr to Nov 1953.
40 Squadron
Canberra B2; formed Oct 1953 to Feb 1954.
Care & Maintenance 1954 to 1956.
57 Squadron
Canberra B2; Nov 1956, disbanded Dec 1957.
249 Squadron
Detachment, Canberra B2; formed Aug 1957 to Oct 1957.
45 Squadron
Detachment, Canberra B2; formed Oct 1957 to Nov 1957.
Bomber Command Aircrew Holding Unit
Canberra T4; formed Dec 1957, disbanded Apr 1959.
9 Squadron
Canberra B6; Jun 1959, disbanded Jul 1961.
12 Squadron
Canberra B2, B6; Jul 1959, disbanded Jul 1961.
Rebuilding 1961 to 1962.

9 Squadron
Vulcan B2; formed Mar 1962 to Nov 1964.
12 Squadron
Vulcan B2; formed Jul 1962 to Nov 1964
35 Squadron
Vulcan B2; formed Dec 1962 to Nov 1964. Rebuilding for TSR2.
No5 School of Technical Training
Formed Mar 1967, disbanded Aug 1968.
228 Operational Conversion Unit
Phantom FGR2; formed Aug 1968 to Apr 1987.
6 Squadron
Phantom FGR2; formed May 1969, disbanded Sep 1974.
54 Squadron
Phantom FGR2; formed Sep 1969, disbanded Jun 1974
41 Squadron
Phantom FGR2; formed Apr 1972, disbanded Mar 1977.
111 Squadron
Phantom FGR2; formed Oct 1974 to Nov 1975.
29 Squadron
Phantom FGR2; formed Jan 1975, disbanded Mar 1987.
23 Squadron
Phantom FGR2; formed Nov 1975 to Feb 1976.
56 Squadron
Phantom FGR2; formed Jun to Jul 1976.
Battle of Britain Memorial Flight
Lancaster, Hurricane, Spitfire, Dakota, Devon, Chipmunk; Mar 1976 to present (2004).

Coningsby was the first, and only, station to operate the Tornado F2, one of which is seen here serving with 229 Operational Conversion Unit in 1985. The F2 was used for training only and was soon replaced by the more advanced F3. Author

219 Field Squadron, Royal Engineers
Formed 1984, disbanded Jun 1999.
229 Operational Conversion Unit
Tornado F2, F3; formed Jul 1985, became **56 (Reserve) Sqn**, Tornado F3; formed Jul 1992 to March 2003
Tornado F3 Operational Evaluation Unit
Formed Jun 1987 to present (2004)
29 Squadron
Tornado F3; formed Apr 1987, disbanded Oct 1998.
5 Squadron
Tornado F3; Jan 1988, disbanded Sept 2002 Still open. BBMF Visitor's Centre. Closed Mar–Oct 2003 for runway resurfacing. Strike/Attack OEU to amalgamate April 2004 with Tornado F3 OEU to form Fast Jet OEU, April 2004.

CRANWELL
OS sheet 130. 000490. 1m W of village, north of A17.
Opened Apr 1916. Naval Air Service
Royal Naval Air Service Training Establishment
Various types, plus airships; Apr 1916 to Mar 1918.

201 Training Depot Station
Hamble Baby Convert, Camel, Avro 504, RE7, Pup, F2b, Cuckoo; formed Apr 1913, became **56 TDS**, plus DH9, Snipe; formed Jul 1918, disbanded Mar 1919.
202 Training Depot Station
DH4, DH9, BE2e, RE8, O/400; formed Apr 1918, became **57 TDS**, plus DH6, Camel, Avro 504; formed Jul 1918, disbanded Mar 1919.
213 Training Depot Station
0/400; formed Apr 1918, became **58 TDS**, plus DH6, Avro 504; formed Jul 1918, disbanded Mar 1919.
59 Training Wing
formed Jul 1918, disbanded Jun 1919.
Airship Training Wing
Apr 1918, disbanded 1920.

A Sea Scout Class airship over Market Rasen c1918; the three crew sat in the Farman aeroplane fuselage suspended beneath the gas bag, with the engine at the rear driving a pusher propeller. This is almost certainly a Cranwell ship and appears to be carrying a USA star on its ventral fin, signifying the training of US Navy airship crews at Cranwell. Mrs Barraclough

Cranwell's East Camp under construction in February 1918. The light railway is much in evidence and the railway station, today the main guardroom, is at bottom right. Apart from that few, if any, of these buildings remain. RAF Cranwell

The magnificent College buildings provide the backdrop for this RAF College de Havilland Chipmunk T10 formation, c1955.
RAF Cranwell

Boy's Training Wing
Apr 1918 became **2 School of Technical Training (Boys)**, formed Mar 1920, became **Boy's Wing**, formed Apr 1921 to 1926.

Wireless Operator's School
Formed Apr 1918, disbanded Jun 1919.

12 Group
Formed Apr 1918, disbanded Nov 1919.

Royal Air Force Cadet College
Formed Dec 1919, became **RAF College**, formed Feb 1929, disbanded Sep 1939.

RAF College Band 1920 to present (2004).

Fire & Rescue Training Unit
Formed 1922 to Jul 1940.

RAF Hospital 1922 to 1940.

Electrical & Wireless School
Aug 1929 became **No1 EWS** formed Nov 1938, became **No1 Radio School**, formed Mar 1941 to Jan 1943, became **No8 Radio School**, formed Jan 1943, disbanded Jun 1946.

School of Store Accounting and Storekeeping
formed Jul 1934, became **Equipment Training School**. formed Dec 1936 to Jun 1941.

Supply Depot
Formed Oct 1936 to Nov 1949.

21 Group and its **Communications Flight**
Formed Dec 1938 to Jul 1944.

RAF College Flying Training School
Oxford, Blenheim I, Master; formed Sep 1939 to Mar 1944, became **17 SFTS**, formed Mar 1944 to May 1945.

School of Clerks Accounting
Formed 1939 to 1941.

26 Group
Formed Feb 1940 to Mar 1940.

2 Flying Instructor's School
Oxford, Tutor; formed Sep 1940 became **2 Central Flying School**, formed Nov 1940 to Jun 1941.

2806 Squadron RAF Regiment, 1941.

3 Operational Training Unit
Whitley, Wellington; Jul 1941 to Jun 1943.

1 Radio School
Dominie, Hudson; formed Mar 1941 became **8 Radio School** to Oct 1950.

Officer's Advanced Training School
Formed Feb 1944 became **1 OATS**, formed Nov 1944 to Aug 1945.

19 Flying Training School
Harvard & Tiger Moth; formed May 1945 to Apr 1947.

RAF College
Formed Oct 1946 to present (2004).

3 Initial Training School
Formed Dec 1950, disbanded Mar 1953.

Aircrew Transit Unit
Dec 1951 to Oct 1953.

HQ, University Air Squadrons
Formed Nov 1971, became **HQ, UAS and Air Cadets**, formed Jul 1995, became **HQ Elementary Flying Training** 1998 became **1 EFTS** 2003.

Central Flying School HQ
Apr 1976 to Sep 1977.

Basic Flying Training School
Jet Provost T3, T5, formed Aug 1979, became **3 FTS**, formed Feb 1989, JPT3, T5, Tucano (1991), Dominie, Jetstream, Bulldog (95), kingair (04); to present (2004).

Officer and Aircrew Selection Centre
Sep 1992 to present (2004).

RAF College Air Squadron
Bulldog, Tutor (99); formed Apr 1992 to present (2004).

HQ Air Cadets
Formed 1998 to present (2004).

Central Flying School Bulldog Squadron
Mar 1995 to Dec 2000 became **CFS Tutor Sqn** to present. (2004).

Central Flying School HQ
Jun 1995 to present (2004)

RAF Regiment Band
To present (2004)

Air Warfare Centre
Detachment, 1995 to present (2004)

RAF Aerobatic Team
Hawk T1, Feb 1996 to Dec 2000

HQ Provost and Security (Central Region)
? to present (2004)

East Midlands UAS/7 Air Experience Flight
Tutor, 2000 to present (2004)
Still open.
RAF Cranwell Visitor Centre on the A17.

CROWLAND
OS sheet 131. 262114.
USAF/RAF Communications link mast, 1960s to present (2004).

CUXWOLD
OS sheet 113. 177008. 1m E of village on minor road.
WW1 Emergency Landing Ground
1916-19 for 33 Squadron.

DIGBY/SCOPWICK
OS sheet 121. 038565. 2m NW of village, W of B1191.
Opened Sep 1918.
59 Training Depot Station
DH9, F2b, BE2e; Oct 1918 became **59 Training Sqn**, formed Mar 1919, became **3 FTS**, F2b, formed Apr 1920, disbanded Apr 1922.
209 Squadron
Cadre; Feb 1919, disbanded Jun 1919.
210 Squadron
Cadre; Feb 1919, disbanded Jun 1919.
213 Squadron
Cadre; Mar 1919, disbanded Dec 1919.
11 Squadron
Cadre, Sep 1919, disbanded Dec 1919.
25 Squadron
Cadre, Dec 1919, disbanded Jan 1920.
203 Squadron
Cadre; Dec 1919, disbanded Jan 1920.
205 Squadron
Cadre, Dec 1919, disbanded Jan 1920.
2 Squadron
F2b; Feb to Jun 1922.
2 Flying Training School
Avro 504, DH9a, Vimy, Snipe, Atlas, Siskin, Grebe; Jun 1924 to Jul 1933.
2 Flying Training School
Hart T, Fury, Tutor; formed Oct 1934 to Sep 1937.
46 Squadron
Gauntlet, Hurricane I (39); Nov 1937 to Dec 1939.
73 Squadron
Gladiator, Hurricane (38); Nov 1937 to Sep 1939.
504 Squadron
Hurricane I; Aug to Oct 1939.
229 Squadron
Blenheim If; Hurricane I (40); Oct 1939 to Jun 1940.
611 Squadron
Spitfire I; IIa (40) Oct 1939 to Dec 1940.
46 Squadron
Hurricane I; Jan to May 1940.
111 Squadron
Hurricane I; May to May 1940.
222 Squadron
Spitfire I, May to May, 1940.
56 Squadron
Hurricane I; May to Jun 1940.

79 Squadron
Hurricane I; May to Jun 1940.
46 Squadron
Hurricane I; Jun to Sep 1940.
29 Squadron
Blenheim If; Jun to Jul 1940.
151 Squadron
Hurricane I; Sep to Nov 1940.
46 Squadron
Hurricane; Dec 1940 to Feb 1941.
2 RCAF Squadron
Hurricane I; formed Dec 1940 became **402 Sqn**, Hurricane I, IIa, IIb, formed Mar to May 1941.
1 RCAF Squadron
Hurricane I, IIa, Feb 1941 became **401 Sqn**, Spitfire IIa, formed Mar 1941, to Oct 1941.
409 (Canadian) Squadron
Defiant I; formed Jun 1941 to Jul 1941.
411 (Canadian) Squadron
Spitfire I, IIa, Vb; formed Jun 1941 to Nov 1941.
121 Squadron
Hurricane I; Sep to Oct 1941.
412 (Canadian) Squadron
Spitfire IIa; Jun to Oct 1941.
92 Squadron
Spitfire Vb; Oct 1941 to Feb 1942.
609 Squadron
Spitfire Vb; Nov 1941 to Mar 1942.
12 Group Anti-Aircraft Co-operation Flight
Blenheim IV, Lysander; formed May 1941 became **288 Sqn**, plus Hudson & Hurricane; formed Nov 1941 to Dec 1942.
601 Squadron
Spitfire Vb; Mar to Apr 1942.
421 (Canadian) Squadron
Spitfire Va; Apr to May 1942.
411 (Canadian) Squadron
Spitfire Vb; Jun to Aug 1942, Aug 1942 to Mar 1943.
242 Squadron
Spitfire Vb; Sep to Oct 1942.
198 Squadron
Typhoon Ia, Ib; formed Dec 1942 to Jan 1943.
288 Squadron
Various types; Jan to Nov 1943.
402 (Canadian) Squadron
Spitfire Vb, Vc; Mar to Aug 1943.
411 (Canadian) Squadron
Spitfire Vb, IX, Mar to Mar 1943.
19 Squadron
Spitfire Vb; May to Jun 1943.
167 Squadron
Spitfire Vc; Apr to May 1943.
416 (Canadian) Squadron
Spitfire Vb, Vc; Jun to Aug 1943.
350 (Belgian) Squadron
Spitfire Vc; Aug to Oct 1943.
402 (Canadian) Squadron
Spitfire Vb, Vc; Sep to Dec 1943.
416 (Canadian) Squadron
Spitfire Vc, IX; Oct 1943 to Feb 1944.
288 Squadron
Various types; Nov 1943 to Jan 1944.
438 (Canadian) Squadron
Hurricane IV; formed Nov 1943 to Dec 1943.

402 (Canadian) Squadron
Spitfire IX; Jan to Feb 1944
441 (Canadian) Squadron
Spitfire Vb, IX; formed Feb to Mar 1944.
442 (Canadian) Squadron
Spitfire Vb, IX; formed Feb to Mar 1944.
443 (Canadian) Squadron
Spitfire Vb, IX; formed Feb to Mar 1944.
504 Squadron
Spitfire Vb; Apr to Jul 1944.
527 Squadron
Blenheim IV, Hurricane II; Apr 1944 to Nov 1945.
2815, 2882, 2892, 2894, 2896 Squadrons
RAF Regiment, Apr 1944.
528 Squadron
Blenheim IV; May, disbanded Sep 1944.
310 (Czech) Squadron
Spitfire Vb; Jul to Aug 1944.
441 (Canadian) Squadron
Mustang III; May to Jul 1945.
442 (Canadian) Squadron
Mustang III; May to Jul 1945.
Lincolnshire Sector
Formed Jul 1945 to Aug 1945.
No1 Officer's Advanced Training School
Spitfire XI, Mustang IV, Master II, Proctor; Aug 1945 to Apr 1947.
Relief Landing Ground for Cranwell, Jan 1946 to Jan 1951.
107 Gliding School
Cadet; Dec 1946, disbanded Oct 1949.
Equipment & Secretarial Section of RAF College
Apr 1947 to Nov 1953.
Aircrew Transit Unit
Sep to Nov 1949.
No2 Wing of 1 Initial Training School
Nov 1949 to Apr 1950.
2 Initial Training School
formed Oct 1950 to Aug 1951.
Aircrew Grading School
Tiger Moth; formed Aug 1951 became **No1 Grading Unit (Airwork)**, formed Jun 1952, became **No1 Grading School**, disbanded Mar 1953.
No3 Wing of 2 Initial Training School
Formed Jan to Jul 1952.
Aircrew Transit Unit
Oct 1953, disbanded Oct 1953.
399 Signals Unit
Jan 1955, became **Joint Service Signals Unit**, formed 1999 to present (2004).
591 Signals Unit
Jul 1955 to present (2004)
Aerial Erectors School
Sep 1959 to present (2004).
Wireless Operators School
Sep 1959 to Oct 1964.
54 Signals Unit
Feb 1969 to 1974.
Still open.
Digby Sector Operations Room Museum.

DONNA NOOK
OS sheet 113. 425979. 1.5m NE of North Somercotes, on coast.
Opened 1940.
Relief Landing Ground for Manby 1940.

Target Number IV at Donna Nook range was old aircraft wings, and the gunner of Fairey Gordon I K2686, of 35 Squadron, is drawing a bead on them, c1932. P H T Green

Relief Landing Ground for North Coates 1940 to 1945.
PoW Camp 1945.
Master Provision Office 1945.
61 Maintenance Unit Sub-site
Oct 1945 to Dec 1947.
Closed 1948.
403002. WW2 **Night and Day Decoy** for North Coates.

DONNA NOOK RANGE
Opened 1926.
Bombing and Gunnery Range to 1946.
Closed 1946.
Re-opened Aug 1976.
Air Weapons Range to present (2004)
Still open.

DORRINGTON
OS sheet 121. 095543.
WW2 Night Decoy for Digby

DUNHOLME LODGE
OS sheet 121. 993776. 1.5m SSW of village, W of A46.
Opened 1942.
Relief Landing Ground for 14 (P) AFU, Ossington, Apr to Aug 1942.
Air Bomber Training Flight (5 Group)
Aug to Oct 1942.
1485 Target Towing and Gunnery Flight
Manchester; Aug to Oct 1942.
Runways built Oct 1942 to May 1943.
52 Base Sub-station
May 1943 to Oct 1944.
15 Base Sub-station
Oct 1944 to Jun 1945.
44 Squadron
Lancaster; May 1943 to Sep 1944.
619 Squadron
Lancaster; Apr to Sep 1944.
170 Squadron
Lancaster; Oct to Nov 1944.
2799 Squadron RAF Regiment
Nov to Dec 1944.
General Aircraft Ltd
Work on Hamilcar gliders, Nov 1944 to 1945.
No3 Polish Resettlement Unit
Formed 1946, disbanded 1949.

Polish Record Office
Feb 1948, disbanded 1949?
Closed 1949.
141 Squadron
Bloodhound SAM 1; formed Apr 1959, disbanded Mar 1964.
Closed 1964.

EAST HALTON
OS sheet 113. 137229
Night Dummy Oil Refinery Decoy
for Killingholme.
138231. **WW2 Night Decoy** for Immingham Docks.

EAST KIRKBY
OS sheet 122. 341607. SE of village, S of A155.
Opened Aug 1943.
57 Squadron
Lancaster, Lincoln (45); Aug 1943 disbanded Nov 1945.
630 Squadron
Lancaster; formed Nov 1943 disbanded Jul 1945.
55 Base
Formed Apr 1944 disbanded Nov 1945.
460 (Australian) Squadron
Lancaster; Jul 1945 disbanded Oct 1945.
93 Maintenance Unit Sub-site to Dec 1950.
USAF 3931 Air Base Squadron
C-47 Dakota; Apr to Nov 1954.
3917 Air Base Squadron
C-47, SC-47; Nov 1954 to Aug 1958.
Closed Aug 1958.
Lincolnshire Aviation Heritage Centre.

EASTOFT
OS sheet 112. 789167.
WW2 Night Decoy for Finningley.

ELSHAM
OS sheet 112. 055138. NE of village, 0.5m E of A15.
Opened Dec 1916.
33 Squadron C Flight
BE2c, BE12, BE2e (17), FE2b (17), BE12a (17), FE2d (17); Dec 1916 to Jun 1918.
Closed Jul 1918.

ELSHAM WOLDS
OS sheet 112. 035135. Straddles A15 NE of village.
Opened Jul 1941.
103 Squadron
Wellington Ic, Halifax II (42), Lancaster (42); Jul 1941 disbanded Nov 1945.
103 Conversion Flight
Halifax II; formed May disbanded Oct 1942.
1656 Heavy Conversion Unit, B Flight
Halifax II, Oct to Nov, 1942
576 Squadron
Lancaster; formed Nov 1943 to Oct 1944.
13 Base
Formed Dec 1943 disbanded Dec 1945.
100 Squadron
Lancaster; Apr to Nov 1945.
57 Squadron
Lancaster; formed from 103 Sqn Nov to Dec 1945.

21 Heavy Glider Conversion Unit, Albemarle, Dakota, Horsa & Hadrian
Dec 1945 to Dec 1946.
93 Maintenance Unit Sub-site to Dec 1950.
Closed 1951.
USAF comms link 1950s to 1970s.

FALDINGWORTH
OS sheet 121. 030847. 2m W of village, N of minor road to Spridlington.
Opened Oct 1943.
1667 Heavy Conversion Unit
Halifax II & V; Oct 1943 to Feb 1944.
No1 Lancaster Finishing School C Flight
Nov 1943 to Jan 1944.
14 Base Sub-station
Dec 1943 to Oct 1945.
300 (Polish) Squadron
Wellington X, Lancaster; Mar 1944 disbanded Jan 1947.
1546 Beam Approach Training Flight
Oxford; formed May 1944 disbanded Jan 1945.
305 (Polish) Squadron
Mosquito FB6; Oct 1946 disbanded Jan 1947.
93 Maintenance Unit Sub-site
Feb 1949 to Dec 1950.
92 Maintenance Unit Sub-site
Aug 1955 to Jul 1956.
93 Maintenance Unit Sub-site
Jul 1956 to Oct 1957.
92 Maintenance Unit
Formed Oct 1957 disbanded Nov 1972.
Closed 1973.

FENTON
OS sheet 121. 848776. NW of village on Fossdyke Canal.
WW2 Bombing Range for 5 Group.

FISKERTON
OS sheet 121. 040725. N of village straddling minor road to Reepham.
Opened Jan 1943.
49 Squadron
Lancaster; Jan 1943 to Oct 1944.
52 Base Sub-station
May 1943 to Oct 1944.
15 Base Sub-station
Oct 1944 to Oct 1945.
1514 Beam Approach Training Flight
Oxford; formed Jan 1944 disbanded Jan 1945.
1690 Bomber Defence Training Flight det
Spitfire II & Hurricane II; Aug 1944 to Sep 1944.
576 Squadron
Lancaster; Oct 1944 disbanded Sep 1945.
150 Squadron
Lancaster; formed Nov to Nov 1944.
2753 Squadron RAF Regiment, 1944 to 1945.
2799 Squadron RAF Regiment, 1945.
61 Maintenance Unit Sub-site
Nov 1945 to Nov 1948.
255 Maintenance Unit Sub-site
Nov 1945 to Nov 1948.

93 Maintenance Unit Sub-site
Nov 1948 to Dec 1950.
Closed 1951.
HQ 15 Group ROC
1960 disbanded Sep 1991.
HQ Midland Area, ROC & UK Warning and Monitoring Organisation to Sep 1991.
Closed Sep 1991.

FOLKINGHAM
OS sheet 130. 040290. 2m ESE of village, S of minor road to Lenton.
Opened 1943.
Station 484 USAAF
313th Troop Carrier Group
C-47, GC-4a, C-46 (45); Feb 1944 to Feb 1945
RAF Regiment Sub-Depot
1945 to Aug 1946.
2704, 2709, 2737, 2791, 2830, 2847, 2875, 2949 Squadrons RAF Regiment, 1945, disbanded 1945.
16 Maintenance Unit Sub-site
Jun 1945 to Mar 1948.
Relief Landing Ground for Cranwell, Sep 1957 to Aug 1959.
223 Squadron
Thor ICBM; formed Dec 1959 disbanded Aug 1963 (North Luffenham complex).
Closed 1963.
064325. **WW2 Night and Day Decoy** for Grantham.

FOSTON
OS sheet 130. 872408.
WW2 Night Decoy for Bottesford

FRIESTON
OS sheet 131. 385405. 2m S of village, now HMP North Sea Camp.
Opened Sep 1917.
RNAS Armament School for Cranwell, Sep 1917 to Apr 1918.
No4 School of Aerial Fighting and Gunnery
Various types; formed May 1918 became **No4 Fighting School**, Camel, Avro 504K, Snipe (19); May 1918 disbanded Mar 1920.
Closed 1920.

FRISKNEY
OS sheet 122. 493545.
Opened May 1944.
5 Group Anti-Aircraft Gunnery School
May to Oct 1944.
Closed 1944.

FRITHVILLE
OS Sheet 131. 298496.
WW2 Night Decoy for Coningsby and Manby.

FULBECK
OS sheet 121. 890503. 3m W of village, W of minor road from Brant Broughton to Marston.
Opened Nov 1940.
Relief Landing Ground for Cranwell Nov 1940 to Oct 1942.
Runways built.

Air Bomber Training Flight (5 Gp)
Oct 1942 disbanded Mar 1943.
1485 Target Towing and Gunnery Flight
Manchester, Lysander, Martinet & Oxford; Oct 1942 to Aug 1943.
1506 Beam Approach Training Flight
Oxford; Feb to Aug 1943.
Station 488. USAAF
434th Troop Carrier Group
C-47; Oct to Dec 1943.
29 Glider Servicing Section RAF
Horsa; dates unknown.
442nd Troop Carrier Group
C-47; Mar to Jun 1944.
440th Troop Carrier Group
C-47; Aug and Sep 1944.
RAF, 56 Base Sub-station
Oct 1944 to Apr 1945.
49 Squadron
Lancaster; Oct 1944 to Apr 1945.
189 Squadron
Lancaster; Nov 1944 to Apr 1945.
Automatic Gun Laying Turret Trials Flight
Lancaster; Mar to Mar 1945.
Bomber Command Film Flight Unit
Lancaster & Mosquito; Apr to Apr 1945.
4 Equipment Disposal Depot
Formed Jun 1945 became **255 MU** Jun 1945 disbanded Nov 1948.
93 Maintenance Unit Sub-site
Dec 1948 to Apr 1956.
Air Historical Branch Store
1953 to late 1950s.
Relief Landing Ground for Cranwell Feb 1956 to 1969.
Closed 1969, but used occasionally for Army and RAF exercises to present (2004).

GAINSBOROUGH
OS sheet 112. 818885.
Opened Dec 1916.
HQ 33 Squadron
In 'The Lawn' workshops on Lea Road, aerodrome across the Trent in Notts, Dec 1916 to Jun 1918.
HQ 48 Home Defence Wing
In 'North Sandsfield', formed Feb 1918 disbanded Apr 1919.
Closed 1919.

GAUTBY
OS sheet 121. 170714.
WW2 Night Decoy for Waddington.

GAYTON TOP
OS sheet 122. 418830. 1m E of S Reston on A157.
Opened 1943, as receiver station for Louth.
Closed 1945.

GIBRALTAR POINT
OS sheet 122. 560583.
WW2 RAF Regiment Gunnery Range and Battle Training Area.

GLENTHAM
OS sheet 122. 011893
WW2 Night Decoy for Hemswell.

GOSBERTON
OS sheet 130. 174295. 4m W of village, N of B1397.
WW1 Emergency Landing Ground for 38 Sqn.

GOXHILL
OS sheet 113. 107210. E of village.
Opened Jun 1941.
1 Group Target Towing Flight
Lysander; formed Sep to Nov 1941.
Relief Landing Ground for Kirton-in-Lindsey, Nov 1941 to May 1942.
Relief Landing Ground for 15 (Pilots) Advanced Flying Unit, Kirmington, Oxford; May to Jun 1942.
USAAF Station 345
1st Fighter Group
P-38 Lightning; Jun to Aug 1942.
52nd Fighter Group
Spitfire Vb; Aug to Oct 1942.
81st Fighter Group
P-38; Oct to Nov 1942.
358th Fighter Group
P-47 Thunderbolt; Oct to Nov 1942.
78th Fighter Group
P-38, P-47; Dec 1942 to Apr 1943.
No2 Gunnery & Target Towing Flight
Feb to Nov 1943.
353rd Fighter Group
P-47; Jun to Aug 1943.
356th Fighter Group
P-47; Aug to Oct 1943.
No3 Gunnery and Target Towing Flight
Oct 1943 to Jan 1944.
496th Fighter Training Group
P-38 & P-51; Dec 1943 to Feb 1945.
USAAF out.
233 Maintenance Unit Sub-site
May 1945 to Dec 1948.
35 Maintenance Unit Sub-site
May 1947 to Sep 1950.
93 Maintenance Unit Sub-site
Dec 1948 to Dec 1950.
92 Maintenance Unit Sub-site
Sep to Dec 1957.
Closed 1958.

GRANTHAM/SPITTLEGATE/SPITALGATE
OS sheet 130. 935345. 1.5m E of town, N of A52.
Opened Nov 1916.
49 Training Squadron
Shorthorn & Grahame-White, FK3 (17); Nov 1916 to Sep 1917.
87 (Canadian) Reserve Squadron
Various types; formed Jan 1917.
83 Squadron
Various types; Jan to Sep 1917.
24 Training Wing HQ
Mar 1917 to Apr 1918.
11 Training Squadron
Various types; Apr to Sep 1917.
20 Training Squadron
Various types; Sep to Nov 1917.
37 Training Squadron
Various types, BE2e (18), FK8 (18), DH9 (18); Sep 1917 to Aug 1918.

Instructors and aircraft of 3 FTS Grantham, 1932, with Atlas TMs in the foreground and Tutors beyond. Flight International

91 Squadron
Various types; formed Sep to Sep 1917.
106 Squadron
Various types; formed Sep 1917 to Oct 1917.
50 Training Squadron
Various types; Nov 1917 to Jul 1918.
39 Training Depot Station
FK8, BE2e, FE2b; formed Oct 1918, disbanded Mar 1919 became **39 TS**, Avro 504K, became **6 Flying Training School**, Apr to Sep 1920.
29 Squadron
Cadre; Aug 1919, disbanded Dec 1919.
43 Squadron
Cadre; Aug 1919, disbanded Dec 1919.
70 Squadron
Cadre; Aug 1919, disbanded Jan 1920.
202 Squadron
Cadre; Dec 1919, disbanded Jan 1920.
39 Squadron
DH9a; Mar 1921 to Jan 1928.

100 Squadron
DH9a & Vimy; Feb 1922 to May 1924.
HQ 3 Group
Formed Apr 1923 to Apr 1926.
HQ 23 Group
Formed Apr to Aug 1926.
3 Flying Training School
Avro 504N & Siskin IIIa, Tutor, Atlas, Hart T (all 30s); formed Apr 1928 to Aug 1937.
113 Squadron
Hind; Aug 1937 to Apr 1938.
211 Squadron
Hind; Sep 1937 to May 1938.
HQ 23 Group and Comms Flight
Oct 1937 to Oct 1939.
106 Squadron
Battle; Sep to Oct 1938.
185 Squadron
Battle; Sep to Oct 1938.
No5 Group Comms Flight
Various types; formed 1938 to Nov 1943.
12 Flying Training School
Harvard I, Oxford (39), Hart T (39), Anson (40), Battle T (40), Oxford (41); formed Dec 1938 to 1942 became 12 (Pilots) Advanced Flying Unit Blenheim I, IV, V, Oxford (44); 1942 to Feb 1945.

2749 & 2793 Squadrons RAF Regiment, 1941.
1536 Beam Approach Training Flight
Oxford; formed Mar 1943, disbanded Feb 1945.
1544 Beam Approach Training Flight
Oxford; Mar 1944, disbanded Aug 1944.
HQ 21 Group and Comms Flight
Various types; Jul 1944 to Mar 1946.
17 Service Flying Training School
Harvard, Oxford, Spitfire, Blenheim; May 1945 to Jun 1946 became **17 FTS**, Jun 1946 disbanded Jun 1947, became **1 FTS**, Harvard; formed Jun 1947, disbanded Feb 1948.
25 Group Comms Flight
Various types; Apr 1947, disbanded Apr 1948.
Officer Cadet Training Unit
Formed Jun 1948, became **2 OCTU**, Jun 1948 to Mar 1953.
RAF Mess Staff School
Sep 1949 to Aug 1957.
Officer Cadet Training Unit
Jan 1951, disbanded Mar 1953.
Relief Landing Ground for Cranwell, Jan 1951 to Mar 1961.

Relief Landing Ground for 7 FTS, Cottesmore, Nov 1952 to Apr 1954.
RAF School of Education
Aug 1954 to Nov 1958.
44 Gliding School
Cadet & Sedburgh; Jul 1955, disbanded Sep 1955 became **644 Volunteer Gliding School**, formed Sep 1955 to Jan 1975.
RAF Central Library
Aug 1955 to Nov 1958.
Secretarial Officer's School
1959 to 1959.
HQ 3 Police District became **HQ Provost and Security Service,** 1959 to unknown date.
USAF comms link mast, 1950s to 1970s.
Women's RAF Depot
1960 to Mar 1974.
No2 Gliding Centre
Cadet; Oct 1965, disbanded Aug 1970 became **Central Gliding School,** various types; Aug 1970 to Jan 1975.
Army took over 1975.

GRANTHAM MILL HOUSE
OS sheet 130. 937358. ENE of town centre.
HQ 24 Training Wing
Apr 1918 disbanded Apr 1919.

GRANTHAM ST VINCENT'S
OS sheet 130. 925351. 0.25m SE of town centre, N of A52.
Opened Oct 1937.
HQ 5 Group
Oct 1937 to Nov 1943.
HQ 9th Troop Carrier Command USAAF
Nov 1943 to Nov 1944.
HQ 7 Group
Nov 1944 to 1945.
HQ 21 Group
Mar 1946 to May 1947.
HQ 25 Group
Apr 1947, disbanded Apr 1948.
Closed 1948.

GREAT LIMBER
OS sheet 113. 140074.
WW2 Night Decoy for Elsham Wolds.

GREENLAND TOP
OS sheet 113. 180115. 1.5m S of Immingham, west of minor road to Keelby.
Opened 1916
Emergency Landing Ground for 33 Sqn to 1918.
251 Squadron, 505 Flight
DH6; May 1918 to Jan 1919.
Closed 1919.

GRIMSBY
OS sheet 113. 340048.
WW2 Night Decoy for Grimsby.

GRIMSBY/WALTHAM
OS sheet 113. 273020. 3.5m S of town, W of A16 at Holton-le-Clay.
Civil aerodrome in 1930s, RAF in Jun 1938.
25 Elementary & Reserve FTS
Magister, Hind, Hart T; formed Jun 1938, disbanded Sep 1939.
Runways built.
142 Squadron
Wellington II, IV, III (42); Nov 1941 to Dec 1942.
100 Squadron
Lancaster; formed Dec 1942 to Apr 1945.
No7 Anti-Aircraft Calibration Unit det
Various types; Mar 1942 to May 1943.
776 Squadron, Fleet Air Arm det
Roc, Skua, Sea Hurricane, Defiant; Jan 1943 to Dec 1944.

12 Base Sub-station
Mar 1943 to Mar 1945.
550 Squadron
Lancaster; formed Nov 1943 to Jan 1944.
35 Maintenance Unit Sub-site
May 1947 to Mar 1953.
107 Gliding School
Cadet; Dec 1948, disbanded Oct 1949.
22 Gliding School det
Cadet; Nov 1949 to May 1950, became **22 GS**, formed May 1950 to Aug 50.
Closed 1953.

GRIMSBY TIDAL BASIN
OS sheet 113. 278115. Mouth of docks.
Opened 1941.
22 Air Sea Rescue Unit/Motor Launch Unit
1941, disbanded Dec 1945.
Air Dept Moorings & Salvage Branch, No2 Area (Civilian manned)
1939 to 1962.
Closed 1946.

This mansion, St Vincent's, stands near the bottom of Spittlegate Hill, Grantham, below the airfield, and was commandeered by the RAF to become the HQ of No5 Group, Bomber Command, in 1937. The operations block, seen on the right in this 1970s view, has since been demolished. Ogden, Dodd and Welch

GRIMSTHORPE
OS sheet 130. 030210. SW of village.
WW2 Bombing Range for 7 Group.

HABROUGH
OS sheet 113. 145175. 2m N of village in North Killingholme Rectory.
Opened Jun 1918.
HQ 18 Group
Formed Jun 1918, disbanded Oct 1919.
Closed 1919.

HAGNABY
OS sheet 122. 352618.
WW2 Day and Night Decoy for Coningsby.

HAMILTON HILL
OS sheet 113. 123901. 1m E of Market Rasen, S of B1203.
WW2 Gunnery Range.

HARLAXTON
OS sheet 130. 900320. 1.25m E of village, W of A1.
Opened Nov 1916.
44 Training Squadron
Avro 504, DH4, BE2c; Nov 1916 to Nov 1917.
68 Squadron
DH5, formed Jan to Sep 1917.
54 Training Squadron
Avro, DH5; Mar to Dec 1917.
98 Squadron
Various types; formed Aug to Aug 1917.
26 Training Squadron
BE2, RE8, DH6; Sep 1917 to Feb 1918.
20 Training Squadron
Avro 504, DH6; Nov 1917 to Jul 1918.
64 Training Squadron
RE8, Avro 504, DH6; Dec 1917 to Jul 1918.
53 Training Squadron
RE8, Avro 504, DH6; Dec 1917 disbanded Aug 1918
40 Training Depot Station
DH6, Avro 504, RE8, FK8; formed Aug 1918, disbanded May 1919.
Closed 1919.
Re-opened 1939.
Relief Landing Ground for 12 FTS Oct 1939 to Feb 1945.
Relief Landing Ground for 17 SFTS May 1945 to Jun 1947.
Closed 1947.

HARPSWELL
OS sheet 112. 938903. 0.25m E of village, E of B1398.
Opened Jun 1918.
199 Night Training Squadron
FE2b; Jun 1918, disbanded May 1919.
200 Night Training Squadron
FE2b; Nov 1918, disbanded Jun 1919.
Closed 1919.

HEMSWELL
OS sheet 112. 938903.
Opened Jan 1937 on site of Harpswell.
144 Squadron
Audax, Blenheim I, Hampden (39); Feb 1937 to Jul 1941.

61 Squadron
Audax, Anson, Blenheim I (38), Hampden (39); formed Mar 1937 to Jul 1941.
New Zealand Training Flight
Wellington I, Ia; Sep 1939 to Jan 1940.
2717 Squadron RAF Regiment, 1941.
300 (Polish) Squadron
Wellington Ic, IV, III (42); Jul 1941 to May 1942.
301 (Polish) Squadron
Wellington IC, IV; Jul 1941, disbanded Apr 1943.
305 (Polish) Squadron
Wellington II, IV, X (43); Jul 1942 to Jun 1943.
2706 Squadron RAF Regiment, 1943 to 1944.
Runways built Jun 1943 to Jan 1944.
No1 Lancaster Finishing School
Jan 1944, disbanded Nov 1944.
Night Bomber Training School
May to Dec 1944.
150 Squadron
Lancaster; Nov 1944, disbanded Nov 1945.
170 Squadron
Lancaster; Nov 1944, disbanded Nov 1945.
15 Base Sub-station
Dec 1944 to Jun 1945.
2799 Sqn
RAF Regiment, Dec 1944 to Apr 1945.
1687 Bomber Defence Training Flight
Spitfire II, VB, Hurricane II; Apr 1945, disbanded Oct 1946.
109 Squadron
Mosquito B16; Nov 1945 to Nov 1946.
139 Squadron
Mosquito B16, B25; Feb to Nov 1946.
100 Squadron
Lincoln; Oct 1946 to Mar 1950.
83 Squadron
Lincoln; Nov 1946 to Jan 1956 became **Antler Squadron**, Lincoln; formed Jan 1956, disbanded Oct 1957.
97 Squadron
Lincoln; Nov 1946 to Jan 1956 became **Arrow Squadron**, Lincoln; formed Jan 1956, disbanded Oct 1957.
12 Squadron
Lincoln; Jan to Mar 1948.
109 Squadron
Mosquito B35; Mar 1950 to Jan 1956.
139 Squadron
Mosquito B35; Apr 1950 to Jan 1956.
199 Squadron
Lincoln, Mosquito NF36, Canberra B2 (54); Apr 1952 to Oct 1957.
Bomber Command Jet Conversion Unit
Meteor, Canberra B2; Jul 1952 to Apr 1953.
Bomber Command Bombing School
det, 1955 to 1957.
Lincoln Conversion Flight
Jan 1956, disbanded Feb 1957.
Bomber Command Modification Centre
Aug 1956, disbanded Oct 1962.
76 Squadron
Canberra B6; Apr 1957 to Jul 1958.
542 Squadron
Canberra B2, B6, PR7; Apr 1957 to Aug 1958.
1321 Flight
Lincoln, Canberra B2; formed Oct 1957 to

Jan 1958.
1439 Flight
Varsity, Whirlwind HAR2; formed May 1957 to Aug 1957, Nov 1957, disbanded Nov 1957.
Rebuilt.
97 Squadron
Thor ICBM and Hemswell Complex HQ; formed Dec 1958, disbanded May 1963.
No7 School of Recruit Training 2 Wing
1964 to May 1967.
Closed 1968.
Bomber County Aviation Museum.
643 Volunteer Gliding School
Cadet; Oct 1965 to Apr 1974.

HIBALDSTOW
OS sheet 112. 976004. 1m S of village, E of B1206.
Opened May 1941.
255 Squadron
Defiant; May to Sep 1941.
253 Squadron
Hurricane IIa, IIb, IIc (42); Sep 1941 to May 1942.
1459 Flight
Boston, Havoc; Sep 1941 to Sep 1942 became **538 Sqn**, Havoc; formed Sep 1942, disbanded Jan 1943.
253 Squadron
Hurricane IIc; May to Jun 1942, Jul to Aug 1942 and Aug to Nov 1942.
532 Squadron
Havoc, Hurricane IIc; Nov 1942, disbanded Jan 1943.
Relief Landing Ground
for Kirton-in-Lindsey, May 1943 to Aug 1948.
Closed Aug 1948.

HOLBEACH
OS sheet 131. 450310. 6m E of town on coast, N of Gedney Drove End.
Opened 1928.
Bombing and Gunnery Range
(with small landing ground up to end of WW2)
Air Weapons Range
To present (2004)

HOLTON-LE-MOOR
OS sheet 112. 093970. 0.5m ESE of village by railway.
WW2 AMWD Depot. Also a W/T **Aspirin Station**, opened Oct 1940 to Jun 1941 (exact location not known)

HONINGTON
OS sheet 130. 943437. 0.5m NW of village on railway.
WW2 AMWD Depot.

HUMBERSTON
OS sheet 113. 328055. Seaward end of South Sea Lane near Humberston Fitties, now site of Humberston Residential Centre.
Opened Dec 1941.
CHL Radar Station to 1950s.
Closed late 1950s.

255 Squadron replaced its Defiants with the more potent Beaufighter IIfs in July 1941. R2402, at Hibaldstow in 1941, shows its AI-IV radar aerials underwing and on the leading edge. MAP via P H T Green

HUTTOFT
OS sheet 122. 534773.
WW2 Night Decoy for area.

IMMINGHAM DOCK
OS sheet 113. 195130. 1m E of village in docks.
Opened 1917.
8 Kite Balloon Section
RNAS 1917 to Apr 1918, became **8 Balloon Station**, disbanded 1919.
Closed 1919.
Opened 1946.
1110 MCU
1946, disbanded Feb 1958.
Closed Feb 1958.

IMMINGHAM RANGE
OS sheet 113. 235136.
Night Decoy for Immingham Docks.

INGHAM/CAMMERINGHAM
OS sheet 121. 958830. 1m E of village, W of A15.
Opened May 1942.
300 (Polish) Squadron
Wellington IV; May 1942 to Jan 1943.
199 Squadron
Wellington III, X; Feb to Jun 1943.

300 (Polish) Squadron
Wellington X; Jun 1943 to Mar 1944.
305 (Polish) Squadron
Wellington X; Jun to Sep 1943.
Relief Landing Ground for 16 (Polish) FTS Hucknall, Dec 1943 to Feb 1944.
1687 Bomber Defence Training Flight
Spitfire II, Vb, Hurricane II; Feb to Dec 1944.
1481 Target Towing and Gunnery Flight
Wellington, Martinet, Hurricane; Mar 1944, disbanded Dec 1944.
Night Bomber Tactics School
Mar to May 1944.
15 Base Sub-station
Dec 1944 to Jun 1945.
2799 Squadron RAF Regiment, Apr to Jun 1945.
Polish Technical Training School
Formed Jun 1945 became **16 Polish School of Technical Training**, formed Jul 1945, disbanded Dec 1946.
No4 Personnel Holding Unit (Polish)
Formed Nov 45, became **No1 Polish Resettlement Unit**, 1946, disbanded Feb 1948.
Polish Record Office
Formed 1945 to Feb 1948. Closed 1948.

INGOLDMELLS
OS sheet 122. 560690 approx. Exact location unknown.
Opened 1942.
CHL Radar Station, but bad location meant used for training only, closed 1945. Also a **Bombing Range** for 5 Group on sands.

KELSTERN
OS sheet 113. 262914. 1m NNE of village on minor road to Ludborough.
Opened 1916.

WW1 Emergency Landing Ground for 33 Sqn, 1916-1918.
WW2 Night Decoy for Binbrook.
Re-opened Oct 1943.
12 Base Sub-station
Mar 1943 to Mar 1945.
625 Squadron
Lancaster; Oct 1943 to Apr 1945.
170 Squadron
Lancaster; formed Oct to Oct 1944.
Closed 1945.

KILLINGHOLME
OS sheet 113. 166203. 1m NNE of East Halton on coast.
Opened Aug 1914.
RNAS Training Base
Various types, Aug 1914 to Mar 1918.
RNAS Flying Boat Patrol Base
Curtiss H-12 and Felixstowe F2a; 1916 to Apr 1918.
RAF, 320-322 Flying Boat Flights
H-12, F2a; formed May to Jul 1918.
403 Seaplane Flight
Short 184 & 320, Hamble Baby; formed May to Aug 1918.
404 Seaplane Flight
Short 184; formed May to Aug 1918.
United States Navy
Flying boats, H-12; Jul 1918 to Jan 1919.
251 Squadron
DH6; formed Jan 1919 disbanded Jun 1919; (comprised 506, 507, 510, 527 and 528 Flts).
256 Squadron
DH6; Jan 1919, disbanded Jun 1919.
229 Squadron
Short 184; Mar 1919, disbanded Dec 1919.

228 Squadron
Short 184, 320, Fairey IIIc; Jun 1919, disbanded Jun 1919.
249 Squadron
Short 184; Aug 1919, disbanded Oct 1919.
Closed 1920.

KIRMINGTON
OS sheet 112. 092095. 1m SE of village, S of A18.
Opened Mar 1942.
Relief Landing Ground for 15 (P) AFU, Oxford, from Leconfield; Mar to Oct 1942.
150 Squadron
Wellington Ic, III; Oct to Dec 1942.
142 Squadron
Wellington III; Dec 1942, disbanded Jan 1943.
166 Squadron
Wellington III, X, Lancaster; formed Jan 1943, disbanded Nov 1945.
13 Base Sub-station
Jan 1944 to Dec 1945.
153 Squadron
Lancaster; formed Oct to Oct 1944.
Closed 1946. Now Humberside Airport.

KIRTON-IN-LINDSEY/MANTON
OS sheet 112. 942015. 2m N of village, E of B1398.
Opened Dec 1916.
33 Squadron B Flight
BE2c, BE12, FE2b (17), Avro 504K (19); Dec 1916 to Jun 1919.
HQ 33 Squadron
Jun 1918 to Jun 1919.
Closed 1919.

KIRTON-IN-LINDSEY
OS sheet 112. 943965. 1M SE of village, E of B1398.
Opened May 1940.
222 Squadron
Spitfire I; May to May 1940.
65 Squadron
Spitfire I; May to Jun 1940.
253 Squadron
Hurricane I; May to Jul 1940.
222 Squadron
Spitfire I; Jun to Aug 1940.
264 Squadron
Defiant; Jul to Aug 1940, Aug to Oct 1940.
74 Squadron
Spitfire IIa; Aug to Sep 40.
307 (Polish) Squadron
Defiant; formed Sep 1940 to Nov 1940.
616 Squadron
Spitfire I, IIa (41); Sep 1940 to Feb 1941.
85 Squadron
Hurricane I; Oct to Nov 1940.
71 (Eagle) Squadron
Hurricane I; Nov 1940 to Apr 1941.
255 Squadron
Defiant; formed Nov 1940 to May 1941.
No7 Anti-Aircraft Calibration Unit det
Various types; 1940 to Jan 1941.
65 Squadron
Spitfire IIa, IIb; Feb to Sep 1941, Oct to Oct 1941.

No6 AACU det
Various types; Mar to May 1941.
452 (Australian) Squadron
Spitfire I, IIa; formed Apr 1941 to Jul 1941.
121 (Eagle) Squadron
Hurricane I, IIB; formed May to Sep 1941.
12 Group AAC Flight
Blenheim IV, Lysander; May to Nov 1941.
136 Squadron
Hurricane IIa, IIb; formed Aug to Nov 1941.
121 (Eagle) Squadron
Hurricane I, IIb, Spitfire IIa, Vb; Oct to Dec 1941.
616 Squadron
Spitfire Vb; Oct 1941 to Jan 1942.
133 (Eagle) Squadron
Spitfire IIa, Va, Vb; Dec 1941 to Jan 1942.
486 (NZ) Squadron
Hurricane IIb; formed Mar to Apr 1942.
306 (Polish) Squadron
Spitfire Vb; May to Jun 1942.
457 (Australian) Squadron
Spitfire Vb; May to Jun 1942.
303 (Polish) Squadron
Spitfire Vb; Jun to Aug 1942, Aug 1942 to Feb 1943.
1st Fighter Group, USAAF
P-38; Jun to Aug 1942.
43 Squadron
Hurricane I; Sep to Oct 1942.
169 Squadron
Mustang I; Oct to Nov 1942.
1489 Target-Towing & Gunnery Flight det
Blenheim IV, Lysander; Dec 1942 to Apr 1943.
302 (Polish) Squadron
Spitfire Vb; Feb to Apr 1943.
317 (Polish) Squadron
Spitfire Vb; Feb to Apr 1943.
53 Operational Training Unit
Spitfire, Master; May 1943, disbanded May 1945.
2733 Squadron RAF Regiment, 1943 to 1944.
7 Service Flying Training School
Harvard; Apr 1946, became **7 Flying Training School**, formed Jan to Apr 1948.
Aircrew Transit Unit
May 1948 to Sep 1949.
Central Synthetic Training Establishment
formed Jun 1948, disbanded Aug 1949, became **Link Trainer School**, formed Aug 1949-51.
Satellite of OCTU at Grantham, 1948 to 1954.
Relief Landing Ground for Flying Refresher School, Finningley, Harvard; Jun 1949 to Apr 1950.
Aircrew Educational School
1949 to 1950.
Relief Landing Ground for 101 RFS, Finningley, Harvard; Jun 1950 to Oct 1951.
22 Gliding School
Cadet; Aug 1950 to Sep 1955, became **643 VGS**, Cadet; formed Sep 1955 to Oct 1965.
No4 Initial Training School
Tiger Moth; formed May to Aug 1951.

No2 Initial Training School
Tiger Moth; Aug 1951 to Oct 1953.
No2 Grading Unit
Tiger Moth; formed Jun 1952, disbanded Mar 1953.
1 Initial Training School
Prentice, Chipmunk; formed Oct 1953 to Jul 1957.
Adult Supply Training School
Formed Jan 1959, became **7 School of Technical Training**, formed 1960 to Dec 1965.
No2 Gliding Centre
Cadet, Prefect, Sedbergh, Sep 1959 to Oct 1965.
Air Movements School
Jan to Dec 1963.
To the Army 1965.

LANGTOFT
OS sheet 130. 138109. 1m SE of village, on minor road, camp. 154130 Rotor site, on minor road to Sixscore Farm.
Opened 1941.
GCI Radar Station to 1958. Semi-sunk 1953-1958
Closed 1958

LEA MARSH
OS sheet 112. 810870. W of village on Trent.
WW2 Bombing Range for 1 Group.

LEADENHAM
OS sheet 121. 970520. 1m E of village, E of minor road to Welbourn.
Opened Sep 1916.
38 Squadron A Flight
BE12, BE2e, Fe2b, FE2d (17); Sep 1916 to May 1918.
90 Squadron A Flight
Fe2b, Avro 504K; May 1918, disbanded Jun 1919.
Closed 1919.

LEGBOURNE
OS sheet 122. 367843. Opposite old village school, later to Gayton Top.
Opened Mar 1941 as **Receiver Station** for Louth to 1943 (?)
Closed 1943 (?).

LEVERTON
OS sheet 131. 450480. 2m E of village on coast.
WW2 Bombing Range for 1 Group.

LINCOLN LONGDALES ROAD
OS sheet 121. 980730. N of city centre.
No6 (Lincoln) Store Park, RFC/RAF in WW1.

LINCOLN WEST COMMON
OS sheet 121. 960720. 1m W of city, N of A57.
Opened 1916 as airfield for Ruston Proctor.
No4 Aircraft Acceptance Park
RFC, formed 17, became **4 (Lincoln) AAP** 1918 to 1919.
Closed 1919.

LONDONTHORPE
OS sheet 130. 962376. E of B6403 near Londonthorpe turn.
Transmitting Station for Grantham St Vincent's, WW2.

LOUTH
See Legbourne,
Gayton Top and South Elkington.

LUDBOROUGH
OS sheet 113. 290942. E of A16.
WW2 ELG for heavy bombers. Little if any use.
284960. **WW2 Night Decoy** for Binbrook.

LUDFORD MAGNA
OS sheet 113. 202871. 0.5m S of village, E of B1225.
Opened Jun 1943.
101 Squadron
Lancaster; Jun 1943 to Oct 1945.
2702 Squadron RAF Regiment, 1943 to 1944.
14 Base
Formed Dec 1943, disbanded Oct 1945. FIDO equipped.
61 Maintenance Unit Sub-site
Dec 1945 to 1950.
90 Maintenance Unit Sub-site
May 1946 to Dec 1950.
93 Maintenance Unit Sub-site
Dec 1950 to Sep 1952.
92 Maintenance Unit Sub-site
Sep 1952 to Jun 1956.
93 Maintenance Unit Sub-site
Jun 1956 to Oct 1958.
104 Squadron
Thor ICBM; formed Jul 1959, disbanded May 1963 (Hemswell complex).
Closed 1963.

MABLETHORPE
OS sheet 122. 477845.
WW2 Night decoy for Manby.

MANBY
OS sheet 122. 383862. W of village, S of B1200.
Opened Aug 1938.
No1 Air Armament School
Various types; Aug 1938, became **Empire AAS**, formed Apr 1944, became **RAF Flying College**, formed Jun 1949, became **RAF College of Air Warfare**, formed Jul 1962, disbanded Apr 1974.
2782 Squadron RAF Regiment, 1941.
Handling Flight
All new types; formed Jul 1949 to Apr 1954.
HQ 25 Group and Comms Flight
Mar 1951 to Jan 1961.
School of Refresher Flying
Jet Provost T3; formed Jul 1962 to Dec 1973.
Closed 1974.

MANTON
See Kirton-in-Lindsey.

MANTON COMMON
OS sheet 112. 929035.
WW2 Bombing Range.

MARKET DEEPING
OS sheet 130. 170110. 1.5m ESE of town, E of B1525.
WW1 ELG for 38 & 51 Squadrons.

MARKET STAINTON
OS sheet 122. 228802. Centre of village.
Opened Jun 1943.
233 Maintenance Unit
Formed Jun 1943, disbanded Sep 1948.
Closed 1948.

MARSHCHAPEL
OS sheet 113. 403002.
WW2 Night Decoy for Donna Nook
Closed Feb 1962.

MERE
OS sheet 121. 014640. 1m E of Waddington airfield, W of minor road to Scopwick.
No2 Direction Finding Station WW2 and after.
'Y' Service outstation by 1947, **3 Direction Finding Station** by 1951, became **661 SU** Nov 1951, became part of **399 SU** Digby Oct 1957 until Feb 1962.

METHERINGHAM
OS sheet 121. 100600. 2.5m E of village, E of B1189.
Opened Oct 1943.
106 Squadron
Lancaster; Nov 1943, disbanded Feb 1946.
54 Base Sub-station
Jan 1944 to Dec 1945.
1690 Bomber Defence Training Flight
Spitfire II, Hurricane; Sep 1944 to Jun 1945. FIDO equipped.
467 (Australian) Squadron
Lancaster; Jun 1945, disbanded Sep 1945.
189 Squadron
Lancaster; Oct 1945, disbanded Nov 1945.
93 Maintenance Unit Sub-site
Dec 1948 to Dec 1950.
Closed 1951.
Metheringham Airfield Visitor Centre.

MOORBY
OS sheet 122. 300655. 0.5m N of village.
WW1 **ELG** for 38 and 90 Squadrons.

MORTON HALL
OS sheet 121. 879642. 0.5m W of village on minor road to Eagle. Now HMP Morton Hall.
Opened 1942 (?)
Aircrew Commando School
Mar 1942 to Nov 1943.
HQ 51 Base
Formed Mar to Oct 1943.
No5 Group HQ
Nov 1943, disbanded Dec 1945.
HQ 21 Group
1947 to 1955.
Closed 1955 (?)

NETTLETON
OS sheet 113. 120001. Exact location unknown.

GEE Station
from Feb 1944 to Jul 1945.

NEW HOLLAND
OS sheet 112. 078237. 0.5m W of village.
WW1 Emergency Landing Ground for 33 Sqn.

NOCTON HALL
OS sheet 121. 065640. In village.
WW2 US Army hospital
Casualties flown in via Metheringham.
RAF took over Nov 1947.
RAF Hospital to Mar 1983.
USAF Emergency Hospital
Mar 1983 to 1995.
Closed 1996.

NORMANBY-BY-SPITAL
OS sheet 121. 988882. N of minor rd from A15 to village.
Opened June 1940. **Transmitting Station** for Hemswell, Scampton and Kirton-in-Lindsey.
Bomber Command/Strike Command No 1 Gp Transmitting Station, 1950s to 1990(?).

NORTH COATES
OS sheet 113. 366018. 1.5m NE of village, on coast.
Opened 1916.
Emergency Landing Ground for 33 Sqn
1916 to Sep 1918.
248 Squadron 404 Flight
DH6; Sep 1918 to Mar 1919.
Closed 1919.
Re-opened 1927.
Summer only **Armament Training Camp** to Jan 1932.
No2 Armament Training Camp
Hart, Fairey IIIf, Gordon; formed Jan 1932, became **Air Observer's School**, Wallace, Anson I; formed Nov 1936, became **2 Air Armament School**, formed Nov 1937, became **1 Air Observer's School**, Wallace, Henley, Battle, formed Mar 1938 to Sep 1939.
No2 Recruit Training Pool 1939-1940
No1 Ground Gunner's School
Wallace, Hart; formed Nov 1939 to Jul 1940.
Digby Forward Base 1939 to 1940.
235 Squadron
Blenheim IVf; Feb to Apr 1940.
236 Squadron
Blenheim If; Feb to Apr 1940.
248 Squadron
Blenheim If, IVf; Feb to Apr 1940.
22 Squadron
Beaufort; Apr 1940 to Jun 1941.
42 Squadron det
Beaufort; Apr to Jun 1940.
812 Squadron
FAA, Swordfish; May to May 1940, May to Jun 1940, Jun to Aug 1940, Sep to Oct 1940, Oct to Nov 1940.
431 Flight
Maryland; formed Aug to Sep 1940.
No2 Mobile Torpedo Servicing Unit
Formed Dec 1940 to Sep 1942.

Westland Wallace I target towers of the Air Observer's School, North Coates, formate over Donna Nook sands, c1936. P H T Green

407 (Canadian) Squadron
Hudson III, IV; Jul 1941 to Feb 1942.
816 Squadron
FAA, Swordfish; Mar to Jul 1941.
No6 Anti-Aircraft Co-operation Unit det
Lysander; May 1941 to Feb 1942.
278 Squadron det
Lysander, Walrus; 1941 to 1942.
No7 AACU det
Mar to Mar 1942.
59 Squadron
Hudson V, VI; Jan to Aug 1942.
53 Squadron
Hudson V; Feb to May 1942.
415 (Canadian) Squadron
Hampden TB; Jun to Aug 1942.
236 Squadron
Beaufighter Ic, VIc, X (43); Sep 1942, disbanded May 1945.
143 Squadron
Beaufighter Ic, IIf, VIc, XI (43); Aug 1942 to Aug 1943.

254 Squadron
Beaufighter VIf, X (43), Mosquito XVIII (45); Nov 1942 to Jun 45.
2705 & 2802 Sqns RAF Regiment, 1942 to 1943.
No7 AACU det
May to May 1943.
2790, 2831 & 2899 Sqns RAF Regiment, 1943.
143 Squadron
Beaufighter X, XI; Feb to May 44, plus Mosquito II; Sep to Oct 1944.
2778 & 2854 Squadrons RAF Regiment, 1944.
61 Maintenance Unit Sub-site
Oct 1945 to May 1950.
No1 Initial Training School
Formed May to Dec 1945.
School of Explosive Handling
May to Oct 1948, became **15 School of Technical Training**, formed Oct 1948, disbanded Sep 1959.
Bomb Disposal School
Aug to Oct 1948, became **15 SoTT**.
54 Maintenance Unit
Aug 1953 to july 1956
Closed 1955.
Re-opened 1958.

264 Squadron
Bloodhound SAM1; formed Dec 1958, disbanded Nov 1962.
148 (SAM) Wing
Formed May 1960, disbanded May 1964.
25 Squadron
Bloodhound SAM2; formed Oct 1963 to Jan 1971.
SAM Operational Training School
Formed Oct 1963 to 1964.
17 Joint Services Trials Unit
Bloodhound SAM2; formed Oct 1963, disbanded Nov 1966.
Closed Feb 1971.
Re-opened 1976
85 Squadron B Flight
Bloodhound SAM2; Jan 1976, disbanded Apr 1990.
Closed Nov 1990. Civil airfield.

NORTH KILLINGHOLME
OS sheet 113. 124167. W of village.
Opened Nov 1943.
550 Squadron
Lancaster; Nov 1943, disbanded Oct 1945.
13 Base Sub-station
Jan 1944 to Dec 1945.

35 Maintenance Unit Sub-site
Jan 1946 to Sep 1950.
93 Maintenance Unit Sub-site
Dec 1948 to Dec 1950.
Closed 1951.

NORTH WITHAM
OS sheet 130. 943220. 1m ENE of village, E of
A1.
Opened Dec 1943.
1st Tactical Air Depot USAAF
Dec 1943 to 1945. Station 479.
**9th Troop Carrier Command Pathfinder
   Group School**
C-47, Mar 1944 to Sep 1945.
RAF Regiment Sub-depot
1945 to Aug 1946.
259 Maintenance Unit
Formed Jul to Aug 1945.
259 Maintenance Unit Sub-site
Aug 1945 to Aug 1948.
93 Maintenance Unit Sub-site
Dec 1950 to Apr 1956.
Closed 1956.

NORTON DISNEY
OS sheet 121. 868643. 3m NW of village at
   railway station.
Opened as Swinderby Sep 1939.
No3 Air Ammunition Park
Formed Sep 1939, became **93 MU**, formed
   Oct 1939 to Oct 1948.
Name changed 1940.
93 Maintenance Unit Sub-site
Dec 1948 to Jun 1956.
Closed 1956.

ORBY
OS sheet 122. 526679. 1.5m E of village on
   minor road to Addlethorpe. Now site of
   Skegness Raceway.
Opened Mar 1941.
GCI Radar Station
Mar 1941 to Aug 1945.
Closed 1945.

PICKWORTH
OS sheet 130. 002122.
WW2 Night Decoy for Woolfox Lodge.

POTTERHANWORTH
OS sheet 121. 079667.
WW2 Night Decoy for Waddington.

RAND
OS sheet 121. 133796.
WW2 Night decoy for Scampton.

RAUCEBY
OS sheet 130. 040440. 1m SE of South
   Rauceby, S of A153.
Taken over by RAF 1940.
RAF Hospital 1940 to 1947.
Closed 1947.
NHS hospital, now closed.

RISBY
OS sheet 112. 929158.
Night Decoy for Scunthorpe.

ROMAN HOLE
OS sheet 113. 154961. 0.5m NW of
   Thoresway.
WW2 Gunnery Range.

RUSKINGTON
OS sheet 121. 111514
WW2 Night Decoy for Digby.

SANDTOFT
OS sheet 112. 752072. E of village, S of M180.
Opened Feb 1944.
11 Base Sub-station
Feb to Nov 1944.
1667 Heavy Conversion Unit
Halifax V, Lancaster; formed Feb 1944, dis-
   banded Nov 1945.
71 Base Sub-station
Nov 1944 to Oct 1945.
35 Maintenance Unit Sub-site
Dec 1945 to Feb 1946.
61 Maintenance Unit Sub-site
Feb 1946 to May 1947.
Closed 1947. Now a civil airfield.

SCAMPTON/BRATTLEBY (WW1)
OS sheet 121. 957789. E of village, W of A15.
Opened Oct 1916.
33 Squadron A Flight
BE12, BE12a (17), BE2e (17), FE2b, 2d (17);
   Oct 1916 to Jun 1919.
49 Training Squadron
Shorthorn, Longhorn; Oct to Nov 1916.
37 Training Squadron
Avro 504, FK3, DH6 (17); Nov 1916 to Sep
   1917.
11 Training Squadron
Avro 504, JN4, BE12, Pup, Camel (18), DH4
   (18); Sep 1917, disbanded Jul 1918.
60 Training Squadron
Avro 504, Pup, 1½ Strutter, Camel (18), BE2e
   (18); Apr 1917 to Jul 1918.
81 Squadron
Various types; Jan 1917 to Apr 1918.
34 Training Depot Station
Pup, Dolphin, Camel, Avro 504; formed Jul
   1918, disbanded Mar 1919.
Closed 1920.
Re-opened Aug 1936.
9 Squadron
Heyford III; Oct 1936 to Mar 1938.
214 Squadron
Virginia X, Harrow (37); Oct 1936 to Apr
   1937.
148 Squadron
Audax, Wellesley; formed Jun 1937 to Mar
   1938.
49 Squadron
Hind, Hampden, Manchester (42), Lancaster (42); Mar 1938 to Jan 1943.
83 Squadron
Hind, Hampden, Manchester (41), Lancaster (42); Mar 1938 to Aug 1942.
Recruit Training Depot
1938 to 1939.
98 Squadron
Battle; Mar to Mar 1940.
2724 Squadron RAF Regiment, 1941.

No5 Group Training Flight
Various types; Aug to Oct 1941.
1518 Beam Approach Training Flight
Oxford; formed Nov 1941 to Jun 1943.
57 Squadron
Lancaster; Sep 1942 to Aug 1943.
467 (Australian) Squadron
Lancaster; formed Nov to Nov 1942.
83 Conversion Flight
Manchester, Lancaster; formed Apr to Aug
   1942.
49 Conversion Flight
Manchester, Lancaster; formed May 1942,
   disbanded Nov 1942.
52 Base
Formed May 1942, disbanded Oct 1943.
Air Bomber Training Flight, (5 Group)
Formed Jun to Aug 1942.
617 Squadron
Lancaster; formed May to Aug 1943.
2749 Squadron RAF Regiment, 1943.
Runway building Aug 1943 to Oct 1944.
Re-opened Oct 1944.
153 Squadron
Lancaster; Oct 1944, disbanded Sep 1945.
15 Base
Formed Oct 1944, disbanded Oct 1945.
1690 Bomber Defence Training Flight
Spitfire II, Hurricane II; Jul to Sep 1944.
1687 Bomber Defence Training Flight
Spitfire V, Hurricane II; Dec 1944 to Apr 1945.
625 Squadron
Lancaster; Apr 1945, disbanded Oct 1945.
57 Squadron
Lancaster, Lincoln; Dec 1945 to May 1946.
100 Squadron
Lancaster; Dec 1945 to May 1946.
Lincoln Service Trials Flight
Formed Nov 1945, disbanded May 1946.
No1 Group Major Servicing Unit
May 1946, disbanded Jun 1948.
Bomber Command Instructor's School
Lancaster, Lincoln; Jan 1947, became **BC
   Instrument Rating and Examination Flt**,
   Lincoln; formed Jun 1948, disbanded Mar
   1952.
28th Bomber Wing USAF
B-29; Jul to Oct 1948.
301st Bomber Wing USAF
B-29; Oct 1948 to Feb 1949.
230 Operational Conversion Unit
Lincoln; Feb 1949, disbanded Oct 1952.
Bomber Command Bombing School
Lincoln; formed Oct to Nov 1952.
10 Squadron
Canberra B2; formed Jan 1953 to May 1955.
27 Squadron
Canberra B2; formed Jun 1953 to May 1955.
18 Squadron
Canberra B2; formed Aug 1953 to May 1955.
21 Squadron
Canberra B2; formed Sep 1953 to Jun 1955.
Closed for rebuilding.
Re-opened 1958.
617 Squadron
Vulcan B1, B2 (61); formed May 1958, dis-
   banded Dec 1981.

83 Squadron
Vulcan B2; formed Oct 1960, disbanded Aug 1969.
27 Squadron
Vulcan B2; formed Apr 1961, disbanded Mar 1972.
No4 Joint Services Trials Unit
Blue Steel; Oct 61, became **18 JSTU**, formed Dec 1961, disbanded Aug 1964.
230 Operational Conversion Unit
Vulcan B1, B2, Hastings T5; Dec 1969, disbanded Aug 1981.
Strike Command Avionics Development and Servicing Unit
Formed Dec 1971 to ?
Strike Command Bombing School
Sep 1972, disbanded Jul 1974.
27 Squadron
Vulcan B2; formed Nov 1973, disbanded Mar 1982.

35 Squadron
Vulcan B2; Jan 1975, disbanded Mar 1982.
2503 Squadron
RAuxAF Reg., formed Jul 1979 to Feb 1985.
643 Volunteer Gliding School
Viking; Mar 1982 to Jun 1991.
RAF Aerobatic Team (Red Arrows)
Hawk T1; Mar 1983 to Feb 1996.
Central Flying School
Jet Provost T3, T5, Bulldog T1, Tucano T1 (88); Sep 1984 to May 1995.
Trade Management Training School
Exact date not known to 1996.
Joint Arms Control Implementation Group
Formed Jul 1990 to May 1996.
27 Squadron
RAF Regiment, Rapier; ? to 1996. Closed Jun 1996 except as training airfield for Red Arrows at Cranwell.
Re-opened 2000.
RAF Aerobatic Team
Hawk T1, Dec 2000 to present, (2004). Still open.
Dambusters Museum.

SCOPWICK See Digby.

SIBSEY
OS sheet 122. 367528.
WW2 Night Decoy for Coningsby & East Kirkby.

SKEGNESS
OS sheet 122. 556643. S of Burgh road.
Opened Aug 1914.

RNAS Mobile Squadron
Various types; Aug to Aug 1914.
Closed Aug 1914.

SKEGNESS
OS sheet 122. 565630.
Various billets in town centre.
Opened Feb 1941.
11 Recruit's Centre
Feb 1941 to Oct 1944.
Closed Oct 1944.

SKELLINGTHORPE
OS sheet 121. 925688. 1.5m SE of village, E of A46. Now site of Birchwood estate.
Opened Nov 1941.
50 Squadron
Hampden, Manchester (42), Lancaster (42); Nov 1941 to Jun 1942.
Relief Landing Ground for 14 PAFU, Ossington, Oxford; Apr 1942.
50 Conversion Flight
Manchester, Lancaster; formed May to Jun 1942.

45 Training Squadron
Shorthorn, FB5, FB9, DH5; Nov 1916, disbanded Jul 1918.
HQ 23 Training Wing
Formed Nov 1916, disbanded May 1919.
69 (Australian) Squadron
Various types, RE8 (17); formed Dec 1916 to Aug 1917.
39 Training Squadron
BE2, Avro 504, RE8; Sep 1917, disbanded Jul 1918.
61 Training Squadron
DH4, DH6; Sep 1917, disbanded Jul 1918.
96 Squadron
Various types; formed Oct to Oct 1917.
109 Squadron
Various types; formed Nov to Nov 1917.
43rd Aero Squadron US Army
DH4; 1918 to Oct 1918.
46 Training Depot Station
Camel, Dolphin, Avro 504, Pup; formed Jul 1918, disbanded Jul 1919.
57 Squadron
Cadre ; Aug 1919, disbanded Dec 1919.
25 Squadron
Cadre; Sep to Dec 1919.
46 Training Squadron
Avro 504, Camel; formed Jul 1919, disbanded Apr 1920.
Closed 1920.

SOUTH ELKINGTON
OS sheet 113. 312870. 1m ESE of village, N of A157.
Opened Mar 1941.
W/T transmitter for Louth radio station.
Closed 1945.

SOUTH FERRIBY
OS sheet 112. 000203.
WW2 Night Decoy for Elsham Wolds.

SOUTH WITHAM
OS sheet 130. 955185. 1.25m ESE of village at Stocken Hall.
Opened Mar 1942.
100 Maintenance Unit
Formed Mar 1942, disbanded Dec 1948.
Closed 1949.

SPILSBY
OS sheet 122. 450645. 2m E of town, N of B1195.
Opened Oct 1943.
207 Squadron
Lancaster, Oct 1943 to Oct 1945.

Relief Landing Ground for Swinderby, 1942.
97 Conversion Flight
Manchester, Lancaster; Sep to Oct 1942.
50 Squadron
Lancaster; Oct 1942 to Jun 1945.
1485 Bombing & Gunnery Flight
Wellington, Martinet; Aug to Nov 1943.
1506 Beam Approach Training Flight
Oxford; Aug 1943, disbanded Oct 1943.
53 Base Sub-station
Nov 1943 to Nov 1945.
61 Squadron
Lancaster; Nov 1943 to Jan 1944. Apr 1944 to Jun 1945.
619 Squadron
Lancaster; Jun 1945, disbanded Jul 1945.
463 (Australian) Squadron
Lancaster; Jul 1945, disbanded Sep 1945.
58 Maintenance Unit
Nov 1945 to Apr 1947.
92 Maintenance Sub-site
1952 to Dec 1955.
Closed 1956.

SKENDLEBY
OS sheet 122. 441708. 0.5m NE of village, E of A1028.
Opened 1941.
CHL Radar Station
1941 to 1951.
Rotor Radar Station
1951 to 1957, underground 1953
Closed 1957.
Sub-Regional HQ
Home Office, 1960s to 1992.
Closed 1992.

SKIDBROOKE
OS sheet 113. 440920. Exact location unknown.
Opened Feb 1944.
USAAF Fixer Radio Station
Feb 1944 to May 1945.
Closed May 1945.

SOUTH CARLTON
OS sheet 121. 965762. 1m E of village, W of A15.
Opened Nov 1916.

55 Base Sub-station
Apr 1944 to Nov 1945.
2751 Squadron RAF Regiment, 1944.
44 Squadron
Lancaster; Sep 1944 to Jul 1945.
75 (NZ) Squadron
Lancaster; Jul 1945, disbanded Oct 1945.
Armament Practice Station
Martinet; Dec 45, disbanded Aug 1946.
129 Squadron
Spitfire IXe; Jan to Feb 1946.
264 Squadron
Mosquito NF30; Jan to Feb 1946.
65 Squadron
Spitfire XVI; Feb to Mar 1946.
29 Squadron
Mosquito NF30; Feb to Mar 1946.
222 Squadron
Meteor F3; Mar to Apr 1946.
219 Squadron
Mosquito NF30; Mar to Apr 1946.
Highball Trails Flight
Mosquito, Sea Mosquito TR33; Apr to Jun 1946.
Closed 1946.
Re-opened 1955.
7536th Materials Squadron
USAF det, Jul 1955 to Nov 1958.
Closed 1958.

SPITALGATE/SPITTLEGATE See Grantham.

STENIGOT
OS sheet 122. 257825. 1m NE of village, S of minor road to Withcall.
Opened 1938/39.
CH Radar Station to 1952.

GEE Station Jun 1941 to Mar 1970.
NATO Forward Scatter Site
? to 1990s.
Mast training for Aerial Erectors School, 1959 to present (2004).

STRUBBY
OS sheet 122. 440810. S of village, S of A157.
Opened Apr 1944.
280 Squadron
Warwick ASR1; May to Sep 1944.
144 Squadron
Beaufighter X; Jul to Sep 1944.
404 (Canadian) Squadron
Beaufighter X; Jul to Sep 1944.
Relief Landing Ground for Manby.
55 Base Sub-station
Sep 1944 to Nov 1945.
619 Squadron
Lancaster; Sep 1944 to Jul 1945.
2735 Squadron RAF Regiment, 1944 to 1945.
227 Squadron
Lancaster; Apr to Jun 1945.
381 MU, 382 MU, 383 MU and **384 MU** for Tiger Force, all formed Jul to Sep 1945.
35 Maintenance Unit Sub-site
Nov 1945 to Sep 1950.
Relief Landing Ground for Manby, Jun 1949 to Sep 1972.
Closed 1972.

STURGATE
OS sheet 121. 873873. S of Heapham village, E of minor road to Springthorpe.
Opened Apr 1944.

Relief Landing Ground for No1 Lancaster Finishing School Hemswell, Apr to Nov 1944.
Night Bomber Training School
May to Dec 1944.
1520 Beam Approach Training Flight
Oxford; Sep 1944, disbanded May 1945.
No1 Aircrew School
Nov 1944 to May 1945.
71 Base Sub-station
Dec 1944 to Oct 1945.
FIDO equipped.
50 Squadron
Lancaster; Jun 1945 to Jan 1946.
61 Squadron
Lancaster; Jun 1945 to Jan 1946.
Care & Maintenance.
3928th Air Base Group USAF
Jun 1953 to Aug 1959.
7513th Air Base Squadron det
1959 to 1964.
Closed 1964.
Now civil airfield.

SUTTON BRIDGE
OS sheet 131. 476194. SE of town across river, S of A17.
Opened 1926 as **Armament Practice Camp,** summer only, to 1932.
No3 Armament Training Camp
Fairey IIIf, Gordon, Hart (33), Wallace (33), Audax (33); formed Jan 1932, became **3 Armament Training Station,** Gordon, Wallace, Henley; formed Apr 1938, disbanded Sep 1939.
64 Squadron
Blenheim If; Aug to Aug 1939.

RAF Sutton Bridge, home of 3 Armament Training Camp, c1934. Hawker Demon fighters of an AuxAF squadron are at top and bottom, Bulldogs are by the large hangar, two Wallace target towers are on the concrete apron, and two Avro 504Ns are close to the hangars. The River Nene runs alongside, with the village by the swingbridge – under which, it is reputed, 'Batchy' Atcherley flew his Gloster Gamecock in July 1930. J A Richardson

264 Squadron
Defiant; Oct to Dec 1939.
266 Squadron
Battle, Spitfire I (40); formed Oct 1939 to Mar 1940.
254 Squadron
Blenheim If; Dec 1939 to Jan 1940.
Target Towing Flight
Wallace; formed Jan 1940, disbanded Apr 1940.
No6 Operational Training Unit
Gladiator, Hurricane I; formed Mar 1940, became **56 OTU**, Hurricane I, Master, Lysander, Battle; formed Nov 1940 to Mar 1942.
12 Group Target Towing Flight
Lysander; Oct 1941 to Apr 1942.

2717 Squadron, RAF Regiment, 1942.
Central Gunnery School
Various types; Apr 1942 to Feb 1944.
2750 & 2884 Squadrons RAF Regiment, 1943.
Relief Landing Ground for 16 (Polish) FTS, Hucknall, Oxford, Harvard; Feb to May 1944.
Satellite of 7 (Pilots) Advanced Flying Unit, Peterborough, Oxford, Harvard; May 1944 to Apr 1946.
Care & Maintenance.
58 Maintenance Unit
Jul 1954, disbanded Nov 1957.
Closed 1957.

SWAYFIELD
OS sheet 130. 995225. N of village.
WW2 RAF Regiment Battle Training Area. 979218. **WW2 Night Decoy** for Cottesmore.

SWINDERBY BOMB DUMP
See Norton Disney.

SWINDERBY
OS sheet 121. 873615. 1m E of village, E of A46.
Opened Jul 1940.
300 (Polish) Squadron
Battle, Wellington Ic; Aug 1940 to Jul 1941.

301 (Polish) Squadron
Battle, Wellington Ic; Aug 1940 to Jul 1941.
2726 Squadron RAF Regiment, 1941.
455 (Australian) Squadron
Hampden; formed Jun 1941 to Feb 1942.
50 Squadron
Hampden; Jul to Nov 1941.
1654 Heavy Conversion Unit
Manchester and Lancaster; formed May to Jun 1942.
50 Squadron
Lancaster; Jun to Oct 1942.
50 Conversion Flight
Manchester, Lancaster; Jun to Aug 1942.
61 Conversion Flight
Manchester, Lancaster; Aug 1942, disbanded Oct 1942.
207 Conversion Flight
Lancaster; Aug 1942, disbanded Oct 1942.
97 Conversion Flight
Manchester, Lancaster; Oct 1942, disbanded Oct 1942.
106 Conversion Flight
Manchester, Lancaster; Oct 1942, disbanded Oct 1942.
1660 Heavy Conversion Unit
Manchester, Lancaster, Halifax, Stirling I, III (43); formed Oct 1942, disbanded Nov 1946.

51 Base
Oct 1943, disbanded Nov 1944.
5 Group Communications Flt
Various types; Nov 1943, disbanded Dec 1945.
75 Base
Formed Nov 1944, disbanded Oct 1945.
13 Aircraft Modification Unit
formed Sep 1945, disbanded Aug 1946.
17 Operational Training Unit
Wellington III, X; formed Oct 1946, became **201 Advanced Flying School**, Wellington T10, Varsity T1 (50), formed Mar 1947, became **11 Flying Training School**, Varsity T1; formed Jun 1954, disbanded Jun 1955.
21 Group Comms Flight
Various types; May 1947, disbanded Mar 1955.
204 Advanced Flying School
Mosquito T3, FB6; Jun 1950 to Feb 1952.
8 Flying Training School
Vampire FB(T)5, T11; Aug 1955, disbanded Mar 1964.
No7 School of Recruit Training
Jan 1964, became **The School of Recruit Training**, formed Jul 1970 to 1993.
Flying Selection Squadron
Chipmunk; formed Jul 1979, became **Elementary Flying Training Squadron**, Chipmunk; formed Jun 1987, disbanded Apr 1993.
Closed Jul 1993.

SWINSTEAD
OS sheet 130. 013220. S of village, W of B1176.
WW1 ELG for 38/90 Sqns, 1916 to 1918.
019236. **WW2 Night Decoy** for Woolfox Lodge.

TATTERSHALL THORPE/TUMBY
OS sheet 122. 226591. 0.5m E of village on minor road to Kirkby on Bain.
WW2 Radio Station; Radar Bombing Unit 1966 to 1981
RAF Police Dog Kennels for Coningsby, 1981 to present (2004).

THEDDLETHORPE
OS sheet 113. 469905. 1m N of village on coast.
Opened 1935.
Bombing and Gunnery Range
With small landing ground (to 1945).
Closed Dec 1973.

TOFT GRANGE
OS sheet 121. 033869.
WW2 Day and Night Decoy for Hemswell.

TUMBY See Tattershall Thorpe.

TWIGMOOR
OS sheet 112. 921058.
WW2 Night Decoy for Scunthorpe.

A group of trainee pilots and navigators pose in front of a 204 Advanced Flying School Mosquito T3, at Swinderby c1950. Ted Hooton

TYDD ST MARY
OS Sheet 131. 460192. 1m E of village.
Opened Aug 1916.
Emergency Landing Ground for 51 Sqn, BE2c, BE12, FE2b, Aug 1916 to Aug 1917.
51 Squadron B Flight
Martinsyde G100, BE12b (18) Camel (18); Aug 1917 to May 1919.
Closed May 1919.

WADDINGTON
OS sheet 121. 982630. E of village, W of A15.
Opened Nov 1916.
47 Training Squadron
Shorthorn, RE8 (17), FK3 (17), DH6 (17); Nov 1916, disbanded Jul 1918.
48 Training Squadron
Grahame White, Shorthorn (17), DH6 (17); Nov 16, disbanded Jul 18.
82 Squadron
FK8; formed Mar to Jul 1917.
51 Training Squadron
BE2c, DH6; May 1917 to Oct 1918.
HQ 27 Training Wing
Formed May 1917, disbanded Apr 1919.

105 Squadron
Various types; formed Sep to Oct 1917.
44 Training Squadron
Avro 504, DH4; formed Nov 1917, disbanded Mar 1919.
75 Training Squadron
DH4, DH6, BE2e; formed Nov to Dec 1917.
97 Squadron
Various types; formed Dec 1917 to Jan 1918.
117 Squadron
Various types; formed Jan to Apr 1918.
123 Squadron
Various types; formed Feb to Mar 1918.
48 Training Depot Station
Avro 504k, RE8; formed Jul 1918, disbanded Mar 1919.
48 Training Squadron
Avro 504K; formed Mar 1919, disbanded Nov 1919.
23 Squadron
Cadre; Mar 1919, disbanded Dec 1919.
203 Squadron
Cadre; Mar to Dec 1919.
204 Squadron
Cadre; Feb 1919, disbanded Dec 1919.
Closed 1920.
Re-opened 1926.

503 Squadron
Fawn, Hyderabad (29), Hinaidi (33), Wallace (35), Hart (36), Hind (38); formed Oct 1926, disbanded Nov 1938.
No1 Aircraft Storage Unit
Feb 35, became **'H' Maintenance Unit**, formed Oct 1938 to Mar 1939.
110 Squadron
Hind, Blenheim I (38); formed May 1937 to May 1938.
50 Squadron
Hind, Hampden (38), formed May 1937 to Jul 1940.
44 Squadron
Hind, Blenheim I, Anson I (39), Hampden (39), Lancaster (41); formed Jun 1937 to May 1943.
88 Squadron
Hind; formed Jun to Jul 1937.
3 Group Practice Flight
Tutor; formed Jun to Oct 1937.
'F' Temporary Maintenance Unit
Apr 1939 to December 1942.
No3 Group Target Towing Flight
Lysander; Jan to Feb 1940.
142 Squadron
Battle; Jun to Jul 1940.

A Fairey Fawn II bomber of 503 Squadron attracts the attention of local children after it crashed at Metheringham, near Sleaford, in March 1929. Via P H T Green

207 Squadron
Manchester, Hampden (41), Manchester (41); formed Nov 1940 to Nov 1941.
DB7 Flight
Boston; formed Dec 1940, disbanded Feb 1941.
97 Squadron
Manchester; formed Feb to Mar 1941.
6 Beam Approach Training Flight
Blenheim, Anson, Hampden; formed Jan 1941, became **1506 BATF**, Oxford; formed Oct 1941 to Feb 1943.
2729 Squadron RAF Regiment, 1941.
420 (Canadian) Squadron
Hampden; formed Dec 1941 to Aug 1942.
44 Conversion Flight
Manchester, Lancaster; formed Jan 1942, disbanded Nov 1942.

420 Conversion Flight
Manchester; formed May 1942, disbanded Jun 1942.

9 Conversion Flight
Manchester, Lancaster; formed Aug 1942, disbanded Nov 1942.

9 Squadron
Lancaster; Aug 1942 to Apr 1943.

2890 Squadron
RAF Regiment, formed Oct 1942 to ?

1661 Heavy Conversion Unit
Manchester, Lancaster; formed Nov 1942 to Jan 1943.
Runway building Jan to Nov 1943.

2956 Squadron RAF Regiment, 1943.
Re-opened Nov 43.

53 Base
Formed Nov 1943, disbanded Nov 1945.

463 (Australian) Squadron
Lancaster; formed Nov 1943 to Jul 1945.

467 (Australian) Squadron
Lancaster; Nov 1943 to Jun 1945.

617 Squadron
Lancaster; Jun 1945 to Jan 1946.

9 Squadron
Lancaster; Jul 1945 to Jan 1946.

50 Squadron
Lancaster, Lincoln; Jan 1946, disbanded Jan 1951.

61 Squadron
Lancaster, Lincoln; Jan 1946 to Aug 1953.

12 Squadron
Lancaster, Lincoln; Jul to Sep 1946.

57 Squadron
Lincoln; Oct 1946 to Apr 1951, Jun 1951 to Apr 1952.

307th Bomber Wing USAF
B-29; Jul to Oct 1948.

301st Bomber Wing USAF
B-29; Oct 1948 to Feb 1949.

374th Reconnaissance Squadron USAF
B-29; Dec 1948 to Jan 1949.

100 Squadron
Lincoln; Mar 1950 to Mar 1953.

3914th Air Base Squadron USAF
C-47; May 1951 to 1953.

49 Squadron
Lincoln; Jun 1952 to Aug 1953.

Lincoln Conversion Flight
Formed 1953 to Aug 1953.
Rebuilding. Re-opened May 1955.

27 Squadron
Canberra B2; May 1955, disbanded Dec 1957.

21 Squadron
Canberra B2; Jun 1955, disbanded Jun 1957.

230 Operational Conversion Unit
Vulcan B1; formed May 1956 to Jun 1961.

83 Squadron
Vulcan B1; formed May 1957 to Oct 1960.

44 Squadron
Vulcan B1, B2 (66); formed Aug 1960, disbanded Dec 1982.

101 Squadron
Vulcan B1, B2 (67); Jun 1961, disbanded Aug 1982.

50 Squadron
Vulcan B1, B2 (66), B2K (82); Aug 1961, disbanded Mar 1984.

9 Squadron
Vulcan B2; Jan 1975, disbanded May 1982.

Vulcan Display Flight
Formed Apr 1984, disbanded Sep 1994.

Nimrod AEW Joint Trials Unit
Nimrod AEW3; formed Dec 1984, disbanded Apr 1987.

2503 (RAuxAF Regiment) Squadron
Feb 1985 to present (2004).

2729 (RAuxAF Regiment) Squadron
Formed Apr 1985, disbanded Apr 1994.

1339 (RAuxAF Regiment) Wing
Formed 1986, disbanded Apr 1994.

267 Field Squadron, Royal Engineers (TA)
Apr 1987, disbanded 1999.

2890 (RAuxAF Regiment) Squadron
Formed 1989, disbanded Apr 1994.

Air Combat Manouevring Installation
1990 to present (2004).

Sentry Training Squadron
Formed Jun 1990, disbanded Jan 1993.

8 Squadron
Sentry AEW1; formed Jul 1991 to present (2004).

Sentry Standards Unit
Formed Jan 1993 to present (2004).

Air Warfare Centre
Sep 1995 to present (2004).

Electronic Warfare Avionics Dept
Apr 1995 to present (2004).

51 Squadron
Nimrod R1; Apr 1995 to present (2004)

23 Squadron
Sentry AEW1; formed Apr 1996 to present (2004).

Sentry Operational Evaluation Unit
Formed Jun 1996 to present (2004).

27 Squadron RAF Regiment Rapier, Apr 1996, disbanded Sep 1998.

48 Squadron RAF Regiment, Rapier; Jul 1996, disbanded Sep 1998.

7644 (Media) Squadron
RAuxAF, ? to 2000

26 Squadron RAF Regiment, Rapier; Dec 1998 to present (2004).

7006 (Int)
2000 to present (2004)

7010 (PI)
2000 to present (2004)

Tornado F3 OEU
Mar 2003-Apr 2004
Still open.
Aircraft Viewing Area.

WAINFLEET
OS sheet 122. 525565. 2m S of village on coast.
Opened Aug 1938.

Bombing and Gunnery Range
1938 to present (2000).
Still open.

WALTHAM See Grimsby.

WELLINGORE/WELBOURN
OS sheet 121. 983540. 1m S of village, E of minor road to Fulbeck.

Opened as Welbourn LG in the 1930s as a **Relief Landing Ground** for Cranwell to 1940.

Relief Landing Ground for Digby, 1940.

29 Squadron
Blenheim If, Beaufighter If; Jul 1940 to Apr 1941.

412 (Canadian) Squadron
Spitfire IIa, Vb; Oct 1941 to May 1942.

54 Squadron
Spitfire Vb; Jun 1942.

154 Squadron
Spitfire Vb; Sep to Nov 1942.

81 Squadron
Spitfire Vb; Oct 1942.

288 Squadron
Defiant, Hurricane II, Spitfire Vb; Dec 1942 to Jan 1943.

2953 Squadron RAF Regiment, 1943.

613 Squadron
Mustang I; Mar to May 1943.

416 (Canadian) Squadron
Spitfire IX; May to Jun 1943.

349 (Belgian) Squadron
Spitfire Va; Aug 1943.

416 (Canadian) Squadron
Spitfire Vb, Vc; Sep to Oct 1943.

309 (Polish) Squadron
Mustang I; Nov 1943.

439 (Canadian) Squadron
Hurricane IV; formed Jan to Jan 1944.

402 (Canadian) Squadron
Spitfire Vb, Vc; Feb to Apr 1944, Apr 1944.

Relief Landing Ground for 16 (Polish) FTS Hucknall Oxford, Harvard; Jan to Feb 1944.

Relief Landing Ground for Cranwell, Apr 1944 to Jun 1946.
Closed Jun 1946.

WICKENBY
OS sheet 121. 088803. 0.5m S of village, N of B1399.
Opened Sep 1942.

12 Squadron
Lancaster; Sep 1942 to Sep 1945.

626 Squadron
Lancaster; formed Nov 1943, disbanded Oct 1945.

14 Base Sub-station
Dec 1943 to Oct 1945.

109 Squadron
Mosquito XVI; Oct to Nov 45.

233 Maintenance Unit
Formed Sep 1948, became **93 MU**, formed Dec 1948 to Jan 1951.

93 Maintenance Unit Sub-site
Jan 1951 to Sep 1952.

92 Maintenance Unit
Formed Sep 1952, disbanded Sep 1956.
Closed 1956.
Civil airfield and museum.

WILLOUGHBY HILLS
OS sheet 131. 355455. E of Boston, N of A52.
WW1 ELG for 38/90 Sqns, 1916 to 1918.

WILLOUGHBY WALKS
OS sheet 130. 035409.
WW2 Night Decoy for Cranwell and Barkston.

WINTERTON
OS sheet 112. 942195. 1m E of village, E of minor road to Winteringham.
WW1 ELG for 33 Sqn, 1916 to 1918.

WOODHALL SPA
OS sheet 122. 203610. 1.5m SE of village, E of B1192.
Opened Feb 1942.
97 Squadron
Lancaster; Feb 1942 to Apr 1943.
1514 Beam Approach Training Flight
Oxford; Mar to Aug 1943.
619 Squadron
Lancaster; formed Apr 1943 to Jan 1944.
617 Squadron
Lancaster; Jan 1944 to Jun 1945.
54 Base Sub-station
Jan 1944 to Nov 1945.
627 Squadron
Mosquito IV, XX, XXV, B16 (45); Apr 1944, disbanded Oct 1945.

1317 Flight
Mosquito B9, B16, Lancaster; formed Jun 1945, disbanded Jun 1945.
109 Squadron
Mosquito B16; formed Oct to Oct 1945.
92 Maintenance Unit Sub-site
1945 to Jun 1953.
93 Maintenance Unit Sub-site
Nov 1951 to Mar 1958.
222 Squadron
Bloodhound SAM1; formed May 1960, disbanded Jun 1964.
112 Squadron
Bloodhound SAM2; formed Nov 1964 to Oct 1967.
Engine Overhaul and Test Facility for Coningsby, 1969 to 2003.
Closed 2003.
Thorpe Camp Visitor Centre at Tattershall Thorpe.

WYHAM
OS sheet 113. 258939.
WW2 Night Decoy for Binbrook.

Wellingore had an exciting day in late 1941 when contaminated fuel caused several abandoned take-offs, as with Spitfire Vb AB792 shown here, and grounded the rest of 412 (RCAF) Squadron; AB792 was repaired.
Public Archives of Canada

Bibliography

Many personal reminiscences published over the years include references to Lincolnshire, and it is impossible to list them all here. The works listed below deal specifically with units based in Lincolnshire, or have proved most useful to the author, and are additional to those quoted in the text.

44 (Rhodesia) Squadron on Operations: A N White; Author, 1977.

83 Squadron 1917-1969: R C Low & F E Harper; Authors, 1992.

101 Squadron: R Alexander; CMH, 1979.

Action Stations 2: B B Halpenny; Patrick Stephens, 1981. (revised edition 1991)

The Air Force Memorials Of Lincolnshire: M Ingham; Midland Publishing Ltd, 1995.

Aircraft Made In Lincoln: J Walls & C S Parker; SLHA, 2000.

The Airfields of Lincolnshire since 1912: R Blake, M Hodgson & W Taylor; Midland Counties, 1984.

At First Sight: A B Webb; Author, 1991. (627 Sqn)

Attack to Defence! – The History of RAF Binbrook: S Scott & J Jackson; GMS, 1990.

The Battle of Britain Memorial Flight: Midland Publishing Ltd; 1995.

Battlebags – British Airships of The First World War: C Mowthorpe; Sutton, 1995.

Beware The Dog At War: J Ward; Author, 1998. (Fiskerton)

Big Skies Over Lincolnshire: P Washbourn; Breedon, 2001

The Black Swan: S Finn; Newton, 1989. (103 Sqn)

Bomber Group At War: C Bowyer; Ian Allan, 1981.

Bomber Intelligence: W E Jones, 1983.

Bomber Squadron At War: A Brookes; Ian Allan, 1983.

Bomber Squadrons at War: G D Copeman; Sutton, 1997. (57 and 630 Sqns)

Bomber Squadrons of The RAF and Their Aircraft: P J R Moyes; Macdonald; 1976.

Broken Wings – Post-War RAF Accidents: J Halley; Air-Britain, 1999.

Coastal, Support and Special Squadrons of the RAF and Their Aircraft: Jane's; 1982.

Combat Ready!: A Goodrum; GMS, 1997. (Sutton Bridge).

Cranwell – RNAS & RAF Photographs: P Green & M Hodgson; Midland Publishing Ltd, 1994.

The Dambusters Squadron: A Cooper; Arms & Armour, 1993.

Fields of Deception: C Dobinson; Methuen, 2000.

Fifty Years of Cranwell: RAF College; 1970.

Fighter Squadrons of the RAF and Their Aircraft: J D R Rawlings; Macdonald, 1976.

Flight Cadet: R M Hancock; Pentland, 1996.

For Faith and Freedom: J F Hamlin; GMS, 1996. (Waddington)

Goxhill at War: L Dixon & R Parker; Authors, 1994.

Great Britain Ministry of Defence – RAF Nuclear Deterrent Forces and the RAF Strategic Nuclear Deterrent Force: HMSO; 1996.

Guy Gibson. J Morris; 1994.

Hagnaby: G Hall & D Feary; Authors, 1996.

A History of RAF Scampton 1917-1968: C G Jefford; Delta, 1968.

A History of Royal Air Force Cranwell: E B Haslam; HMSO, 1982.

In the Middle of Nowhere (Metheringham): R Bailey; Tucann, 1999.

Lancaster Operations (100 Squadron): I Reid; Ashlea Thomas, 2003

Lincolnshire Air War, 1939-1945: Aero Litho; 1973.

Lincolnshire Air War 1939-1945 Book 2: Control Column, 1984.

Lincolnshire Airfields in the Second World War: P Otter; Countryside; 1996.

Maximum Effort – The Story of the North Lincolnshire Bombers: P Otter; Archive; 1990.

Maximum Effort 2 – One Group at War: P Otter; Hutton; 1991.

Maximum Effort 3 – The Untold Stories: P Otter; Hutton; 1993.

Military Airfields of The British Isles, 1939-1945: S Willis & B Hollis; Enthusiast Pub, 1987.

No 5 Bomber Group RAF (1939-1945): W J Lawrence; Chivers, 1970.

North Coates: B Taylor; GMS, 1994.

On Wings of War: J Wright; 166 Sqn Assoc, 1996.

Paths in the Woods (Nth Witham): M Chorton; Old Forge Oub, 2003

The Poacher's Brats: F E Whitehouse; RAF Cranwell Apprentice's Assoc, 1988.

The Polish Air Force in Lincolnshire: N. Ingham; 1988.

RAF Beam Benders: L Brettingham; Midland Publishing Ltd, 1997.

RAF Squadrons: C G Jefford; Airlife; 1988. (revised 2001)

Red Arrows – The Inside Story: T Cunnane; Woodfield, 2002.

Royal Air Force Flying Training and Support Units: R Sturtivant, J J Halley & J Hamlin; Air-Britain, 1997.

The Royal Observer Corps in Lincolnshire 1936-1991: C S Parker; Author. 1991.

Scampton: S Scott; GMS, 1994.

A Short History of RAF Digby 1918-1973: B G Montgomery; RAF Digby, 1974.

Silksheen: G D Copeman; Midland Counties; 1989. (East Kirkby)

Spittlegate: G Gardiner; GMS, 1994.

The Squadrons of the Royal Air Force and Commonwealth 1918-1988: Air-Britain; 1989.

The Story of 11 Group, Royal Observer Corps: John Newton; 1946.

Swinderby: GMS; 1997.

The V-Force: Jane's; 1982.

Thundering Through The Clear Air – 61 Squadron at War: D A Brammar; Author, 1997.

To Fly over Waltham: I Reid; Ashridge, 1997. (Grimsby)

A WAAF in Bomber Command: P Beck; Goodall. 1989.

Wings Over Lincolnshire: P Green, M Hodgson & W Taylor; Midland Publishing Ltd, 1994.

Abbreviations

AAC	Army Air Corps	ELG	Emergency Landing Ground	OCTU	Officer Cadet Training Unit
AACU	Anti-Aircraft Co-operation Unit	ERFTS	Elementary and Reserve Flying Training School	OCU	Operational Conversion Unit
AAM	Air-to Air Missile			OTU	Operational Training Unit
AAP	Aircraft Acceptance Park	EWAD	Electronic Warfare and Avionics Detachment	PAFU	Pilot's Advanced Flying Unit
AAR	Air-to-Air Refuelling			P/O	Pilot Officer
AAS	Air Armament School	FAA	Fleet Air Arm	PRU	Photographic Reconnaissance Unit
ABC	Airborne Cigar	FFI	Free From Infection		
ABS	Air Base Squadron	FG	Fighter Group	QFI	Qualified Flying Instructor
AC	Aircraftsman	FIS	Flying Instructor's School	QRA	Quick Reaction Alert
ACMI	Air Combat Manoeuvring Installation	Flt	Flight	RAAF	Royal Australian Air Force
		F/Lt	Flight Lieutenant	RAuxAF	Royal Auxiliary Air Force
AEF	Air Experience Flight	F/O	Flying Officer	RAF	Royal Air Force
AF	Air Force	FS	Fighter Squadron	RAFC	Royal Air Force College
AFS	Advanced Flying School	F/Sgt	Flight Sergeant	RAFFC	Royal Air Force Flying College
A-M	Air Marshal	FSS	Flying Selection Squadron	RAFVR	Royal Air Force Volunteer Reserve
AMWD	Air Ministry Works Dept	FTG	Fighter Training Group		
AOC	Air Officer Commanding	FTR	Failed To Return	RCAF	Royal Canadian Air Force
AOS	Air Observer' School	FTS	Flying Training School	RE	Royal Engineers
ASRMCU	Air-sea-rescue Marine Craft Unit	G/C	Group Captain	RFC	Royal Flying Corps
		GCI	Ground controlled Interception	RFS	Reserve Flying School
ATS	Armament Training School			RLG	Relief Landing Ground
AuxAF	Auxiliary Air Force	Gp	Group	RN	Royal Navy
AWC	Air Warfare Centre	GS	Gliding School	RNAS	Royal Naval Air Service
BATF	Beam Approach Training Flight	HCU	Heavy Conversion Unit	ROC	Royal Observer Corps
BDTF	Bomber Defence Training Flight	HDU	Hose Drum Unit	RS	Reserve Squadron
		HE	High Explosive	SAM	Surface-to Air Missile
BFTS	Basic Flying Training School	HGCU	Heavy Glider Conversion Unit	SFTS	Service Flying Training School
BW	Bomber Wing	HQ	Head Quarters	Sgt	Sergeant
Capt	Captain	HSL	High-Speed Launch	S/Ldr	Squadron Leader
CAW	College of Air Warfare	JARIC	Joint Air Reconnaissance Intelligence Centre	SoTT	School of Technical Training
Cdr	Commander			Sqn	Squadron
CF	Conversion Flight	JEFTS	Joint Elementary Flying Training School	Sqn Cdr	Squadron Commander
CFE	Central Fighter Establishment			SSQ	Station Sick-Quarters
CFS	Central Flying School	JSSU	Joint Services Signals Unit	SU	Signals Unit
CGS	Central Gliding School	ICBM	Intercontinental Ballistic Missile	Sub-F/Lt	Sub Flight Lieutenant
CH	Chain Home			TA	Territorial Army
CHL	Chain Home Low	ITS	Initial Training School	TCC	Troop Carrier Command
CO	Commanding Officer	LACW	Leading Aircraftswoman	TCG	Troop Carrier Group
Col	Colonel	LCP	Launch Control Point	TDS	Training Depot Station
COTU	Coastal Operational Training Unit	Lt	Lieutenant	Trng	Training
		Lt Col	Lieutenant Colonel	TS	Training Squadron
det	Detachment	MCU	Marine Craft Unit	TTF	Target Towing Flight
DGST	Department of Specialist Ground Training	MLU	Motor Launch Unit	UAS	University Air Squadron
		MU	Maintenance Unit	USAF	United States Air Force
DIOT	Department of Initial Officer Training	NATO	North Atlantic Treaty Organization	USAAF	United States Army Air Force
				USN	United States Navy
DP	Descent Point	NCO	Non-Commissioned Officer	VC	Victoria Cross
DRS	Directorate of Recruitment and Selection	NZ	New Zealand	WAAF	Women's Auxiliary Air Force
		OAFU	Observer's Advanced Flying Unit	W/C	Wing Commander
EAAS	Empire Air Armament School			WRAF	Women's Royal Air Force
ECM	Electronic Counter Measures	OASC	Officer and Aircrew Selection Centre		
EFTS	Elementary Flying Training School	OC	Officer Commanding		

Index